Q: Skills for Success ⑤
READING AND WRITING

Nigel A. Caplan

Scott Roy Douglas

SERIES CONSULTANTS

Marguerite Ann Snow

Lawrence J. Zwier

VOCABULARY CONSULTANT

Cheryl Boyd Zimmerman

OXFORD

UNIVERSITY PRESS

OXFORD
UNIVERSITY PRESS

198 Madison Avenue

New York, NY 10016 USA

Great Clarendon Street, Oxford, OX2 6DP, United Kingdom

Oxford University Press is a department of the University of Oxford.
It furthers the University's objective of excellence in research, scholarship,
and education by publishing worldwide. Oxford is a registered trade
mark of Oxford University Press in the UK and in certain other countries

General Manager, American ELT: Laura Pearson
Publisher: Stephanie Karras
Associate Publishing Manager: Sharon Sargent
Senior Development Editor: Andrew Gitzy
Associate Development Editors: Rebecca Mostov, Keyana Shaw
Director, ADP: Susan Sanguily
Executive Design Manager: Maj-Britt Hagsted
Associate Design Manager: Michael Steinhofer
Electronic Production Manager: Julie Armstrong
Production Artist: Elissa Santos
Cover Design: Molly Scanlon
Image Manager: Trisha Masterson
Image Editors: Liaht Pashayan
Production Coordinator: Elizabeth Matsumoto

ISBN: 978-0-19-475642-6 Reading Writing 5 Student Book Pack
ISBN: 978-0-19-475626-6 Reading Writing 5 Student Book
ISBN: 978-0-19-475621-1 Q Online Practice Student Access Code Card

Printed in China

This book is printed on paper from certified and well-managed sources

ACKNOWLEDGMENTS

Authors

Nigel A. Caplan holds an M.S.Ed. in TESOL from the University of Pennsylvania. He is an assistant professor at the University of Delaware English Language Institute. Previously, he was an ESL specialist at the University of North Carolina at Chapel Hill and a teacher in the Intensive English Programs at Michigan State University and the University of Pennsylvania and at schools in the U.K., France, and Germany. He has presented at numerous conferences on the topics of academic writing and teaching language through drama.

Scott Roy Douglas holds a Ph.D. in Education from the University of Calgary with a specialization in Teaching English as a Second Language. Over the years, he has had the privilege of working with learners of all ages and abilities throughout the world, from the Middle East to Asia. His research primarily looks at the vocabulary use and academic achievement of non-native English speaking students at the post-secondary level. His other research interests include English for Academic Purposes curriculum design and using online technology as a tool for fostering English language proficiency.

Series Consultants

Marguerite Ann Snow holds a Ph.D. in Applied Linguistics from UCLA. She is a professor in the Charter College of Education at California State University, Los Angeles where she teaches in the TESOL M.A. program. She has published in *TESOL Quarterly*, *Applied Linguistics*, and *The Modern Language Journal*. She has been a Fulbright scholar in Hong Kong and Cyprus. In 2006, she received the President's Distinguished Professor award at Cal State L.A. In addition to working closely with ESL and mainstream public school teachers in the United States, she has trained EFL teachers in Algeria, Argentina, Brazil, Egypt, Japan, Morocco, Pakistan, Spain, and Turkey. Her main interests are integrated content and language instruction, English for Academic Purposes, and standards for English teaching and learning.

Lawrence J. Zwier holds an M.A. in TESL from the University of Minnesota. He is currently the Associate Director for Curriculum Development at the English Language Center at Michigan State University in East Lansing. He has taught ESL/EFL in the United States, Saudi Arabia, Malaysia, Japan, and Singapore. He is a frequent TESOL conference presenter and has published many ESL/EFL books in the areas of test-preparation, vocabulary, and reading, including *Inside Reading 2* for Oxford University Press.

Vocabulary Consultant

Cheryl Boyd Zimmerman is associate professor of TESOL at California State University, Fullerton. She specializes in second-language vocabulary acquisition, an area in which she is widely published. She teaches graduate courses on second-language acquisition, culture, vocabulary, and the fundamentals of TESOL and is a frequent invited speaker on topics related to vocabulary teaching and learning. She is the author of *Word Knowledge: A Vocabulary Teacher's Handbook*, and Series Director of *Inside Reading*, both published by Oxford University Press.

REVIEWERS

We would like to acknowledge the advice of teachers from all over the world who participated in online reviews, focus groups, and editorial reviews. We relied heavily on teacher input throughout the extensive development process of the Q series, and many of the features in the series came directly from feedback we gathered from teachers in the classroom. We are grateful to all who helped.

UNITED STATES Marcarena Aguilar, North Harris College, TX; Deborah Anholt, Lewis and Clark College, OR; Robert Anzelde, Oakton Community College, IL; Arlys Arnold, University of Minnesota, MN; Marcia Arthur, Renton Technical College, WA; Anne Bachmann, Clackamas Community College, OR; Ron Balsamo, Santa Rosa Junior College, CA; Lori Barkley, Portland State University, OR; Eileen Barlow, SUNY Albany, NY; Sue Bartch, Cuyahoga Community College, OH; Lora Bates, Oakton High School, VA; Nancy Baum, University of Texas at Arlington, TX; Linda Berendsen, Oakton Community College, IL; Jennifer Binckes Lee, Howard Community College, MD; Grace Bishop, Houston Community College, TX; Jean W. Bodman, Union County College, NJ; Virginia Bouchard, George Mason University, VA; Kimberley Briesch Sumner, University of Southern California, CA; Gabriela Cambiasso, Harold Washington College, IL; Jackie Campbell, Capistrano Unified School District, CA; Adele C. Camus, George Mason University, VA; Laura Chason, Savannah College, GA; Kerry Linder Catana, Language Studies International, NY; An Cheng, Oklahoma State University, OK; Carole Collins, North Hampton Community College, PA; Betty R. Compton, Intercultural Communications College, HI; Pamela Couch, Boston University, MA; Fernanda Crowe, Intrax International Institute, CA; Margo Czinski, Washtenaw Community College, MI; David Dahnke, Lone Star College, TX; Gillian M. Dale, CA; L. Dalgish, Concordia College, MN; Christopher Davis, John Jay College, NY; Sonia Delgadillo, Sierra College, CA; Marta O. Dmytrenko-Ahrabian, Wayne State University, MI; Javier Dominguez, Central High School, SC; Jo Ellen Downey-Greer, Lansing Community College, MI; Jennifer Duclos, Boston University, MA; Yvonne Duncan, City College of San Francisco, CA; Jennie Farnell, University of Connecticut, CT; Susan Fedors, Howard Community College, MD; Matthew Florence, Intrax International Institute, CA; Kathleen Flynn, Glendale College, CA; Eve Fonseca, St. Louis Community College, MO; Elizabeth Foss, Washtenaw Community College, MI; Duff C. Galda, Pima Community College, AZ; Christiane Galvani, Houston Community College, TX; Gretchen Gerber, Howard Community College, MD; Ray Gonzalez, Montgomery College, MD; Alyona Gorokhova, Grossmont College, CA; John Graney, Santa Fe College, FL; Kathleen Green, Central High School, AZ; Webb Hamilton, De Anza College, San Jose City College, CA; Janet Harclerode, Santa Monica Community College, CA; Sandra Hartmann, Language and Culture Center, TX; Kathy Haven, Mission College, CA; Adam Henricksen, University of Maryland, MD; Peter Hoffman, LaGuardia Community College, NY; Linda Holden, College of Lake County, IL; Jana Holt, Lake Washington Technical College, WA; Gail Ibele, University of Wisconsin, WI; Mandy Kama, Georgetown University, Washington, DC; Stephanie Kasuboski, Cuyahoga Community College, OH; Chigusa Katoku, Mission College, CA; Sandra Kawamura, Sacramento City College, CA; Gail Kellersberger, University of Houston–Downtown, TX; Jane Kelly, Durham Technical Community College, NC; Julie Park Kim, George Mason University, VA; Lisa Kovacs-Morgan University of California, San Diego, CA; Claudia Kupiec, DePaul University, IL; Renee La Rue, Lone Star College-Montgomery, TX; Janet Langon, Glendale College, CA; Lawrence Lawson, Palomar College, CA; Rachele Lawton, The Community College of Baltimore County, MD; Alice Lee, Richland College, TX; Cherie Lenz-Hackett, University of Washington, WA; Joy Leventhal, Cuyahoga Community College, OH; Candace Lynch-Thompson, North Orange County Community College District, CA; Thi Thi Ma, City College of San Francisco, CA; Denise Maduli-Williams, City College of San Francisco, CA; Eileen Mahoney, Camelback High School, AZ; Brigitte Maronde, Harold Washington College, IL; Keith Maurice, University of Texas at Arlington, TX; Nancy Mayer, University of Missouri-St. Louis, MO; Karen Merritt, Glendale Union High School District, AZ; Holly Milkowart, Johnson County Community College, KS; Eric Moyer, Intrax International Institute, CA; Gino Muzzatti, Santa Rosa Junior College, CA; William Nedrow, Triton College, IL; Eric Nelson, University of Minnesota, MN; Rhony Ory, Ygnacio Valley High School, CA; Paul Parent, Montgomery College, MD; Oscar Pedroso, Miami Dade College, FL; Robin Persiani, Sierra College, CA; Patricia Prenz-Belkin, Hostos Community College, NY; Jim Ranalli, Iowa State University, IA; Toni R. Randall, Santa Monica College, CA; Vidya Rangachari, Mission College, CA; Elizabeth Rasmussen, Northern Virginia Community College, VA; Lara Ravitch, Truman College, IL; Deborah Repasz, San Jacinto College, TX; Andrey Reznikov, Black Hills State University, SD; Alison Rice, Hunter College, NY; Jennifer Robles, Ventura Unified School District, CA; Priscilla Rocha, Clark County School District, NV; Dzidra Rodins, DePaul University IL; Maria Rodriguez, Central High School, AZ; Maria Ruiz, Victor Valley College, CA; Kimberly Russell, Clark College, WA; Irene Sakk, Northwestern University, IL; Shaeley Santiago, Ames High School, IA; Peg Sarosy, San Francisco State University, CA; Alice Savage, North Harris College, TX; Donna Schaeffer, University of Washington, WA; Carol Schinger, Northern Virginia Community College, VA; Robert Scott, Kansas State University, KS; Suell Scott, Sheridan Technical Center, FL; Shira Seaman, Global English Academy, NY; Richard Seltzer, Glendale Community College, CA; Kathy Sherak, San Francisco State University, CA; German Silva, Miami Dade College, FL; Andrea Spector, Santa Monica Community College, CA; Karen Stanely, Central Piedmont Community College, NC; Ayse Stromsdorfer, Soldan I.S.H.S., MO; Yilin Sun, South Seattle Community College, WA; Thomas Swietlik, Intrax International Institute, IL; Judith Tanka, UCLA Extension–American Language Center, CA; Priscilla Taylor, University of Southern California, CA; Ilene Teixeira, Fairfax County Public Schools, VA; Shirl H. Terrell, Collin College, TX; Marya Teutsch-Dwyer, St. Cloud State University, MN; Stephen Thergesen, ELS Language Centers, CO; Christine Tierney, Houston Community College, TX; Arlene Turini, North Moore High School, NC; Suzanne Van Der Valk, Iowa State University, IA; Nathan D. Vasarhely, Ygnacio Valley High School, CA; Naomi S. Verratti, Howard Community College, MD; Hollyahna Vettori, Santa Rosa Junior College, CA; Julie Vorholt, Lewis & Clark College, OR; Laura Walsh, City College of San Francisco, CA; Andrew J. Watson, The English Bakery; Donald Weasenforth, Collin College, TX; Juliane Widner, Sheepshead Bay High School, NY; Lynne Wilkins, Mills College, CA; Dolores "Lorrie" Winter, California State University at Fullerton, CA; Jody Yamamoto, Kapi'olani Community College, HI; Ellen L. Yaniv, Boston University, MA; Norman Yoshida, Lewis & Clark College, OR; Joanna Zadra, American River College, CA; Florence Zysman, Santiago Canyon College, CA;

ASIA Rabiatu Abubakar, Eton Language Centre, Malaysia; Wiwik Andreani, Bina Nusantara University, Indonesia; Mike Baker, Kosei Junior High School, Japan; Leonard Barrow, Kanto Junior College, Japan; Herman Bartelen, Japan; Siren Betty, Fooyin University, Kaohsiung; Thomas E. Bieri, Nagoya College, Japan; Natalie Brezden, Global English House, Japan; MK Brooks, Mukogawa Women's University, Japan; Truong Ngoc Buu, The Youth Language School, Vietnam; Charles Cabell, Toyo University, Japan; Fred Carruth, Matsumoto University, Japan; Frances Causer, Seijo University, Japan; Deborah Chang, Wenzao Ursuline College of Languages, Kaohsiung; David Chatham, Ritsumeikan University, Japan; Andrew Chih Hong Chen, National Sun Yat-sen University, Kaohsiung; Christina Chen, Yu-Tsai Bilingual Elementary School, Taipei; Jason Jeffree Cole, Coto College, Japan; Le Minh Cong, Vungtau Tourism Vocational College, Vietnam; Todd Cooper, Toyama National College of Technology, Japan; Marie Cosgrove, Daito Bunka University, Japan; Tony Cripps, Ritsumeikan University, Japan; Daniel Cussen, Takushoku University, Japan; Le Dan, Ho Chi Minh City Electric Power College, Vietnam; Simon Daykin, Banghwa-dong Community Centre, South Korea; Aimee Denham, ILA, Vietnam; Bryan Dickson, David's English Center, Taipei; Nathan Ducker, Japan University, Japan; Ian Duncan, Simul International Corporate Training, Japan; Nguyen Thi Kieu Dung, Thang Long University, Vietnam; Nguyen Thi Thuy Duong, Vietnamese American Vocational Training College, Vietnam; Wong Tuck Ee, Raja Tun Azlan Science Secondary School, Malaysia; Emilia Effendy, International Islamic University Malaysia, Malaysia; Robert Eva, Kaisei Girls High School, Japan; Jim George, Luna International Language School, Japan; Jurgen Germeys, Silk Road Language Center, South Korea; Wong Ai Gnoh, SMJK Chung Hwa Confucian, Malaysia; Peter Goosselink, Hokkai High School,

WELCOME TO Q:Skills for Success

Q: Skills for Success is a six-level series with two strands,
Reading and Writing and *Listening and Speaking*.

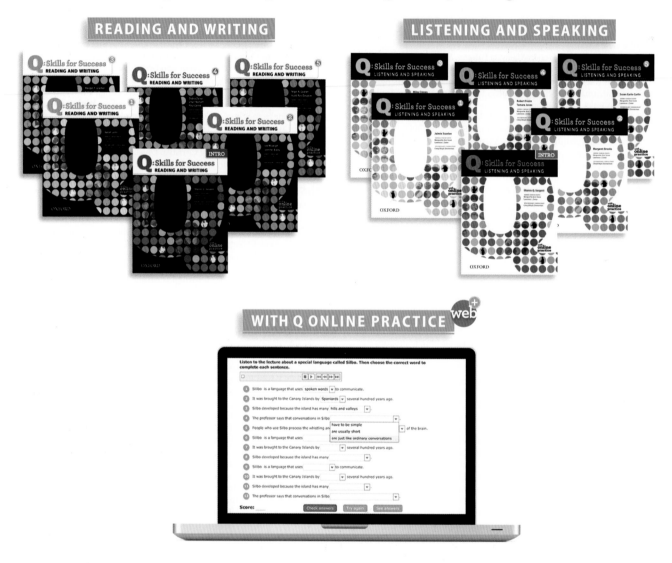

READING AND WRITING

LISTENING AND SPEAKING

WITH Q ONLINE PRACTICE

STUDENT AND TEACHER INFORMED

Q: Skills for Success is the result of an extensive development process involving thousands of teachers and hundreds of students around the world. Their views and opinions helped shape the content of the series. *Q* is grounded in teaching theory as well as real-world classroom practice, making it the most learner-centered series available.

CONTENTS

Quick Guide viii

Scope and Sequence xiv

Unit 1 **Q: Why do people read and write blogs?** 2
Reading 1: Blogs and journalism need each other
Reading 2: Diary-Keeping Pet Project for Bloggers
web Q Online Practice Reading: On the Road with Apps

Unit 2 **Q: What happens when a language disappears?** 28
Reading 1: History of the Maori Language
Reading 2: When Languages Die
web Q Online Practice Reading: Languages in Switzerland

Unit 3 **Q: What is the difference between work and fun?** 56
Reading 1: Laid-Back Labor: The $140 Homemade Scarf
Reading 2: Video Gamers
web Q Online Practice Reading: The Blurring of Work and Leisure

Unit 4 **Q: How well does a picture illustrate the truth?** 82
Reading 1: How to Lie with Maps
Reading 2: Phototruth or Photofiction?
web Q Online Practice Reading: The Many Lives of Identity Thieves

Unit 5 **Q: Why is global cooperation important?** 108
Reading 1: In Norway, Global Seed Vault Guards Genetic Resources
Reading 2: The Long Countdown: For U.S. Astronauts, a Russian Second Home
web Q Online Practice Reading: Safeguarding the World's Network

Unit 6 **Q: What makes a public place appealing?** 136
Reading 1: The New Oases
Reading 2: A Path to Road Safety with No Signposts
web Q Online Practice Reading: The New Third Places

Unit 7 **Q: How can we turn trash into treasure?** 164
Reading 1: Garbage of Eden
Reading 2: Trash Talker: Garbage Mogul Makes Millions from Trash
web Q Online Practice Reading: From Fast Food to Fast Cars

Unit 8 **Q: Why do people want to change who they are?** 192
Reading 1: Set in Our Ways: Why Change Is So Hard
Reading 2: Kids Want to Tan
web Q Online Practice Reading: Book Review of *The Tipping Point*

Unit 9 **Q: What energizes people?** 222
Reading 1: A Healthy Lifestyle Can Reduce Fatigue, Boost Energy
Reading 2: A Jolt of Caffeine, by the Can
web Q Online Practice Reading: Improving Athletic Performance

Unit 10 **Q: Does the size of a country matter?** 250
Reading 1: "Small Country," Part I
Reading 2: "Small Country," Part II
web Q Online Practice Reading: Land Art

Q connects critical thinking, language skills, and learning outcomes.

LANGUAGE SKILLS

Explicit skills instruction enables students to meet their academic and professional goals.

LEARNING OUTCOMES

Clearly identified **learning outcomes** focus students on the goal of their instruction.

UNIT 2

Language

READING	distinguishing main ideas from details
VOCABULARY	using a thesaurus
WRITING	writing an extended definition
GRAMMAR	contrast and concession connectors

LEARNING OUTCOME

Prepare an extended definition of a word or concept from a different language or culture for which there is no equivalent term or idea in English.

Unit QUESTION

What happens when a language disappears?

PREVIEW THE UNIT

A Discuss these questions with your classmates.

Which languages can you speak? Which is spoken by the most people? What other languages would you like to learn? Why?

Do you think your identity is related to the language you speak? Why or why not?

Look at the photo. Why does the man have a microphone? What is the woman doing?

B Discuss the Unit Question above with your classmates.

Listen to *The Q Classroom*, Track 5 on CD 1, to hear other answers.

28 UNIT 2 Photo is part of the National Geographic "Enduring Language" project

29

CRITICAL THINKING

Thought-provoking **unit questions** engage students with the topic and provide a **critical thinking framework** for the unit.

> " Having the learning outcome is important because it gives students and teachers a clear idea of what the point of each task/activity in the unit is. "
> *Lawrence Lawson, Palomar College, California*

CD 1
Track 9   **Read the article.**

FREAKONOMICS

Laid-Back Labor: The $140 Homemade Scarf

By Stephen J. Dubner and Steven D. Levitt

1 During the late 19th century, piano manufacturing was one of New York City's largest industries. Every right-minded American family, it seemed, wanted to fill its home with music. The advent of the player piano[1]—a music-making machine that required zero talent—drove the **boom** even further. By the 1920s, some 300,000 pianos were being sold in the United States each year, roughly two-thirds of them player pianos.

2 But a pair of newer technologies, the radio and the phonograph,[2] soon began to drive the piano into a deep disfavor that continues to this day. Last year, Americans bought only 76,966 pianos. That's a decrease of 75 percent over a period in which the population more than doubled. As much as people may love music, most

knitting for fun

though just 1 percent of Americans live on a farm today, down from 30 percent in 1920. On a more personal note: one of the authors of this column has a sister who runs a **thriving** yarn[4] store, while the other is married to a knitting devotee who might buy $40 worth of yarn for a single scarf and then spend ten hours knitting it. Even if her **labor** is valued at only $10 an hour, the scarf costs at least $140—or roughly $100 more than a similar machine-made scarf might cost.

Knitting: a way to relax

4 Isn't it puzzling that so many middle-aged Americans are spending so much of their time and money performing **menial** labor when they don't have to? Just as the radio and phonograph proved to be powerful substitutes for the piano, the forces of technology have greatly eased the burden of

Q WHAT DO YOU THINK?

A. Discuss the questions in a group. Then choose one question and write one or two paragraphs in response.

1. Do you like playing video games? Why or why not?

2. After reading the article, do you think that video gaming can be considered a real sport?

Explicit skills instruction prepares students for academic success.

LANGUAGE SKILLS

Explicit instruction and practice in reading, vocabulary, grammar, and writing skills **help students achieve language proficiency.**

LEARNING OUTCOMES

Practice activities allow students to **master the skills** before they are evaluated at the end of the unit.

WHAT DO YOU THINK?

Discuss the questions in a group. Then choose one question and write freely for five to ten minutes in response.

1. Will the global partnerships being formed while working on the Global Seed Vault help the world in other ways? Why or why not?

2. Do you think the scientists and governments in the article on the Global Seed Vault will be successful in preserving seeds and shoots from around the world? What are the consequences for humanity if the Global Seed Vault project is not successful?

3. Does your home country have any unique plants or crops that aren't found anywhere else? Do you feel they should be preserved in the Global Seed Vault? Why or why not?

Reading Skill Making inferences

Writers often use facts and opinions to suggest ideas rather than giving the ideas to the reader directly. The reader has to determine, or **infer**, what the writer is saying. Making an inference is making a logical conclusion about something based on the information that is given. Making inferences while reading a text can improve your overall comprehension and can help you become a more critical reader.

This excerpt is taken from Reading 1:

☐ Bored into the middle of a snow-topped Arctic mountain, the seed vault . . .

The text doesn't need to say exactly what kind of place is best for preserving the world's seeds and shoots. From the information in the excerpt, you can determine that it is a place that needs to be safe and secure, as well as cold and far away. You come to this conclusion because of clues such as *bored, snow-topped, Arctic,* and *middle of a . . . mountain.*

Tip Critical Thinking
When you infer ideas from a text, you are using separate pieces of information as clues or evidence to support a conclusion. This is an analytical process and shows a deeper understanding of the material.

A. Match each excerpt from Reading 1 with the correct inference.

Excerpts

____ 1. With plant species disappearing at an alarming rate, scientists and governments are creating a global network of plant banks to store seeds and sprouts—precious genetic resources that may be needed for man to adapt the world's food supply to climate change. (Paragraph 1)

____ 2. In Leuven, Belgium, scientists are scouring the world for banana samples and cryo-preserving their shoots in liquid nitrogen before they become extinct. (Paragraph 3)

| Reading and Writing 117

A. Read the first two paragraphs in a description of another third place. Then complete the tasks below.

"The Third Place" Coffeehouse

"The Third Place" is the name of a coffeehouse in Raleigh, North Carolina. Raleigh is the home of the state capitol and many businesses. However, many workers have not had options for spending their time in locations other than their first places (downtown offices) and second places (homes in the suburbs). The Third Place is a friendly café that fills this gap.

When you walk into the Third Place, you first see the cozy, inviting chairs. Behind them, on the walls, are colorful rugs, suggesting an international theme. Between the rugs, you will see original works by local artists. The artwork is changed monthly and really helps to develop a sense of community. This feeling of community is enhanced by the customers, who represent the range of Raleigh's inhabitants. Businesspeople, students, and families can be found at the Third Place on any day of the week.

1. If a sentence contains old information, circle the old information.

2. Connect each circled phrase to the new information in the previous sentence.

3. Explain how the last sentence in paragraph 1 is linked to the previous sentence.

_____

_____

4. Compare your answers to 1–3 with a partner.

5. Underline the three passive verbs in the second paragraph. Why is the passive voice used in each case?

   a. _____

   b. _____

   c. _____

| Reading and Writing 159

> ❝ The tasks are simple, accessible, user-friendly, and very useful. ❞
> *Jessica March, American University of Sharjah, U.A.E.*

Q Online Practice provides all new content for additional practice in an easy-to-use online workbook. Every student book includes a *Q Online Practice access code card*. Use the access code to register for your *Q Online Practice* account at www.Qonlinepractice.com.

Vocabulary Skill | Using the dictionary

The main verb controls the pattern of a clause or sentence. Knowing the **complements**, or the types of words and phrases allowed with the verb, i important in improving your writing and speaking. For example, some v be followed by a direct object (transitive verbs), but others cannot (intransitive verbs). The dictionary can help you write better sentences by telling you which

When a verb can be followed by a prepositional phrase, it is especially important to use a dictionary because it is very difficult to guess the correct preposition.

~(with sb): This use of *negotiate* is intransitive, so it does not take a direct object. Use *with* to add the person you are negotiating with.

ne·go·ti·ate /nɪˈɡoʊʃiˌeɪt/ *verb* **1** [i] **~ (with sb) (for/about sth)** to try to reach an agreement by formal discussion: *The government will not negotiate with terrorists.* ◆ *We have been negotiating for more pay.* ◆ *a strong negotiating position* ◆ *negotiating skills* **2** [T] **~ sth** to arrange or agree to something by formal discussion: *to negotiate a deal/ contract/treaty/settlement* ◆ *We successfully negotiated the*

(for/about sth): Use *for* or *about* to say what you are negotiating.

All dictionary entries are taken from the *Oxford Advanced American Dictionary for learners of English*.

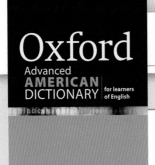

All dictionary entries are taken from the *Oxford Advanced American Dictionary for learners of English*.

LANGUAGE SKILLS

A **research-based vocabulary program** focuses students on the words they need to know academically and professionally, using skill strategies based on the same research as the Oxford dictionaries.

The *Oxford Advanced American Dictionary for learners of English* was developed with English learners in mind, and provides extra learning tools for pronunciation, verb types, basic grammar structures, and more.

The Oxford 3000™ 🔑
The Oxford 3000 encompasses **the 3000 most important words to learn in English.** It is based on a comprehensive analysis of the Oxford English Corpus, a two-billion word collection of English text, and on extensive research with both language and pedagogical experts.

The Academic Word List **AWL**
The Academic Word List was created by Averil Coxhead and contains **570 words that are commonly used in academic English,** such as in textbooks or articles across a wide range of academic subject areas. These words are a great place to start if you are studying English for academic purposes.

Clear learning outcomes focus students on the goals of instruction.

LEARNING OUTCOMES

A culminating unit assignment evaluates the students' **mastery of the learning outcome.**

Unit Assignment | **Write a cause-and-effect essay**

In this assignment, you will write a cause-and-effect essay that examines the best methods for boosting energy levels. As you prepare your essay, think about the Unit Question, "What energizes people?" and refer to the Self-Assessment checklist on page 249. Use information from Readings 1 and 2 and your work in this unit to support your ideas.

For alternative unit assignments, see the *Q: Skills for Success Teacher's Handbook*.

PLAN AND WRITE

A. BRAINSTORM Brainstorm a list of all the different ways of increasing energy that you read about in this unit. Then complete the activities.

1. Use the chart to describe the positive and negative effects each energy booster has on people.

LEARNER CENTERED

Track Your Success allows students to **assess their own progress** and provides guidance on remediation.

Check (✓) the skills you learned. If you need more work on a skill, refer to the page(s) in parentheses.

READING ●	I can organize my notes and annotations in a chart. (p. 230)
VOCABULARY ●	I can use adjective/verb + preposition collocations. (pp. 239–240)
WRITING ●	I can write a cause-and-effect essay. (p. 242)
GRAMMAR ●	I can use cause-and-effect connectors. (p. 245)
LEARNING OUTCOME ●	I can prepare a cause-and-effect essay analyzing two or three methods for boosting energy levels.

Reading and Writing **249**

> Students can check their learning . . . and they can focus on the essential points when they study.
>
> *Suh Yoomi, Seoul, South Korea*

Q Online Practice

For the student

- **Easy-to-use:** a simple interface allows students to focus on enhancing their reading and writing skills, not learning a new software program
- **Flexible:** for use anywhere there's an Internet connection
- **Access code card:** a *Q Online Practice* access code is included with this book—use the access code to register for *Q Online Practice* at www.Qonlinepractice.com

For the teacher

- **Simple yet powerful:** automatically grades student exercises and tracks progress
- **Straightforward:** online management system to review, print, or export reports
- **Flexible:** for use in the classroom or easily assigned as homework
- **Access code card:** contact your sales rep for your *Q Online Practice* teacher's access code

Teacher Resources

Q Teacher's Handbook gives strategic support through:

- specific teaching notes for each activity
- ideas for ensuring student participation
- multilevel strategies and expansion activities
- the answer key
- special sections on 21st century skills and critical thinking
- a *Testing Program CD-ROM* with a customizable test for each unit

For additional resources visit the *Q: Skills for Success* companion website at www.oup.com/elt/teacher/Qskillsforsuccess

Q Class Audio includes:

- reading texts
- *The Q Classroom*

> It's an interesting, engaging series which provides plenty of materials that are easy to use in class, as well as instructionally promising.
> *Donald Weasenforth, Collin College, Texas*

SCOPE AND SEQUENCE | Reading and Writing 5

UNIT	READING	WRITING
1 **New Media** **Q** **Why do people read and write blogs?** **READING 1: Blogs and Journalism Need Each Other** A Magazine Article (Journalism) **READING 2: Diary-Keeping Pet Project for Bloggers** A Newspaper Article (Culture and Media)	• Preview text using a variety of strategies • Annotate a text using various techniques • Summarize main ideas • Read for main ideas • Read for details • Read and recognize different text types • Use glosses and footnotes to aid comprehension	• Use time transitions to write about a process • Plan before writing • Make an outline • Write a process essay • Revise, edit, and rewrite • Give feedback to peers and self-assess
2 **Language** **Q** **What happens when a language disappears?** **READING 1: History of the Maori Language** Web Page (Language and Culture) **READING 2: When Languages Die** A Book Excerpt (Linguistics)	• Preview text using a variety of strategies • Find evidence to distinguish main ideas from details • Read for main ideas • Read for details • Read and recognize different text types • Use glosses and footnotes to aid comprehension	• Plan before writing • Make an outline • Write an extended definition to analyze a concept • Revise, edit, and rewrite • Give feedback to peers and self-assess
3 **Work and Leisure** **Q** **What is the difference between work and fun?** **READING 1: Freakonomics: Laid-back Labor: The $140 Homemade Scarf** A News Magazine Article (Economics and Work) **READING 2: Video Gamers** A Newspaper Article (Sociology and Popular Culture)	• Summarize main ideas • Identify contrasting ideas to follow an author's argument and main ideas • Preview text using a variety of strategies • Read for main ideas • Read for details • Read and recognize different text types • Use glosses and footnotes to aid comprehension	• Use evidence to support an argument • Plan before writing • Make an outline • Write a persuasive essay • Revise, edit, and rewrite • Give feedback to peers and self-assess

VOCABULARY	GRAMMAR	CRITICAL THINKING	UNIT OUTCOME
• Recognize common collocations in order to learn patterns of usage • Match definitions • Define new terms • Learn selected vocabulary words from the Oxford 3000 and the Academic Word List	• Adjective phrases	• Reflect on the unit question • Complete a chart to organize information • Apply knowledge to complete a new task • Connect ideas across texts or readings • Express ideas/reactions/opinions orally and in writing • Apply unit tips and use *Q Online Practice* to become a strategic learner	• Develop a process essay describing how to do an activity with which you are familiar.
• Use a thesaurus to expand vocabulary through the use of synonyms and antonyms • Match definitions • Define new terms • Learn selected vocabulary words from the Oxford 3000 and the Academic Word List	• Contrast and concession connectors	• Reflect on the unit question • Generalize from specific examples to anticipate patterns in text types • Analyze a concept that may be difficult to explain by examining how it is similar to or different from other concepts • Connect ideas across texts or readings • Express ideas/reactions/opinions orally and in writing • Apply unit tips and use *Q Online Practice* to become a strategic learner	• Prepare an extended definition of a word or concept from another language or culture for which there is no equivalent term or idea in English.
• Recognize and use reporting verbs to show attitudes toward a source • Match definitions • Define new terms • Learn selected vocabulary words from the Oxford 3000 and the Academic Word List	• Noun clauses	• Reflect on the unit question • Complete charts to organize information • Paraphrase another's ideas to show understanding • Use evidence in support of an argument • Connect ideas across texts or readings • Express ideas/reactions/opinions orally and in writing • Apply unit tips and use *Q Online Practice* to become a strategic learner	• Develop a persuasive essay arguing why a particular leisure activity should or should not be considered work.

UNIT	READING	WRITING
4 Deception ? **How well does a picture illustrate the truth?** **READING 1:** How to Lie with Maps A Book Excerpt (Geography and Advertising) **READING 2:** Phototruth or Photofiction? A Textbook Excerpt (Ethics and Media)	• Preview text using a variety of strategies • Read captions and figures to see connections to the text • Locate main ideas in a text • Read for main ideas • Read for details • Read and recognize different text types • Use glosses and footnotes to aid comprehension	• Use unity to be clear, interesting, and persuasive • Write a proposal describing an ad • Plan before writing • Make an outline • Revise, edit, and rewrite • Give feedback to peers and self-assess
5 Global Citizenship ? **Why is global cooperation important?** **READING 1:** In Norway, Global Seed Vault Guards Genetic Resources A Newspaper Article (Agriculture) **READING 2:** The Long Countdown: For U.S. Astronauts, a Russian Second Home A Newspaper Article (Space)	• Preview text using a variety of strategies • Make inferences to improve comprehension and understand a text more deeply • Sequence ideas presented in a text • Read for main ideas • Read for details • Read and recognize different text types • Use glosses and footnotes to aid comprehension	• Organize supporting ideas to make writing more coherent • Write an essay • Plan before writing • Make an outline • Revise, edit, and rewrite • Give feedback to peers and self-assess
6 Public Space ? **What makes a public space appealing?** **READING 1:** The New Oases A Magazine Article (Design and Sociology) **READING 2:** A Path to Road Safety with No Signposts A Newspaper Article (Engineering and Urban Planning)	• Preview text using a variety of strategies • Recognize the connections between ideas using pronoun referents • Use an outline to organize main ideas • Locate specific information in a text • Read for main ideas • Read for details • Read and recognize different text types • Use glosses and footnotes to aid comprehension	• Use the passive voice when appropriate to focus information and add variety to writing • Use old-new information structure to connect sentences logically while developing ideas • Use constant information structure to define or explain a complex topic • Plan before writing • Make an outline • Write a descriptive essay • Revise, edit, and rewrite • Give feedback to peers and self-assess

VOCABULARY	GRAMMAR	CRITICAL THINKING	UNIT OUTCOME
• Use knowledge of Latin and Greek roots to determine meaning of new words • Match definitions • Define new terms • Learn selected vocabulary words from the Oxford 3000 and the Academic Word List	• Quantifiers	• Understand how visual information appears in different texts • Use a cluster diagram to organize ideas • Reflect on the unit question • Connect ideas across texts or readings • Express ideas/reactions/opinions orally and in writing • Apply unit tips and use *Q Online Practice* to become a strategic learner	• Create an advertising proposal describing your idea for a print or Web advertisement.
• Use prefixes to expand vocabulary • Match definitions • Define new terms • Learn selected vocabulary words from the Oxford 3000 and the Academic Word List	• Parallel structure and ellipsis	• Reflect on the unit question • Infer ideas from information that is not directly stated • Connect ideas across texts or readings • Express ideas/reactions/opinions orally and in writing • Apply unit tips and use *Q Online Practice* to become a strategic learner	• Prepare an essay describing the importance of global cooperation.
• Use the dictionary to learn correct verb complements • Understand the difference between transitive and intransitive verbs • Match definitions • Define new terms • Learn selected vocabulary words from the Oxford 3000 and the Academic Word List	• Passive voice to focus information	• Use graphic organizers to develop ideas and classify information • Reflect on the unit question • Connect ideas across texts or readings • Express ideas/reactions/opinions orally and in writing • Apply unit tips and use *Q Online Practice* to become a strategic learner	• Develop an analytical essay depicting a public place and ways to make it more appealing.

UNIT	READING	WRITING
7 **Alternative Thinking** **Q** **How can we turn trash into treasure?** **READING 1:** Garbage of Eden A Website (Ecology) **READING 2:** Trash Talker: Garbage Mogul Makes Millions from Trash A Magazine Article (Business and Environmental Science)	• Preview text using a variety of strategies • Anticipate content through questions to be an active reader • Locate support for main ideas • Match subtitles to content • Read for main ideas • Read for details • Read and recognize different text types • Use glosses and footnotes to aid comprehension	• Paraphrase effectively to integrate others' ideas in writing • Plan before writing • Make an outline • Write a business plan • Revise, edit, and rewrite • Give feedback to peers and self-assess
8 **Change** **Q** **Why do people want to change who they are?** **READING 1:** Set in Our Ways: Why Change Is So Hard A Magazine Article (Psychology) **READING 2:** Kids Want to Tan A Magazine Article (Culture and Health)	• Preview text using a variety of strategies • Match content to topic • Identify the author's intent to better analyze texts and become a more critical reader • Read for main ideas • Read for details • Read and recognize different text types • Use glosses and footnotes to aid comprehension	• Summarize to understand and recall main ideas when taking an exam or writing papers • Recognize key indicators and examples that can signal intent • Plan before writing • Make an outline • Write a summary and response essay • Plan before writing • Make an outline • Revise, edit, and rewrite • Give feedback to peers and self-assess
9 **Energy** **Q** **What energizes people?** **READING 1:** A Healthy Lifestyle Can Reduce Fatigue, Boost Energy A Newspaper Article (Health and Lifestyle) **READING 2:** A Jolt of Caffeine, by the Can A Newspaper Article (Business and Nutrition)	• Preview text using a variety of strategies • Organize notes and annotations in a chart • Locate information in a text • Read for main ideas • Read for details • Take notes organized by main ideas and details • Read and recognize different text types • Use glosses and footnotes to aid comprehension	• Learn the difference between the organization of a causal analysis and an effects analysis essay • Combine cause/effect and adjective/verb collocations into complex sentences • Plan before writing • Make an outline • Write a cause-and-effect essay • Revise, edit, and rewrite • Give feedback to peers and self-assess
10 **Size and Scale** **Q** **Does the size of a country matter?** **READING 1:** "Small Country" (Part 1) A Short Story (Fiction) **READING 2:** "Small Country" (Part 2) A Short Story (Fiction)	• Interpret emotions from speech • Understand the elements of narrative structure and analyze the plot • Preview text using a variety of strategies • Read for main ideas • Read for details • Read and recognize different text types • Use glosses and footnotes to aid comprehension	• Use symbols in writing to make it more interesting and meaningful • Plan before writing • Make an outline • Write a short story • Revise, edit, and rewrite • Give feedback to peers and self-assess

VOCABULARY	GRAMMAR	CRITICAL THINKING	UNIT OUTCOME
• Use suffixes to expand vocabulary • Match definitions • Define new terms • Learn selected vocabulary words from the Oxford 3000 and the Academic Word List	• Modals of possibility	• Reflect on the unit question • Use charts to organize information • Develop ideas for a business by synthesizing unit content with firsthand experience • Connect ideas across texts or readings • Express ideas/reactions/opinions orally and in writing • Apply unit tips and use *Q Online Practice* to become a strategic learner	• Prepare a business plan that describes an innovative new garbage recycling company to potential investors.
• Use the dictionary to make word choices appropriate for audience, register, and genre • Match definitions • Define new terms • Learn selected vocabulary words from the Oxford 3000 and the Academic Word List	• Subject-verb agreement	• Assess the effectiveness of summaries • Reflect on the unit question • Connect ideas across texts or readings • Express ideas/reactions/opinions orally and in writing • Apply unit tips and use *Q Online Practice* to become a strategic learner	• Develop a summary and response essay based on an informational text.
• Use adjective/verb + preposition collocations to increase written accuracy and improve reading comprehension • Match definitions • Define new terms • Learn selected vocabulary words from the Oxford 3000 and the Academic Word List	• Cause-and-effect connectors	• Reflect on the unit question • Understand the relationships between causes and effects using a chart • Make text-to-text, text-to-self, and text-to-world connections • Connect ideas across texts or readings • Express ideas/reactions/opinions orally and in writing • Apply unit tips and use *Q Online Practice* to become a strategic learner	• Prepare a cause-and-effect essay analyzing two or three methods for boosting energy levels.
• Use the dictionary to learn sports metaphors and idioms in writing and speaking • Match definitions • Define new terms • Learn selected vocabulary words from the Oxford 3000 and the Academic Word List	• Tense shifts in narratives	• Reflect on the unit question • Use visual information or photos to make inferences about something • Choose a point of view from which to tell a story • Analyze advantages and disadvantages • Connect ideas across texts or readings • Express ideas/reactions/opinions orally and in writing • Apply unit tips and use *Q Online Practice* to become a strategic learner	• Create a short story with an organized plot, interesting characters, and a clear point of view.

UNIT 1

New Media

READING ●	annotating a text
VOCABULARY ●	collocations
WRITING ●	writing about a process
GRAMMAR ●	adjective phrases

LEARNING OUTCOME ●

Develop a process essay describing how to do an activity with which you are familiar.

Unit QUESTION

Why do people read and write blogs?

PREVIEW THE UNIT

(A) **Discuss these questions with your classmates.**

Why do you use the Internet?

Have you ever kept a blog or used a social networking site to tell the world what you are thinking? Why or why not?

Look at the photo. What effects do new forms of media have on social gatherings? Business meetings? Large public events?

(B) **Discuss the Unit Question above with your classmates.**

))) Listen to *The Q Classroom*, Track 2 on CD 1, to hear other answers.

3

C Answer the survey about the news available from different types of media. Rate the news from each medium on a scale of 1 (low) to 5 (high) for each characteristic.

Media Opinion Survey

Media	Trustworthy	Entertaining/ Interesting	Informative	Easy to Access or Use	Total Rating
newspapers					
TV					
radio					
magazines					
news websites					
personal blogs					

D Add the numbers in the chart to get a total rating for each type of media. In a group, discuss these questions.

1. Which type of media scored the highest in each category? Which type of media scored the highest overall?

2. Who creates the content for the form of media with the highest overall rating? What tools are used?

3. Which characteristic from the survey is the most important? Why? Did the media with the highest overall rating score highest in the most important category?

READING

READING 1 | Blogs and Journalism Need Each Other

VOCABULARY

Here are some words from Reading 1. Read the sentences. Circle the answer that best matches the meaning of each bold word.

1. Because bloggers ignore many traditional rules, many people view blogging as a **renegade** form of journalism.
   a. cheaper than the usual way of doing things
   b. against the usual way of doing things

2. A blogger who was at the scene of an accident **relayed** firsthand reports through his blog.
   a. passed on
   b. collected

3. Some blogs aren't about a single clear subject, but are a collection of **random** thoughts.
   a. belonging to other people
   b. lacking a regular objective, pattern, or purpose

4. Today, a lot of the news that people read is **conveyed** through personal media, such as blogs.
   a. communicated
   b. sold

5. People with no journalism training can help to **disseminate** news and information by keeping blogs.
   a. make
   b. spread

6. People write blogs on subjects as **diverse** as personal finance, microbiology, and their favorite desserts.
   a. very different from each other
   b. very similar to each other

7. Blogs are a new form of journalism that is open to anyone who can **establish** and maintain a website.
   a. start something that is meant to last a long time
   b. find or improve something

8. Bloggers often have more freedom than journalists because they are not **confined** by journalism's traditions and values.

    a. limited

    b. satisfied

9. Some newspapers **acknowledge** losing sales because of the Internet, and as a result, they are creating their own websites.

    a. dislike

    b. agree with or admit to

10. In addition to the facts, some bloggers give their own analysis or personal **commentary**.

    a. observations

    b. requests for opinions

11. The **relevance** of a particular blog increases if the blogger's information is current and accurate.

    a. value and usefulness

    b. popularity

12. **Ultimately**, every blogger's goal is to communicate meaningfully with his or her readers.

    a. in the end

    b. certainly

PREVIEW READING 1

 Tip for Success

As you read, circle new vocabulary words that you don't know. After you finish reading, use the dictionary to look up the words to help you better understand the text.

You are going to read an article from Harvard University's quarterly magazine for journalists, *Nieman Reports*, which considers the relationship between blogging and journalism.

Check (✓) the statements that you think the article will support.

☐ It is necessary to be a trained journalist in order to write about the news.

☐ Anyone can write about the news.

☐ Blogs are a good way to get news and information.

☐ Blogs are a bad way to get news and information.

Blogs and journalism need each other

1   Suggest to an old-school[1] journalist that weblogs have anything to do with journalism and you'll be met with howls of derision[2]. Amateur bloggers typically have no editorial oversight, no training in the craft, and no respect for the news media's rules and standards. Does the free-for-all **renegade** publishing form known as blogging really have anything to do with journalism?

2   Well, yes. Consider:

- At technology and media conferences, such as PopTech, South by Southwest, and Digital Hollywood, bloggers in the audience have reported conference events in real time, posting photographs, speaker transcripts, and summaries and analysis of key points a full day before readers could see comparable stories in the daily newspaper.

bloggers at a conference

- On July 16, 2003, blogger Andy Baio reported on the tragedy in which an elderly driver plowed through the Santa Monica Farmers' Market just outside Baio's office window.

He had been walking down that street 20 minutes before. Baio described "the dead and dying" lying in the street and **relayed** firsthand reports from office co-workers who were eyewitnesses. He also posted a map of the accident scene, laid out a detailed chronology of events, and pointed to media coverage and photographs of the bloody scene.

- On Super Bowl Sunday[3], when all other news organizations were focused on football in America, a 22-year-old blogger in Los Angeles named Jessica braved the freezing cold to attend a televised outdoor concert by the British group Coldplay. She came home and blogged it, giving her take on the concert and reporting the band's playlist. Like hundreds of others who watched the show and wanted to learn the names of the songs played, I turned to the Internet. I came up empty when I visited abc.com and coldplay.com. But hundreds of us found them (through Google) on Jessica's blog.

3   Jessica probably didn't know it, but she was committing a **random** act of journalism. And that's the real revolution here: It is a world of micro-content delivered to niche audiences[4]. More and more of the small tidbits of news that we encounter each day are being **conveyed** through personal media—chiefly weblogs.

4   Call it participatory journalism, or journalism from the edges. Simply put, it refers to individuals playing an active role in the process of collecting, reporting, sorting, analyzing, and **disseminating** news and information. This is a task once reserved almost exclusively to the news media.

---

[1] **old-school:** old-fashioned or traditional
[2] **derision:** protest and ridicule

[3] **Super Bowl Sunday:** the championship game of the National Football League (NFL), which is played on a Sunday. It is usually the most-watched American television broadcast of the year.
[4] **niche audience:** a particular group of people with similar interests

5   Weblogs are the most popular expression of this new media form. Blogs have exploded in popularity, fueled by greater access to bandwidth and low-cost, often free software. More than a half million people have taken up the tools of self-publishing to create personal journals on subjects as **diverse** as politics, microbiology, and tropical fish.

6   "Blogs are in some ways a new form of journalism, open to anyone who can **establish** and maintain a website, and they have exploded in the past year." Walter Mossberg wrote this in his *Wall Street Journal* technology column last March. "The good thing about them is that they introduce fresh voices into the national discourse on various topics, and help build communities of interest through their collections of links."

7   Mossberg's description of weblogs as a new kind of journalism might trouble old-fashioned journalists. But it is a journalism of a different sort, one not tightly **confined** by the profession's traditions and values.

8   Citizens are discovering how easy it can be to play reporter and publisher. To practice random acts of journalism, you don't need a big-league publication with a slick website behind you. All you need is a computer, an Internet connection, and an ability to perform some of the tricks of the trade[5]: report what you observe, analyze events in a meaningful way, but most of all, just be fair and tell the truth, as you and your sources see it.

9   Bloggers can do that. Few bloggers fancy themselves journalists, but many **acknowledge** that their blogs take on some of the qualities of journalism. They take part in the editorial function of selecting newsworthy and interesting topics. They add analysis, insight, and **commentary**. Occasionally, they provide a first-person report about an event, a trend, or a subject. Over time, bloggers build up a publishing track record, much as any news publication does when it starts out. Reputation filters—where bloggers gain the respect and confidence of readers based on their reputation for accuracy and **relevance**—and circles of trust in the blogosphere help weed out the unreliable blogs. If the blogs are trustworthy and have something valuable to contribute, people will return.

10   I'm constantly astounded at the amount of knowledge displayed by bloggers on subjects as diverse as wireless networking, sonnet poetry, and much more. All of this is written with a degree of grace and sophistication. Many readers have begun to turn to gifted amateurs or impassioned experts with a deep understanding of niche subjects, rather than to journalists who are generalists and cover topics a mile wide but an inch deep.

11   What's ahead? Certainly there is a much larger role for amateurs in the news process. Weblogs are only one part of the puzzle. For instance, in late June 2003, NHK (the Japan Broadcasting Corporation) carried news of a serious highway accident. The scene was carried live via video from a bystander who was playing the role of journalist by shooting the action with his portable camera phone. Mobloggers—tech-savvy users who post photos, video, and text to weblogs from their mobile devices—held a convention recently in Tokyo, Japan. In Daytona Beach, Florida, a janitor created his own one-man TV station and occasionally webcasts live news events.

12   All of this signifies important changes as journalism expands to include citizen participation. **Ultimately**, bloggers and the phenomenon of grassroots[6] journalism have just as meaningful a role in the future of news on the Net as do the professionals.

---

[5] **tricks of the trade:** clever ways of doing things, known and used by people who do a particular job or activity

[6] **grassroots:** happening at the most basic level of society

MAIN IDEAS

Read the statements. Write *T* (true) or *F* (false). Then correct each false statement to make it true.

_____ 1. Blogs and journalism are connected.

_____ 2. An increasing amount of the information that people receive comes from blogs.

_____ 3. Only the news media are able to collect, report, sort, analyze, and distribute news and information.

_____ 4. It is very difficult for the average person to be a reporter and publisher of news.

_____ 5. Bloggers are able to write quite well on a wide variety of subjects.

_____ 6. In the future, there isn't going to be much of a role for amateurs or average citizens in the news process.

DETAILS

Complete the chart. Then discuss your answers with a partner.

	What did/does this person report?
1. Andy Baio	He reported on a tragedy in which an elderly driver plowed through a farmers' market.
2. Jessica in Los Angeles	
3. Walter Mossberg	
4. bystander in Japan	
5. janitor in Daytona Beach	

Q WHAT DO YOU THINK?

Discuss the questions in a group. Then choose one question and write freely for five to ten minutes in response.

1. Are TV, radio, and newspaper journalism changing because of blogging? What is the future of these forms of journalism?

2. Are blogs a good way to report the news? Are they better than traditional forms of reporting the news? Why or why not?

3. What makes someone want to blog? Would you ever blog about events happening in your community? Why or why not?

Reading Skill | Annotating a text

Become an active reader by annotating the texts you read. **Annotating a text** involves underlining, writing symbols, and taking notes in the margins as you read. These steps can help you to concentrate while you read, increase your understanding, and remember information later.

The margins, between paragraphs, and the space at the end of the text are ideal places to make your notes. The following are popular techniques to use:

- **Circle** new vocabulary and key terms and write out their definitions. Use the symbol = to show words are synonyms.
- **Write questions** you have about the text.
- **Make connections** to your own knowledge and life experience.
- **Summarize main ideas** in only a few words. Use symbols such as = or ≠ to save space.
- **Agree or disagree** with the text and make comments. Use ✓ or X to show your opinion.
- **Number** the steps in a process, supporting details or examples, key points, and so on.
- **Draw symbols** such as stars and arrows to indicate important points, and underline main ideas and important details.

Tip Critical Thinking

Activity B on page 11 asks you to apply what you learned about annotating a text. Applying new information shows you understand the material, and it also helps you to remember it better.

A. The first part of Reading 1 has been annotated on page 11. Work with a partner. Decide which annotation technique from the skill box is used. Then write the correct technique.

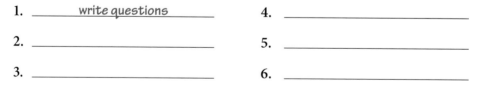

1. _____write questions_____

2. _____

3. _____

4. _____

5. _____

6. _____

Blogs and journalism need each other

① why?

Suggest to an old-school journalist that weblogs have anything to do with journalism and you'll be met with howls of derision. Amateur bloggers typically have no editorial oversight, no training in the craft, and no respect for the news media's rules and standards. <u>Does the free-for-all renegade publishing form known as blogging really have anything to do with journalism?</u> *③*

② traditional journalists think blogging ≠ journalism

Well, yes. Consider:

- At technology and media conferences, such as PopTech, South by Southwest, and Digital Hollywood, bloggers in the audience have reported conference events in real time, posting photographs, speaker transcripts, and summaries and analysis of key points a full day before readers could see comparable stories in the daily newspaper.

④ this is better than newspapers

- On July 16, 2003, blogger Andy Baio reported on the tragedy in which an elderly driver plowed through the Santa Monica Farmers' Market just outside Baio's office window. He had been walking down that street 20 minutes before. Baio described "the dead and dying" lying in the street and (relayed) firsthand reports from office co-workers who were eyewitnesses. He also posted a map of the accident scene, laid out a detailed chronology of events, and pointed to media coverage and photographs of the bloody scene.

⑤ bloggers can sometimes report the news with more in-depth detail than traditional journalists

⑥ relayed = passed on, communicated

B. Read and annotate two or three more paragraphs from Reading 1. Use at least five different annotation techniques.

READING 2 | Diary-Keeping Pet Project for Bloggers

VOCABULARY

Here are some words and phrases from Reading 2. Read the sentences. Then write each bold word or phrase next to the correct definition. You may need to change verbs to their base form.

1. In one recent year, Japanese **accounted for** 37 percent of all blog posts.

2. A team of researchers recently **compiled** a report that summarized how blogs are used in Japan.

3. Many people in the United States and Europe use their blogs to engage with others in political **discourse**.

4. A rapid growth in access to computers and other technology has resulted in a **proliferation** of personal Web journals.

5. Many people find that blogs are a great **medium** for recording their personal journals.

6. Some bloggers seem to enjoy fame and want to be celebrities, but many others want to keep their **anonymity**.

7. Using a computer can **transform** a person's diary from a handwritten paper journal to an electronic blog, complete with photos and music.

8. In their blogs, many people **reveal** personal feelings that they might have kept hidden before starting a journal.

9. A computer failure or power outage can **deny** bloggers the opportunity to update their journals.

10. Bloggers want to develop their own **distinctive** styles.

11. There are three simple steps you need to follow to **register** a new blog.

12. It isn't easy to **improvise** when you are making a speech.

a. _____ (*n.*) a big increase in number

b. _____ (*phr. v.*) to supply the amount of or explain

c. _____ (*n.*) discussion that is long and serious

d. _____ (*v.*) to put together from various information sources

e. _____ (*n.*) secrecy about one's name or who he or she really is

f. _____ (*v.*) put your information on an official list or website

g. _____ (*v.*) to make known

h. _____ (*n.*) a way of communication or an artistic method

i. _____ (*adj.*) unique, special, or uncommon

j. _____ (*v.*) to refuse to allow

k. _____ (*v.*) to completely change

l. _____ (*v.*) to speak or perform without planning in advance

This article from the English edition of the Japanese newspaper *Daily Yomiuri* looks at the phenomenon of Japanese-language blogs and how they differ from blogs in other languages and cultures.

Preview the three charts in the Reading. From the information in the charts, answer these questions.

1. Who blogs the most? _____

2. What do they write about? _____

3. Do they reveal their true identities? _____

CD 1
Track 4   **Read the article.**

Diary-Keeping Pet Project for Bloggers

1   According to U.S. blog survey company Technorati Inc., Japanese became the most common language used in blog posts in the fourth quarter of 2006. Japanese **accounted for** 37 percent of all blog posts. It eclipsed English with 36 percent. This figure is all the more

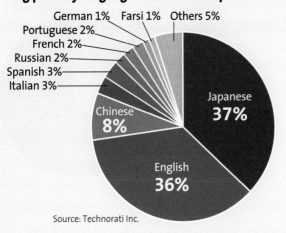

Blog posts by languages in the fourth quarter of 2006

German 1% Farsi 1% Others 5%
Portuguese 2%
French 2%
Russian 2%
Spanish 3%
Italian 3%
Chinese 8%
Japanese 37%
English 36%

Source: Technorati Inc.

remarkable when one considers that Japanese is spoken by only 1.8 percent of the world's population. Also, Japanese people only account for 7.1 percent of the global online population. It speaks volumes of the popularity of blogging in Japan, where many people send barrages of short text messages from their mobile phones.

2   According to Japan's Internal Affairs and Communications Ministry, about 3.35 million people had **registered** blogs as of the end of March 2005. This was also the year when *burogu*, the Japanese word for blog, was chosen as one of the year's top ten buzzwords. The Ministry estimated this number would top 7.8 million within two years, but this prediction ended up being short of the mark. By March 2006, Japanese blogs totalled 8.68 million, it said.

Roots of Japanese blog culture

3   Japan's blogging culture has evolved in a starkly different manner from that in other nations. Japanese bloggers are more into keeping diaries about their daily goings-on, which are mostly trivial matters. According to the "Blog White Paper 2007" **compiled** by Nomura Research Institute Ltd. and Six Apart Ltd., 75 percent of Japanese blog content is about

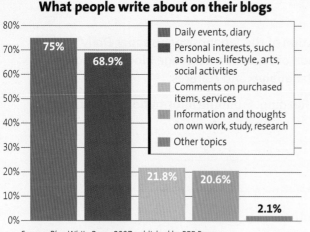

What people write about on their blogs

- Daily events, diary
- Personal interests, such as hobbies, lifestyle, arts, social activities
- Comments on purchased items, services
- Information and thoughts on own work, study, research
- Other topics

75%
68.9%
21.8%
20.6%
2.1%

Source: *Blog White Paper 2007* published by RBB Press

everyday events or diaries. Writing a diary does not require any special skill, knowledge, or experience. This makes it easier for many Japanese to start their own blogs.

4   By contrast, many U.S. and European blogs are journalistic or opinion-oriented. Jason Karlin is an associate professor of cultural history and gender studies at Tokyo University. He commented on this topic in an e-mail. "U.S. blogs appear more journalistic and topical because political **discourse** within the United States has become increasingly more divisive over the last decade." Karlin also said blogs presented information and perspectives that were not usually available in the mainstream media in the United States.

5   Another characteristic of Japanese blogs, according to Karlin, is to use many photos. He said the photos are "an extension of the diary-like desire to document everyday life." They are also a product of the **proliferation** of cell phones equipped with cameras.

6   But why is Japanese blogging culture so different from, say, that of the United States? Many experts believe the answer is deeply embedded in traditions that date back hundreds of years. Senshu University Professor Kiyomi Yamashita says Japan's millennium-old diary culture has a tremendous influence over blogging. "Japanese use diaries as a **medium** for writing down things like changes of season and about nature. This is linked to present-day blogging culture," she said.

7   Japanese diary culture can be traced to the Heian period (794–1192). In the Heian period, women expressed their personal feelings in *kana* characters[1]. They wrote about court lifestyles and romances. Another form of diary was used by court noblemen for keeping records of factual events in *kanji* characters[2].

8   Another traditional element linked to Japanese blogging is the use of **anonymity** when participating in a creative activity. Yuji Wada is the head researcher at the Institute for Future Technology. He said the classical Japanese poetic form of *renga*, in which several people **improvise** lines to create one poem, is similar to the Japanese blogosphere made up of blogs, postings, and interconnections. For example, *Kasagi renga* is a type of linked verse practiced from the Middle Ages. In this type of

Status of Internet users at community sites, such as blogs and social networking sites

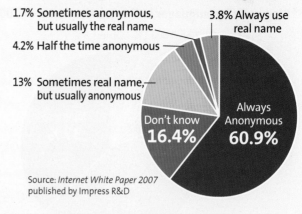

1.7% Sometimes anonymous, but usually the real name

3.8% Always use real name

4.2% Half the time anonymous

13% Sometimes real name, but usually anonymous

Don't know 16.4%

Always Anonymous 60.9%

Source: *Internet White Paper 2007* published by Impress R&D

[1] **kana characters:** symbols that represent syllables in Japanese writing
[2] **kanji characters:** a Japanese system of writing based on Chinese symbols that represent words and ideas

poem, anyone, regardless of rank, can take part in reading a verse while hiding his or her face with a hat. "It's widely believed the Internet has ushered in an anonymous community where anyone can participate freely regardless of . . . social standing, but Japan has had that tradition [for centuries]," Wada said.

Adding a woman's touch

9   The use of kana made it easier for women in the Heian period to write diaries. This is similar to how the increasing availability of personal computers, digital cameras, and other blog tools has **transformed** weblogs into a common medium used by modern Japanese women. According to major Internet service provider Rakuten Inc., women account for 66.2 percent of those using its blog services. "Housewife" is the most common category of Rakuten bloggers.

10   Yamashita is a specialist in cognitive psychology. She said studies of autobiographical memory proved women use more detailed and complicated expressions than men when they remember the past. "Women tend to have a stronger desire to write about and **reveal** their feelings. They also are better at talking about their experiences. This probably encourages women to blog about their daily lives," she added.

11   Karlin said Japan has seen a rising wave of female bloggers. This is because it is the only postindustrial country where large numbers of highly educated women are unemployed after they get married. "Through blogging, these women are expressing the desire to be productive participants in a society that seeks to **deny** them a position outside of their roles as wives and/or mothers," he said.

. . .

Blending cultures

12   Since the term *weblog* was first used in the United States a decade ago, the concept of blogging has become deeply rooted in Japanese society. Japanese are said to have a penchant[3] for adopting foreign cultures. They blend them with their own traditions and then develop a **distinctive** mix of both.

13   "Naturally, there are many Japanese who are keen to express themselves, but there was no place where they could do so," Wada said. "In the same way [Heian] people developed kana from kanji introduced from China, Japan adapted the Internet, which developed in the United States, to create its own blogging style. Blogging has flourished with a distinctive cultural trait. It is a unique feminine style of expressing oneself."

[3] **penchant**: a special liking for something

MAIN IDEAS

Go back and skim the article. Annotate the text by underlining the main ideas for each section of Reading 2. Then write a sentence summarizing each main idea.

1. Opening (Paragraphs 1 and 2)

    _____

    _____

2. Roots of Japanese blog culture

_____

_____

3. Adding a woman's touch

_____

_____

4. Blending cultures

_____

_____

DETAILS

Answer these questions.

1. According to the first chart, what were the top three languages for blog posts in the fourth quarter of 2006?

_____

_____

2. Why is it surprising that there are more blog posts in Japanese than in any other language?

_____

_____

3. Was Japan's Internal Affairs and Communications Ministry correct in estimating there would be more than 7.8 million registered Japanese blogs by 2007? Why or why not?

_____

_____

4. What is the difference between most Japanese blogs and many U.S. or European blogs?

_____

_____

5. What historical aspects of Japanese culture have influenced Japanese blogging the most?

_____

_____

6. According to Professor Yamashita, how do women differ from men when they remember the past?

_____

_____

7. Generally, how are women in Japan unique compared to women in other post-industrial countries?

_____

_____

 WHAT DO YOU THINK?

Tip for Success

Evaluate your own learning by asking yourself how well you have done on an activity. Identify your areas of weakness so you can focus on these areas in the future.

A. Discuss the questions in a group. Then choose one question and write one or two paragraphs in response.

1. Have you ever written a blog? Is its content public or private? Why?

2. In your opinion, why are the bloggers in the article allowing the world to read about their daily lives?

3. Why do you think so many people who write blogs wish to remain anonymous? What are the pros and cons of remaining anonymous?

B. Think about both Reading 1 and Reading 2 as you discuss the questions.

1. What are popular blogs in your community or among your friends? Are they more similar to those described in Reading 1 or those described in Reading 2? How?

2. Is the quality of news, information, and literature available in blogs of a higher quality than in traditional media? Explain your answer.

Language is often remembered and used in groups of words called **collocations**. Using collocations will make your writing more natural. However, if words are put together that are not collocations, your writing may not sound natural. Consider the example below. The words *strong* and *powerful* each collocate with some words, but not with others.

	coffee	computer	man
strong	✓	✗	✓
powerful	✗	✓	✓

✓ This is a **strong cup of coffee**.
✗ This is a **powerful cup of coffee**.
✓ I have a **powerful computer**.
✗ I have a **strong computer**.

Use a dictionary and look for patterns to help recognize collocations. Some common collocation patterns with nouns include:

Adjective + noun
Blogs have given the **silent majority** the ability to create works of literature.

Noun + noun
All you need is a computer with an **Internet connection** to become a blogger.

Verb + noun
Many young women **keep a diary** about the daily events of their lives.

A. Choose a word from the box to form a common collocation with each word below. Skim Reading 1 and Reading 2 to confirm your answers.

cold	device	media	ten
coverage	discourse	points	wave

1. top _____

2. rising _____

3. political _____

4. key _____

5. media _____

6. freezing _____

7. news _____

8. mobile _____

B. Circle the word that forms a common collocation. Skim Reading 1 and Reading 2 to confirm your answers.

1. Blogs often contain information and stories that are not found in the

   ___ media.
   a. mainstream
   b. normal
   c. ordinary

2. People using the Internet have the ability to report events in ___ time.
   a. real
   b. actual
   c. true

3. Many ordinary people are now playing a(n) ___ role in citizen journalism

   on the Internet.
   a. energetic
   b. busy
   c. active

4. My favorite blog reports on ___ acts of kindness.
   a. unsystematic
   b. random
   c. accidental

5. Bloggers and journalists share many of the same ___ of the trade.
   a. techniques
   b. tricks
   c. habits

WRITING

Writing Skill | **Writing about a process**

A **process essay** describes how something is done. The following are the parts of a process essay.

The **introduction** contains introductory information such as:

- why the topic is important
- why the process is done (the purpose or reason for it)
- who does it
- what situations it is done in
- the opinion of the writer

The introduction also states the main idea of the essay in the **thesis statement**, which:

- names the process
- shows that there is a series of steps

Each of the **main body** paragraphs usually:

- describes one of the major steps in the process
- uses time words to make the sequence of the steps clear

Common time words	
Transitions **(to introduce a new sentence)**	**Subordinators** **(to introduce an adverb clause)**
afterward	after
eventually	as soon as
the first step	before
gradually	by the time
later	once
now	when
then	while

The **conclusion**:

- restates the main idea of the essay
- may remind readers why the process is important
- may encourage readers to try the process

A. Read the sample essay posted on a "How to" website. Then analyze it by completing the outline on page 22.

How to Create a Blog

Home   Log in

About

Links

Archives

January

February

March

April

May

June

July

August

September

October

November

December

1   People today are turning to the Internet as one of their major sources of news and entertainment, and often they are getting that news through blogs. Blogs are well known as personal websites that can be updated regularly and easily just like a journal or a diary, and they are an essential alternative to traditional media as a source of information. The greatest advantage to blogs is that it is quite simple for almost anybody to set up a blog in just a few easy steps.

2   The first step in creating a blog is deciding on a theme. With a theme, others who are also interested in that topic will be naturally drawn to the blog as a source of information. This is because when people look for information in search engines such as Google, blogs that focus on that topic will be found in the search results. For example, if the blog focuses on Shiba Inu dogs, a search in Google for *Shiba Inu* will likely result in people finding it.

3   After deciding on a theme for the blog, the next step is to register with a blogging website and create the blog. There are many blog creation websites available, and it is an easy process to register a new blog. Usually there is a big button that says "Join Now" or "Create Your Blog Now." The person just has to click that button and follow the on-screen directions. Once the blog is registered, the new blogger will be able to design the blog and create a personal profile to go with it. As soon as the blog is created, the writer can start writing.

4   One of the last things to remember is to maintain the blog on a regular basis. People soon lose interest in blogs that are not up to date. Bloggers should write often and include pictures in their posts. Following a good post, bloggers are sure to receive some interesting comments on what they have written. When a blog is receiving a lot of comments and has many readers, it can be considered successful. Afterward, it's even possible that the blogger could become famous.

5   It is simple to set up a blog, and blogging is an important way for average people to communicate with the world. Writers who have a theme, create an interesting website, and write regularly are sure to have a successful blog. It would be terrible if this important source of up-to-date information on many topics were not available on the Internet to people around the world.

Process essay outline

Introduction	Introductory information
	Thesis statement
Main body	First major step
	Supporting details
	Second major step
	Supporting details
	Third major step
	Supporting details
Conclusion	Restatement of the main idea of the essay
	Added thoughts or comments

B. Work with a partner or in a group. Discuss the sample essay in Activity A by using the completed outline to answer the questions.

1. What is the process described in this essay?

2. What are the major steps in the process? Are they logical? Why or why not?

3. Does the writer tell why this process is important?

C. Look again at the sample process essay in Activity A. With a partner, complete the following steps.

1. Underline the time words.

2. Do you notice grammatical patterns and how they are used? Discuss them.

Grammar   Adjective phrases

Subject adjective clauses* are clauses that describe or modify a noun or noun phrase. They include a relative pronoun (*who*, *which*, or *that*) and a verb or verb phrase. The subject of the clause is the relative pronoun. For example:

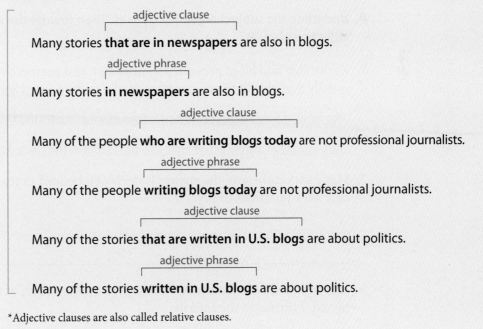

adjective clause

I know a journalist **who writes for an Australian newspaper**.

To avoid wordiness and vary the sentence structure in your writing, you can often reduce subject adjective clauses to **adjective phrases**.

Subject adjective clauses with relative pronoun + *be*

An adjective phrase can be made if the original adjective clause uses a relative pronoun + the verb *be* + either a prepositional phrase, a continuous verb, or a passive verb. Form the adjective phrase by omitting the relative pronoun and the form of *be*.

adjective clause

Many stories **that are in newspapers** are also in blogs.

adjective phrase

Many stories **in newspapers** are also in blogs.

adjective clause

Many of the people **who are writing blogs today** are not professional journalists.

adjective phrase

Many of the people **writing blogs today** are not professional journalists.

adjective clause

Many of the stories **that are written in U.S. blogs** are about politics.

adjective phrase

Many of the stories **written in U.S. blogs** are about politics.

*Adjective clauses are also called relative clauses.

Subject adjective clauses with relative pronoun + verb

If the original adjective clause does not contain the verb *be* and the verb is in the simple present or simple past tense, drop the subject pronoun and change the verb to the *-ing* form.

adjective clause

Blogs **that inform people about the news** are competing with traditional newspapers.

adjective phrase

Blogs **informing people about the news** are competing with traditional newspapers.

adjective clause

Ten years ago there were very few people **who wrote about their lives online.**

adjective phrase

Ten years ago there were very few people **writing about their lives online.**

However, this does not work for subject adjective clauses that are about a single action in the past.

✓ The men **who saw the accident** were old.
✗ The men **seeing the accident** were old.

A. Underline the subject adjective clauses. Then rewrite the sentences with adjective phrases.

1. Karlin also said blogs presented information and perspectives <u>that were not usually available in the mainstream media in the United States.</u>

   <u>Karlin also said blogs presented information and perspectives</u>

   <u>not usually available in the mainstream media in the United States.</u>

2. Many experts believe the answer is deeply embedded in traditions that date back hundreds of years.

   _____

   _____

3. Like hundreds of others who wanted to learn the names of the songs played, I turned to the Internet.

   _____

   _____

4. The scene was carried live via video from a bystander who was playing the role of journalist by shooting the action with his portable camera phone.

_____

_____

B. Underline the adjective phrases. Then rewrite the sentences in your notebook with subject adjective clauses.

1. Japanese became the most common language <u>used in blog posts</u> in the fourth quarter of 2006.

   Japanese became the most common language that was used in blog posts in the fourth quarter of 2006.

2. Does the free-for-all renegade publishing form known as blogging really have anything to do with journalism?

3. It is a world of micro-content delivered to niche audiences.

4. Simply put, it refers to individuals playing an active role in the process of collecting, reporting, sorting, analyzing, and disseminating news and information.

Unit Assignment | Write a process essay

 In this assignment, you will write a process essay for the fictional blog *How to Do It!* As you prepare your essay, think about the Unit Question, "Why do people read and write blogs?" and refer to the Self-Assessment checklist on page 26. Use information from Readings 1 and 2 and your work in this unit to support your ideas.

For alternative unit assignments, see the *Q: Skills for Success Teacher's Handbook.*

PLAN AND WRITE

A. **BRAINSTORM** Follow these steps to help you gather ideas for your process essay.

1. In your notebook, brainstorm a list of activities that you know how to do. You can include anything from cooking a specific dish to playing a sport.

2. Ask and answer questions in a group about how to do these activities.

3. Choose the activity that interests your group the most.

B. PLAN **Follow these steps to plan your essay.**

1. In your notebook, write a list of steps for the activity you have chosen. Try to combine the information into three or four major steps.

2. Organize your essay by writing your ideas in an outline in your notebook. Refer to the process essay outline on page 22 for guidance.

Your Writing Process

For this activity, you could also use Stage 1C, *Writing a First Draft* in *Q Online Practice.*

C. WRITE **Write your essay in your notebook. Use your outline from Activity B, the information in the Writing Skill on page 20, and the vocabulary and grammar you learned in the unit. Look at the Self-Assessment checklist below to guide your writing.**

REVISE AND EDIT

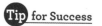 **for Success**

Reading a classmate's work is a great way to learn. Identify what your classmates are doing well in their writing, and apply this to your own work.

A. PEER REVIEW **Read a partner's essay. Answer the questions and discuss them with your partner.**

1. Is the process described easy to follow? If not, where could it be clearer?

2. Are there adequate supporting details for each major step in the process?

3. Are time words used to effectively sequence the process?

4. Would you enjoy trying or doing what the writer has described? Why or why not?

B. REWRITE **Review the answers to the questions in Activity A. You may want to revise and rewrite your essay.**

C. EDIT **Complete the Self-Assessment checklist as you prepare to write the final draft of your essay. Be prepared to hand in your work or discuss it in class.**

SELF-ASSESSMENT		
Yes	No	
☐	☐	Does the introduction contain information such as why the topic is important or who does it?
☐	☐	Does each of the body paragraphs describe one of the major steps in the process?
☐	☐	Does the conclusion restate the main idea?
☐	☐	Are adjective clauses and adjective phrases used correctly?
☐	☐	Are the collocations appropriate and natural?
☐	☐	Did you check the essay for punctuation, spelling, and grammar?

Track Your Success

Circle the words you learned in this unit.

Nouns
anonymity
commentary AWL
discourse
medium 🗝 AWL
proliferation
relevance AWL

Verbs
acknowledge 🗝 AWL
compile AWL
confine AWL
convey
deny 🗝 AWL
disseminate
establish 🗝 AWL
improvise
register 🗝 AWL
relay
reveal 🗝 AWL
transform 🗝 AWL

Phrasal Verb
account for

Adjectives
distinctive AWL
diverse AWL
random AWL
renegade

Adverb
ultimately 🗝 AWL

🗝 Oxford 3000™ words

AWL Academic Word List

For more information on the Oxford 3000™ and the AWL, see page xi.

Check (✓) the skills you learned. If you need more work on a skill, refer to the pages in parentheses.

READING ●	I can annotate a text. (p. 10)
VOCABULARY ●	I can recognize and use collocations. (p. 18)
WRITING ●	I can write about a process. (p. 20)
GRAMMAR ●	I can use adjective clauses and phrases. (pp. 23–24)
LEARNING OUTCOME ●	I can develop a process essay describing how to do an activity with which I am familiar.

UNIT 2

Language

READING ●	distinguishing main ideas from details
VOCABULARY ●	using a thesaurus
WRITING ●	writing an extended definition
GRAMMAR ●	contrast and concession connectors

Prepare an extended definition of a word or concept from a different language or culture for which there is no equivalent term or idea in English.

Unit QUESTION

What happens when a language disappears?

PREVIEW THE UNIT

A Discuss these questions with your classmates.

Which languages can you speak? Which is spoken by the most people? What other languages would you like to learn? Why?

Do you think your identity is related to the language you speak? Why or why not?

Look at the photo. Why does the man have a microphone? What is the woman doing?

B Discuss the Unit Question above with your classmates.

🔊 Listen to *The Q Classroom*, **Track 5 on CD 1,** to hear other answers.

29

C Work with a partner. Read the customs from various countries. Decide where each custom belongs in the chart and write its letter. Then add your own examples.

CUSTOMS QUIZ

a. In Bulgaria, shaking your head back and forth means yes, and up and down means no.

b. In Thailand, yellow is the color for Monday.

c. In South Korea, it is polite to leave some rice at the bottom of your bowl.

d. In France, people kiss on the cheek—sometimes three or four times—when they see each other.

e. In the U.S., it can be threatening to stand closer than 18 inches to someone you don't know very well.

f. In Japan, it is rude to wear your shoes inside someone's house.

Feature of Culture	Custom/Behavior	Your Example
1. Greetings	d	A firm handshake is considered professional in the United States.
2. Styles of dress		
3. Personal space		
4. Gestures		
5. Politeness		
6. Colors		

D With your partner or in a group, discuss these questions.

1. Do you think that any of the various customs listed in Activity C are related to language? Which ones? Why or why not?

2. How does your behavior change when you speak a different language?

READING 1 | History of the Maori Language

VOCABULARY

Here are some words and phrases from Reading 1. Read their definitions. Then complete each sentence. You may need to change the form of the word or phrase to make the sentence grammatically correct.

assimilate (*v.*) to become a part of a country or community rather than remaining in a separate group

confine (*v.*) to keep something inside the limits of an activity, subject, or area

divorced from (*phr.*) appearing not to be affected by something; separate from

ethnicity (*n.*) the fact of belonging to a particular race or culture

initiative (*n.*) a new plan for dealing with a particular problem or for achieving a goal

integral (*adj.*) being an essential part of something

oblige (*v.*) to force someone to do something, sometimes by law

persist (*v.*) to continue to do something despite difficulties; to continue to exist

predominant (*adj.*) having more power or influence than others

revival (*n.*) the process of something becoming or being made popular or fashionable again

suppress (*v.*) to prevent something from growing, developing, or continuing

target (*v.*) to choose or single out for a particular purpose

1. Words or phrases that are out of style sometimes experience a

   _____ and become popular again.

2. The language spoken by most of the people in a country is the

   _____ language of the country.

3. It is hard to _____ a language to a certain community and

   never allow it to be spoken outside that place.

4. A government _____ can help to create new laws, for

   language programs in schools, for example.

5. Many people are proud of their _____, that is, their racial

   and cultural background.

6. In some parts of the United States, some people want to _____ the use of languages other than English in public schools.

7. Learning a new language is one way that people can blend in with, or _____ into, a new society.

8. It takes a long time to learn a new language, so you must _____ by taking classes and practicing speaking.

9. Some people think language lessons should _____ very young children because they learn new languages so fast.

10. When they move to a new place, people often worry that they will forget their old ways of doing things and become _____ their culture.

11. A person's language is such a central and _____ part of her culture that she should try to preserve it.

12. Some parents do not believe their children should _____ to learn a language other than the one they speak at home.

PREVIEW READING 1

The original people of New Zealand are the Maori. They call their language *te reo Maori*. You are going to read a page from the government website New Zealand History Online that describes the history of the Maori language for more than 200 years, from the time Europeans first settled in New Zealand.

Skim the page from the website. Answer these questions.

1. Who is the Web page written for?

2. Where in the text do you expect to find the main ideas?

History of the Maori Language

Decline and revival

1   In the last 200 years, the history of the Maori language (*te reo Maori*) has been one of ups and downs. At the beginning of the 19th century, it was the **predominant** language spoken in *Aotearoa* (the Maori name for New Zealand). As more English speakers arrived in New Zealand, the Maori language was increasingly confined to Maori communities. By the mid-20th century, there were concerns that the language was dying out. Major **initiatives** launched from the 1980s have brought about a **revival** of the Maori language. In the early 21st century, more than 130,000 people of Maori **ethnicity** could speak and understand Maori, one of the three official languages of New Zealand.

Aotearoa (New Zealand)

Maori: A common means of communication

2   For the first half century or so of the European settlement of New Zealand, the Maori language was a common way of communicating. Early settlers[1] had to learn to speak the language if they wished to trade with Maori because settlers were dependent on Maori for many things at this time.

3   Up to the 1870s, it was not unusual for government officials, missionaries, and prominent *Pakeha*[2] to speak Maori.

Their children often grew up with Maori children and were among the most fluent European speakers and writers of Maori. Particularly in rural areas, the interaction between Maori and Pakeha was constant.

Korero Pakeha ("Speak English!")

4   Pakeha were in the majority by the early 1860s, and English became the dominant language of New Zealand. Increasingly, the Maori language **was confined** to Maori communities that existed separately from the Pakeha majority.

5   The Maori language was not understood as an essential expression and envelope of Maori culture, important for the Maori in maintaining their pride and identity as a

---

[1] **settler:** a person who goes to live in a new country
[2] *Pakeha:* Maori word for people who were originally from Europe and also for the English language. Today it refers to any non-Maori.

people. Maori was now officially discouraged. Many Maori themselves questioned its relevance in a Pakeha-dominated world where the most important value seemed to be to get ahead as an individual.

6　The Maori language **was suppressed** in schools, either formally or informally, so that Maori youngsters could **assimilate** with the wider community. Some older Maori still recall being punished for speaking their language. Many Maori parents encouraged their children to learn English and even to turn away from other aspects of Maori custom. Increasing numbers of Maori people learned English because they needed it in the workplace or places of recreation such as the football field. "Korero Pakeha" (Speak English) was seen as essential for Maori people.

A language lives

7　Despite the emphasis on speaking English, the Maori language **persisted**. Until the Second World War[3] most Maori spoke Maori as their first language. They worshipped[4] in Maori, and Maori was the language of the marae[5]. Political meetings were conducted in Maori, and there were Maori newspapers and literature. More importantly, it was the language of the home, and parents could pass on the language to their children.

The lure of the city

8　The Second World War brought about momentous changes for Maori society. There was plenty of work available in towns and cities due to the war, and Maori moved into urban areas in greater numbers. Before the war, about 75 percent of Maori lived in rural areas. Two decades later, approximately 60 percent lived in urban centers.

9　English was the language of urban New Zealand—at work, in school, and in leisure activities. Maori children went to city schools where Maori was unheard of in teaching programs. The new, enforced contact of large numbers of Maori and Pakeha caused much strain and stress, and the language was one of the things to suffer.

10　The number of Maori speakers began to decline rapidly. By the 1980s, less than 20 percent of Maori knew enough of their traditional language to be regarded as native speakers. Even for those people, Maori was ceasing to be the language of everyday use in the home. Some urbanized Maori people became **divorced from** their language and culture. Others maintained contact with their original communities, returning for important hui (meetings) and tangihanga (funerals) or allowing the kaumatua (elders) at home to adopt or care for their children.

Seeds of change

11　From the 1970s, many Maori people reasserted their identity as Maori. An emphasis on the language as an **integral** part of Maori culture was central to this. Maori leaders were increasingly recognizing the dangers of the loss of Maori language. New groups emerged that were committed to strengthening Maori culture and the language.

12　Major Maori language recovery programs began in the 1980s. Many **were targeted**

---

[3] **Second World War:** also called World War II (1939–1945)
[4] **worship:** to pray
[5] **marae:** Maori word for a meetinghouse or a place for formal discussions

at young people and the education system, such as a system of primary schooling[6] in a Maori-language environment.

Legislating for change

13 Efforts to secure the survival of the Maori language stepped up in 1985. In that year the Waitangi Tribunal[7] heard the Te Reo Maori claim, which asserted that the Maori language was a *taonga* (a treasure) that the government **was obliged** to protect under the Treaty of Waitangi. The Waitangi Tribunal agreed with the Maori and recommended a number of laws and policies. In 1987, Maori was made an official language of New Zealand.

14 There are now many institutions working to recover the language. Even so, the decline of the Maori language has only just been arrested. There is a resurgence of Maori, but to survive as a language, it needs enough fluent speakers of all ages as well as the respect and support of the wider English-speaking and multi-ethnic New Zealand community.

[6] **primary school:** elementary school, starting at about age 5 and continuing until age 12 to 14

[7] **Waitangi Tribunal:** a court created to honor the Waitangi Treaty of 1840 between Great Britain and the Maori people. Under the treaty, the Maori accepted British rule, and the British agreed to treat the Maori fairly.

MAIN IDEAS

Tip for Success

Making an outline of the main ideas helps you read actively. You can use subheadings to organize your ideas.

Match each subheading with the correct main idea on page 36.

____ 1. Decline and revival

____ 2. Maori: A common means of communication

____ 3. *Korero Pakeha* ("Speak English!")

____ 4. A language lives

____ 5. The lure of the city

____ 6. Seeds of change

____ 7. Legislating for change

a. After English became the dominant language, Maori was suppressed and many Maori had to learn English.

b. The Maori language has had periods of use and disuse over the last two centuries, but it is currently undergoing a revival.

c. After the Second World War, the majority of Maori lived in cities, and some lost their knowledge of their traditional language and customs.

d. At first, Europeans used Maori to communicate with the local people.

e. The Maori language survived in public and private places.

f. In 1987, Maori became an official language of New Zealand, but more speakers and more support are necessary for its survival.

g. More recently, the Maori have begun to reassert their identity as Maori by learning and speaking the Maori language.

DETAILS

Find two pieces of evidence (examples, facts, or quotations) from Reading 1 that support these statements. Write them below the statement.

1. Europeans who lived in New Zealand before the 1870s learned Maori.

   a. _____

   b. _____

2. Both the Maori and the Pakeha were responsible for the increase in the use of English after 1860.

   a. _____

   b. _____

3. The Maori language survived until the mid-20th century because most Maori lived in rural areas, where Maori was still an important language for communication.

   a. _____

   b. _____

4. As the 20th century progressed, there were fewer native speakers of Maori, but some Maori in the cities maintained a basic knowledge of their language.

   a. _____

   b. _____

5. Starting in the 1970s, the Maori realized that they needed to save their language in order to maintain their cultural identity.

   a. _____

   b. _____

6. The Waitangi Tribunal helped to make Maori an official language and raise its status in New Zealand.

   a. _____

   b. _____

WHAT DO YOU THINK?

Discuss the questions in a group. Then choose one question and write freely for five to ten minutes in response.

1. Do you think the efforts to save the Maori language will continue to be successful? Why or why not?

2. Is it important for society to try to save languages that are in danger of disappearing? Should governments create laws to encourage the protection of endangered languages?

3. What would be the advantages and disadvantages of having one world language?

Main ideas are the major points that support the focus of a piece of writing. If you can find the main ideas and distinguish them from the supporting details, you will understand the purpose and focus of the writing. In most texts, you can find main ideas by:

- paying attention to repeated vocabulary, which may be key words
- looking for words in the headline or title of the text
- reading subheadings and the captions of any graphs or illustrations
- watching for words that introduce conclusions and main ideas, such as *therefore, as a result, so, (more/most) importantly, finally,* and *to conclude*
- focusing on words in bold, italics, or different colors

The position of the main ideas may depend on the **genre**, or **type of text**, because there are different ways of organizing information.

Academic writing is divided into paragraphs that usually contain one main idea. The main idea is often stated near the beginning of the paragraph and summarized at the end, so read the first and last sentences of each paragraph carefully. Remember that all the main ideas in the text are usually connected to the central focus, argument, or thesis of the paper. This is often stated near the end of the introduction.

News articles, whether in print or on the Web, have to catch readers' attention and then keep them reading. They frequently use headlines and subheadings to give main ideas.

Business communication has to be brief, efficient, and persuasive, so main ideas are often stated early and repeated at the end of the text. Bullet points, bold text, and repetition are often used to draw the readers' attention.

A. Read the excerpts. Identify the genre of the writing. Then write the main idea in a sentence.

1.

> When people move to a new culture, they usually experience a series of different feelings as they adjust to their new surroundings. A new culture is not necessarily another country or a place where another language is spoken. Therefore, this adjustment can occur in any situation where a person's normal rules of behavior no longer work. The process of adapting to these differences has four stages and is called culture shock.

Genre: _____

Main idea: _____

_____

2.

> **Solution:** *Say It Again* Language Learning Program
> The company is interested in investing in a language learning program.
> There are two suitable programs available: *Say It Again* and *Language Now*. We recommend *Say It Again* for these reasons:
> · cost—19 percent less
> · technical support—included in price
> *Say It Again* will meet our needs at a lower cost and with better service.

Genre: _____

Main idea: _____

_____

3.

> LANGUAGE RESEARCHER FACES CHALLENGES
> Dr. Wilde's research is certainly exciting. It could change the way we think about the original inhabitants of New Zealand. But it is not without difficulty. "Of course, the greatest challenge will be getting the local chiefs to talk to me," Wilde admitted. "Without their cooperation, my project can't go forward." Gaining the trust of the local population is just one of the many challenges facing Dr. Wilde in his research.

Genre: _____

Main idea: _____

_____

4.

> Languages change through two processes: internal change and language contact. Internal change occurs slowly over time as words or phrases shift in meaning or grammatical structure. For instance, the Old English *a nadder*, meaning a snake, gradually became *an adder*, the modern word, when the *n* became attached to the article. The second source of change is external, and it occurs when another, usually more powerful, language comes into contact with it.

Genre: _____

Main idea: _____

_____

5.

> **New Zealand in the 1830s**
>
> New Zealand was largely a Maori world in the 1830s. There were perhaps 100,000 Maori, divided into major *iwi* or tribes. Relations between groups could be tense, and conflict was common. Maori traditions and social structures prevailed, but more Europeans arrived in New Zealand throughout the decade. There were about 200 in the North Island in the early 1830s. By 1839, there may have been 2,000 throughout the country (including around 1,400 in the North Island), attracted by trade and settlement.

Genre: _____

Main idea: _____

_____

Tip Critical Thinking

In Activity B, you will make generalizations about where main ideas are found in different genres. When you generalize, you use specific information to make general rules. This shows you understand the information in a thorough way.

B. How would you find the main ideas in the following types of writing? Discuss your answers with a partner.

1. an email
2. a business letter
3. an advertisement
4. a newspaper editorial
5. a blog post

READING 2 | When Languages Die

VOCABULARY

Here are some words and phrases from Reading 2. Read the sentences. Then write each bold word or phrase next to the correct definition. You may need to change verbs to their base form and nouns to the singular form.

1. Some researchers hope that plants from the Amazon rain forest can provide a **cure** for cancer.

2. Some drug makers have **exploited** the knowledge that people of the Amazon have about native plants to develop new drugs.

3. The **indigenous** people of the Amazon know more about its native plants than researchers from other countries do.

4. People can still **retain** some traditional knowledge even if they give up some of their old ways of doing things.

5. It can be hard for people to resist doing what others ask, but sometimes we must be strong **in the face of** pressure.

6. Old ways of doing things are **in jeopardy** when the only people who know those traditions grow old and die.

7. People may **abandon** their native languages if they think they are useless.

8. You cannot simply **substitute** words from one language into another.

9. Many groups have made a **shift** away from the traditional hunter-gatherer lifestyle.

10. Many scientists believe that recent changes should be a **wake-up call** that gets the attention of people all over the world.

11. If we take the most negative view of the future, we can picture a disastrous **scenario**.

12. The loss of large parts of the rain forest has reduced the **habitats** of many native Amazon species.

a. _____ (*phr.*) in a dangerous position or situation and likely to be lost or harmed

b. _____ (*n.*) a description of how things might happen in the future

c. _____ (*n.*) a medicine or medical treatment for an illness

d. _____ (*n.*) a place where a particular type of animal or plant is normally found

e. _____ (*phr.*) despite (problems, difficulties, etc.)

f. _____ (*n.*) an event that makes people realize that there is a problem they need to do something about

g. _____ (*v.*) to leave a thing or place; to stop supporting or believing in something

h. _____ (*v.*) to use in place of

i. _____ (*v.*) to use something in order to gain as much from it as possible

j. _____ (*v.*) to keep

k. _____ (*n.*) a change in position or direction

l. _____ (*adj.*) belonging to a particular place rather than coming to it from somewhere else

In his book *When Languages Die*, linguistics professor K. David Harrison examines the traditional knowledge that is lost when a language becomes extinct (that is, when nobody speaks it anymore). What knowledge do you think is lost "when languages die"?

CD 1
Track 7   **Read the book excerpt.**

When Languages Die

**K. David Harrison,
Associate Professor of Linguistics**

1   What exactly do we stand to lose when languages vanish? It has become a cliché[1] to talk about a **cure** for cancer that may be found in the Amazon rain forest, perhaps from a medicinal plant known only to local shamans[2] (Plotkin 1993). But pharmaceutical companies have spared no efforts to get at this knowledge and in many cases have **exploited** it to develop useful drugs. An estimated $85 billion in profits per year is made on medicines made from plants that were first known to **indigenous** peoples for their healing properties (Posey 1990).

2   An astonishing 87 percent of the world's plant and animal species have not yet been identified, named, described, or classified by modern science (Hawksworth & Kalin-Arroyo 1995). Therefore, we need to look to indigenous cultures to fill in our vast knowledge gap about the natural world. But can they **retain** their knowledge **in the face of** global linguistic homogenization[3]?

3   Much—if not most—of what we know about the natural world lies completely outside of science textbooks, libraries, and databases, existing only in unwritten languages in people's memories. It is only one generation away from extinction and always **in jeopardy** of not being passed on. This immense knowledge base remains largely unexplored and uncataloged. We can only hope to access it if the people who possess and nurture it can be encouraged to continue to do so.

4   If people feel their knowledge is worth keeping, they will keep it. If they are told, or come to believe, that it is useless in the modern world, they may well **abandon** it. Traditional knowledge is not always easily transferred from small, endangered languages to large, global ones. How can that be true if any idea is expressible in any language? Couldn't Solomon Islanders talk about the behavior patterns of fish in English just as easily as

---

[1] **cliché:** a phrase or saying that has been used so many times that it no longer has any real meaning or interest
[2] **shamans:** traditional healers or medicine men

[3] **homogenization:** a process in which everything becomes the same

in Marovo, their native language? I argue that when small communities abandon their languages and switch to English or Spanish, there is also massive disruption of the transfer of traditional knowledge across generations. This arises in part from the way knowledge is packaged in a particular language.

5　Consider Western !Xoon, a small language of Namibia (the exclamation mark is a click sound). In !Xoon, clouds are called "rain houses." By learning the word for *cloud*, a !Xoon-speaking child automatically gets (for free) the extra information that clouds contain and are the source of rain. An English child learning the word *cloud* gets no information about rain and has to learn on her own that rain comes from clouds.

6　Languages package and structure knowledge in particular ways. You cannot merely **substitute** labels or names from another language and hold onto all of the implicit, hidden knowledge that resides in a taxonomy, or naming system. Still, each language and indigenous people is unique, and language shift takes place at different speeds and under very different conditions. Can we then predict how much traditional knowledge will successfully be transferred and how much will be lost?

7　Some scientists have tried to do just that. The Bari language (1,500–2,500 speakers) of Venezuela was studied by linguists who asked how much knowledge of the plant world was being lost and how much retained. The Bari live in a close relationship with the rainforest and have learned to use many of its plants for food, material goods, medicine, and construction of houses. One scientist found that the loss of Bari traditional knowledge corresponded with decreasing use of forest resources and a **shift** from the traditional hunter-gatherer lifestyle, along with a shift to speaking Spanish. His conservative estimate of the rate of knowledge loss should be a **wake-up call** to all: "I estimate that the real loss of ethnobotanical[4] knowledge from one generation to the next may be on the order of 40 to 60 percent." (Lizarralde 2001).

8　This is a dire[5] **scenario**: Bari people who have limited connection with the forest have lost up to 45 percent of traditional plant names. Similar patterns of knowledge erosion may be observed among indigenous peoples all around the world as they undergo a cultural shift away from traditional lifestyles and languages.

9　Some researchers offer hope for the persistence and resilience of very basic forms of traditional knowledge. A study by anthropologist Scott Atran (1998) tested residents of Michigan on their knowledge of local animals. He concluded that elements of folk knowledge persist even when people have been schooled in modern scientific classification.

10　Though folk knowledge may persist in modern cultures, we are also losing traditional knowledge at an alarming rate. This loss is accompanied by a severe reduction in number of species and range of **habitats**. Perhaps future technologies hold enough promise that humanity will be able to survive without making use of this accumulated ecological knowledge. Perhaps we will grow plants in greenhouses and breed animals in laboratories and feed ourselves via genetic engineering. Perhaps there are no new medicines to be found in the rain forests. All

---

[4] **ethnobotanical:** describing customs and beliefs about plants and agriculture held by a group of people
[5] **dire:** very serious; terrible

such arguments appeal to ignorance: we do not know what we stand to lose as languages and technologies vanish because much or even most of it remains undocumented. So it is a gamble to think that we will never use it in the future. Do we really want to place so much trust in future science and pay so little attention to our inherited science?

Tip for Success

In Reading 2, the name(s) and year in parentheses form a citation. Citations tell you that an idea comes from another source. You can look in the publication's references list for full information about the source.

References

Atran, Scott (1998). Folk biology and the anthropology of science: Cognitive universals and cultural particulars. *Behavioral and Brain Sciences* 21: 547–609.

Hawskworth, D.L., and M.T. Kalin-Arroyo (1995). Magnitude and distribution of biodiversity. In V.H. Heywood (ed.), *Global Biodiversity Assessment*. Cambridge: Cambridge University Press, pp. 107–192.

Lizarralde, Manuel (2001). Biodiversity and loss of indigenous languages and knowledge in South America. In L. Maffi (ed.), *On Biocultural Diversity*. Washington, D.C.: Smithsonian, pp. 265–281.

Plotkin, Mark (1993). *Tales of a Shaman's Apprentice*. New York: Viking.

Posey, Darrell A. (1990). Intellectual property rights and just compensation for indigenous knowledge. *Anthropology Today* 6(4): 13–16.

MAIN IDEAS

Each statement summarizes the main idea of a paragraph in Reading 2. Write the paragraph number next to the statement that summarizes it.

_7_ 1. As the Bari people become divorced from their surroundings and their language, they lose a lot of traditional knowledge.

____ 2. Some traditional knowledge survives even in modern societies in the United States.

____ 3. Scientists could find new treatments for serious diseases from plants that only indigenous people know about.

____ 4. Information can be lost in translations from indigenous languages.

____ 5. We should not trust science to replace the knowledge that is being lost in indigenous communities.

____ 6. Indigenous people know more about many plant and animal species than scientists.

____ 7. This pattern of knowledge loss exists all over the world.

____ 8. If information is always lost in translation, is it possible to measure how much traditional knowledge is being lost?

____ 9. Traditional knowledge is in danger of disappearing if we do not encourage the people who hold it to preserve it.

____ 10. In some languages, words contain extra information about the things they describe.

DETAILS

Why does the author include these examples and statistics? Circle the answer that best connects each example or statistic to the main idea.

1. An estimated $85 billion in profits per year is made on medicines made from plants that were first known to indigenous peoples for their healing properties. (Paragraph 1)
   a. to show that drug companies make too much money
   b. to show that indigenous knowledge is valuable
   c. to show that drug companies treat indigenous cultures badly

2. An astonishing 87 percent of the world's plant and animal species have not yet been identified, named, described, or classified by modern science. (Paragraph 2)
   a. to support the importance of traditional knowledge for modern science
   b. to criticize scientists for not studying more plants and animals
   c. to explain that the author is surprised about the number of unidentified species

3. Couldn't Solomon Islanders talk about the behavior patterns of fish in English just as easily as in Marovo, their native language? (Paragraph 4)
   a. to suggest that it is impossible to talk about the behavior of fish in English
   b. to suggest that Marovo can be translated into English without any loss
   c. to suggest that English words might not mean the same as words in Marovo

4. In !Xoon, clouds are called "rain houses." (Paragraph 5)
   a. to make fun of the !Xoon word for *clouds*
   b. to show how a language packages information in a word
   c. to suggest that !Xoon is more useful than English

5. Bari people who have limited connection with the forest have lost up to 45 percent of traditional plant names. (Paragraph 8)
   a. to emphasize how cultural changes can lead to loss of traditional knowledge
   b. to demonstrate that 55 percent of traditional plant names have been retained
   c. to criticize the Bari people for forgetting traditional plant names

Q WHAT DO YOU THINK?

A. Discuss the questions in a group. Then choose one question and write one or two paragraphs in response.

1. Have you ever tried to translate directly between two languages or used an online translation program? How accurate was the translation?

2. Can you think of examples of words or idioms that lose meaning when translated into English? How can you express the same word or idioms in English?

3. Harrison clearly does not believe that science can replace all the indigenous knowledge that is being lost. Do you agree with him? Give examples from the text or your experience to support your opinion.

B. Think about both Reading 1 and Reading 2 as you discuss the questions.

1. Why do many traditional communities switch to dominant languages such as English or Spanish?

2. What can be done to save languages such as Bari that are in danger of extinction? Give examples from the text or your experience to support your ideas.

Vocabulary Skill | Using a thesaurus web⁺

A thesaurus is a reference book that gives you **synonyms**, words with similar meanings, and **antonyms**, words with opposite meanings. Learning synonyms and antonyms is a good way to build your vocabulary, and it allows you to use more variety in your writing and speaking. You should always be sure to check the meaning and use of new words carefully. The *Oxford Learner's Thesaurus* lists collocations and appropriate contexts for using each synonym correctly.

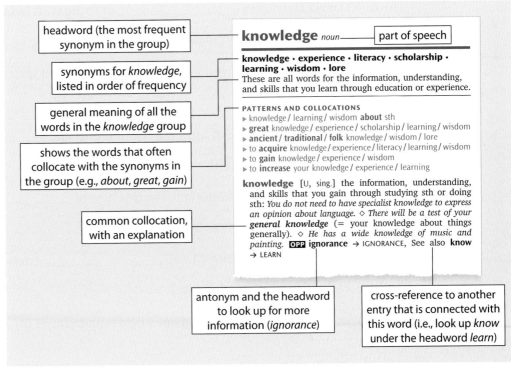

Adapted from *Oxford Learner's Thesaurus: A dictionary of synonyms* by Diana Lea © Oxford University Press 2008.

A. Complete each sentence with a word from the remainder of the thesaurus entry for *knowledge*. Use a different word in each sentence. Discuss your choices with a partner.

knowledge *noun*

knowledge · experience · literacy · scholarship · learning · wisdom · lore
These are all words for the information, understanding, and skills that you learn through education or experience.

PATTERNS AND COLLOCATIONS
▸ knowledge / learning / wisdom **about** sth
▸ **great** knowledge / experience / scholarship / learning / wisdom
▸ **ancient / traditional / folk** knowledge / wisdom / lore
▸ to **acquire** knowledge / experience / literacy / learning / wisdom
▸ to **gain** knowledge / experience / wisdom
▸ to **increase** your knowledge / experience / learning

knowledge [U, sing.] the information, understanding, and skills that you gain through studying sth or doing sth: *You do not need to have specialist knowledge to express an opinion about language.* ◇ *There will be a test of your* **general knowledge** (= your knowledge about things generally). ◇ *He has a wide knowledge of music and painting.* **OPP ignorance** → IGNORANCE, See also **know** → LEARN

experience [U] the knowledge and ability that you have gained through doing sth for a period of time; the process of gaining this: *I have over ten years' teaching experience.* ◇ *Do you have any* **previous experience** *of this type of work?* ◇ *She didn't get paid much but it was all* **good experience.** ◇ *We all* **learn by experience.** **OPP inexperience** → IGNORANCE

literacy [U] the ability to read and write: *The government is running a campaign to promote* **adult literacy** (= the ability of adults to read and write). **OPP illiteracy**

scholarship [U] the serious study of an academic subject and the knowledge and methods involved: *Oxford became one of the great centers of medieval scholarship.*

learning [U] knowledge that you get from reading and studying: *He is a teacher of great intellect and learning.* See also **learned** → INTELLECTUAL 2

wisdom [U] the knowledge that a society or culture has gained over a long period of time: *We need to combine ancient wisdom and modern knowledge.* See also **wise** → WISE

lore [U] knowledge and information related to a particular subject, especially when this is not written down; the stories and traditions of a particular group of people: *an expert in ancient Celtic lore*

Adapted from *Oxford Learner's Thesaurus: A dictionary of synonyms* by Diana Lea © Oxford University Press 2008.

1. K. David Harrison's _____ of living with indigenous people enables him to write persuasively about their cultures.

2. Modern medicine is turning to traditional cultures for their

   _____.

3. The indigenous people of Australia retain traditional _____ about the land and its history.

4. Studying textbooks is important, but this type of _____ can ignore facts that are not written down anywhere.

5. Young people are learning Maori _____ from elders to preserve their songs and dances.

6. Writing a book or article about one's field is an example of

   _____.

7. One way to save the knowledge of the Bari is through _____ campaigns so that it can be written and retained.

Tip for Success

No two words have exactly the same meaning and use. Check the exact meaning of new words in a dictionary or thesaurus before you use them.

B. Write an appropriate synonym for each underlined word. Use your thesaurus or dictionary.

1. _____: Indigenous people in many countries have faced similar <u>problems</u>.

2. _____: The <u>shift</u> from native languages to Spanish can be seen across Central and South America.

3. _____: Multiculturalism is the <u>idea</u> that people of different cultures and ethnicities can live and learn together.

4. _____: One <u>opinion</u> about multiculturalism is that it puts national unity in jeopardy.

5. _____: Linguists <u>say</u> that half of the world's languages are dying.

6. _____: Until recently, native cultures <u>kept</u> knowledge by passing it from one generation to the next.

WRITING

New words or concepts that are complex are often introduced in an **extended definition**. An extended definition is an **analysis** of a concept. It helps the reader understand by focusing on different features of the concept. Extended definitions frequently answer these questions:

Culture shock	
What is it?	Culture shock is a feeling of confusion and anxiety that somebody may feel when he lives in or visits another country.
What is it not?	It is not unusual, and it is not an illness. It is a normal part of the experience of living abroad.
What is it similar/dissimilar to?	If you have ever felt uncomfortable or lost in a new place, such as a new school or a party where you don't know anyone, you have come close to understanding culture shock.
What does it consist of?	Culture shock is divided into four stages, from the initial excitement to complete adjustment. The four stages are . . .
What are its characteristics?	Culture shock can lead to feelings of depression, isolation, and confusion, but ultimately it leaves the traveler with a deeper understanding of his old and new cultures.
What are some examples?	For example, when I lived in France, I was embarrassed to speak. If I used a word incorrectly, I thought people would laugh at me. I felt very alone.
How does it work? How is it used?	Culture shock affects everyone differently, and people go through the stages at different speeds. Most people do reach a comfortable level of adjustment eventually.
Why is it important?	It is important to understand culture shock so that you are not surprised when you encounter these feelings.

Read this extended definition of language. Underline and number (1–5) the information that answers the questions below.

What Is Language?

Language is one of the distinguishing capacities of human beings. The dictionary defines *language* as the system of communication in speech and writing that is used by people of a particular country or area, but in reality, language is much more than communication. A particular language comprises not only grammar and vocabulary, but also aspects of its speakers' culture, their traditional knowledge, their rules of behavior, and their forms of social interaction. For instance, the vocabulary of the Marovo language reflects the Solomon Islanders' understanding of fish behavior. In Japanese, the complex system of honorifics (suffixes added to names that indicate the relationship between speaker and listener) expresses the complex social roles that are important in that country. This deeper definition of language helps explain why translation is often so difficult and why so much human knowledge is lost when a language dies.

1. What is language?

2. What is language not?

3. What does language consist of?

4. What are some examples of language?

5. Why is language important?

Grammar | Contrast and concession connectors | web⁺

Contrast and concession connectors join ideas with different meanings. *Concession* means acknowledging an opposing idea and then showing that it is less important than your idea.

The coordinating conjunctions *but* and *yet* are used to join two contrasting independent clauses of equal importance. *Yet* is stronger than *but* and introduces an unexpected contrast or concession with the first clause. Use a comma between the clauses.

> The Maori language was dying, **but** recent initiatives are now saving it.
> Traditional knowledge could save lives, **yet** modern medicine often ignores it.

The subordinators *although/though/even though* are used in a dependent clause when the main clause is an unexpected contrast or a concession to the idea in the dependent clause; *even though* is stronger than *although* and *though*. *While* introduces a direct contrast or opposition to the idea in the main clause.

Although Europeans learned Maori at first, the English language soon dominated.

The Maori have retained their language **while** the Bari are losing theirs.

Transitions are adverbs and phrases that show the relationship between the ideas in one sentence and the ideas in the next. A period or semicolon is necessary to separate the independent clauses. *However*, the most common transition, can be used to show differences of various kinds.

The Maori language was dying. **However**, recent initiatives are saving it.

On the other hand introduces opposite but not contradictory ideas or qualities of one topic, often with a positive versus negative contrast.

The Maori have successfully saved their language. The Bari, **on the other hand**, are losing theirs.

A. Circle the best connector to complete each sentence.

1. (But /(Although)) some words in French look like English words, they have different meanings.

2. Sign language consists of hand signals instead of words. (However / On the other hand), it is a fully functional language.

3. Many Latin words survive in English (but / even though) the language has not been spoken for centuries.

4. In many countries, an indigenous language is used for daily communication (while / even though) a more powerful language is used for official business.

5. The word *algebra* looks like a Latin or Greek word, (yet / however) it comes from Arabic.

6. Some immigrants keep their native language, (but / however) more lose theirs.

7. Speaking two languages is sometimes seen as a disadvantage for young children, (but / yet) most believe that the opposite is true.

8. (Although / Yet) some governments officially protect native languages, their survival is not guaranteed.

B. In your notebook, combine each pair of sentences into one. Use the connector in parentheses.

1. (although) The children did not all speak the same language. They learned to communicate.

   Although the children did not all speak the same language, they learned

   to communicate.

2. (while) There are more than 6,000 languages in the world. The United Nations operates with only 6 official languages.

   _____

   _____

3. (yet) The translation was accurate. The book was extremely difficult to understand.

   _____

   _____

4. (however) Researchers have studied most of the world's languages. New languages are still being discovered.

   _____

   _____

Unit Assignment | Write an extended definition

 In this assignment, you will write an extended definition of a word or concept from a different language that cannot be translated exactly into English. As you prepare your extended definition, think about the Unit Question, "What happens when a language disappears?" and refer to the Self-Assessment checklist on page 54. Use information from Readings 1 and 2, your work in this unit, and your own experience to support your ideas.

For alternative unit assignments, see the *Q: Skills for Success Teacher's Handbook*.

PLAN AND WRITE

A. **BRAINSTORM** Think of one or two words, phrases, or concepts from a language you know that lose their meaning when translated. Then follow these steps.

1. In your notebook, write about the words, phrases, or concepts for ten minutes without stopping. Then read your freewriting and underline the best ideas to develop.

2. Choose one word, phrase, or concept from your freewriting in Step 1. Check (✔) at least four questions you can answer to define it. Make notes.

☐ What is it?   ☐ What are its characteristics?

☐ What is it not?   ☐ What are some examples?

☐ What is it similar to?   ☐ How does it work?

☐ What is it different from? ☐ How is it used?

☐ What does it consist of?   ☐ Why is it important?

_____

_____

_____

_____

_____

Your Writing Process

For this activity, you could also use Stage 1B, *Formal Outline* or *Informal Outline* in *Q Online Practice*.

B. **PLAN** Write a brief outline. Decide how many paragraphs you need and what information you are going to write in each paragraph.

Paragraph 1: _____

_____

Paragraph 2: _____

_____

Paragraph 3: _____

_____

Paragraph 4: _____

_____

C. **WRITE** Write your extended definition. Look at the questions you checked in Step A2, your outline in Step B, and the Self-Assessment checklist below to guide your writing.

REVISE AND EDIT

A. **PEER REVIEW** Read a partner's extended definition. Answer the questions and discuss them with your partner.

1. Does the writing define a word, phrase, or concept that cannot be translated into English?

2. Does the writing explain what would be lost if the language disappeared?

3. Does the writing give enough examples and other details?

4. Are the ideas logically organized?

B. **REWRITE** Review the answers to the questions in Activity A. You may want to revise and rewrite your extended definition.

C. **EDIT** Complete the Self-Assessment checklist as you prepare to write the final draft of your extended definition. Be prepared to hand in your work or discuss it in class.

Yes	No	SELF-ASSESSMENT
☐	☐	Have you used a variety of sentence types and lengths?
☐	☐	Are main ideas arranged appropriately and supported with convincing details?
☐	☐	Are there sentences using appropriate contrast and concession connectors?
☐	☐	Have you checked new words and collocations in a dictionary or thesaurus?
☐	☐	Does the essay include vocabulary from the unit?
☐	☐	Did you check the essay for punctuation, spelling, and grammar?

Circle the words you learned in this unit.

Nouns	Verbs	Adjectives
cure 🔑	abandon 🔑 AWL	indigenous
ethnicity AWL	assimilate	integral AWL
habitat	confine AWL	predominant AWL
initiative 🔑 AWL	exploit AWL	
revival	oblige	**Phrases**
scenario AWL	persist AWL	divorced from
shift 🔑 AWL	retain 🔑 AWL	in the face of
	substitute 🔑 AWL	in jeopardy
	suppress	wake-up call
	target AWL	

🔑 Oxford 3000™ words
AWL Academic Word List

Check (✓) the skills you learned. If you need more work on a skill, refer to the page(s) in parentheses.

READING	○	I can distinguish main ideas from details. (p. 38)
VOCABULARY	○	I can use a thesaurus. (pp. 46–47)
WRITING	○	I can write an extended definition. (p. 49)
GRAMMAR	○	I can use contrast and concession connectors. (pp. 50–51)
LEARNING OUTCOME	●	I can prepare an extended definition of a word or concept from a different language or culture for which there is no equivalent term or idea in English.

UNIT **3**

Work and Leisure

READING ● identifying contrasting ideas
VOCABULARY ● reporting verbs
WRITING ● using evidence to support an argument
GRAMMAR ● noun clauses

LEARNING OUTCOME •

Develop a persuasive essay arguing why a particular leisure activity should or should not be considered work.

Unit QUESTION

What is the difference between work and fun?

PREVIEW THE UNIT

A Discuss these questions with your classmates.

What do you do for fun? Are your leisure activities the same as your parents' or grandparents' were at your age?

Can you think of a job that you would find fun? What would make work fun?

Look at the photo. Do you think the person in the picture is working?

B Discuss the Unit Question above with your classmates.

Listen to *The Q Classroom*, **Track 8** on **CD 1**, to hear other answers.

C Look at the pictures. Would you describe the activities as fun or work? Circle your answers. Then discuss your answers in a group.

1. fun / work

2. fun / work

3. fun / work

4. fun / work

5. fun / work

6. fun / work

7. fun / work

8. fun / work

9. fun / work

D Discuss these questions in a group.

1. Think of your favorite sports. What are the benefits of being a professional athlete in these sports? What are the drawbacks?

2. All of the following are Olympic events. Which do you consider to be sports? Why or why not?

| taekwondo | snowboarding | target shooting | show jumping on a horse |

READING

READING 1 | Laid-Back Labor

VOCABULARY

Here are some words and phrases from Reading 1. Read the sentences. Circle the answer that best matches the meaning of each bold word or phrase.

1. When an activity becomes popular, companies that make equipment for the activity often have a **boom** in their sales.
   a. increase
   b. problem
   c. benefit

2. People who **engage in** gardening often form groups to share their plants and gardening tools with each other.
   a. have to do
   b. enjoy
   c. participate in

3. My sister's knitting store is **thriving** because every knitter in town buys supplies there.
   a. popular
   b. successful
   c. unusual

4. He didn't consider making his own furniture to be **labor** because he enjoyed it so much.
   a. hard work
   b. a waste of time
   c. unnecessary work

5. Gardening, cooking, and knitting used to be considered **menial** tasks, but are now expensive hobbies for many people.
   a. physical or difficult
   b. boring or unskilled
   c. useless or hopeless

6. Although we know how many hours Americans work each week, we still don't know how much **leisure** time they have.
   a. occupied
   b. spare
   c. uninterrupted

7. People pursue so many different hobbies that there is little **consensus** about the best way to spend free time.
   a. agreement
   b. cooperation
   c. argument

8. Some economists say there is a **gray area** between work and hobbies because it can be difficult to identify when a hobby becomes work.
   a. unclear difference
   b. opposition
   c. wide, empty space

9. Fewer Americans live on farms today compared to 1920: 1 percent and 30 percent, **respectively**.
   a. honestly
   b. most likely
   c. in that order

10. I didn't know **the going rate** for professional photographers, so I asked several of my friends how much they paid for such services.
    a. how fast the average person can do something
    b. the lowest price or salary for something
    c. the typical price or salary for something

11. **The odds are** that you prefer playing sports to doing the laundry.
    a. it is true
    b. it is obvious
    c. it is likely

12. People choose to do some types of work because of various **incentives**, such as extra money or some sort of special benefit.
    a. help to make work easier
    b. types of motivation
    c. offers

PREVIEW READING 1

You are going to read an article from the column "Freakonomics" in *The New York Times Magazine*. It was written by Stephen Dubner and Steven Levitt, the authors of the popular *Freakonomics* books, and it talks about how to define work and fun.

Do you think people work more now than in the past?

☐ Yes   ☐ No

FREAKONOMICS

Laid-Back Labor: The $140 Homemade Scarf

By Stephen J. Dubner and Steven D. Levitt

1   During the late 19th century, piano manufacturing was one of New York City's largest industries. Every right-minded American family, it seemed, wanted to fill its home with music. The advent of the player piano[1]—a music-making machine that required zero talent—drove the **boom** even further. By the 1920s, some 300,000 pianos were being sold in the United States each year, roughly two-thirds of them player pianos.

2   But a pair of newer technologies, the radio and the phonograph,[2] soon began to drive the piano into a deep disfavor that continues to this day. Last year, Americans bought only 76,966 pianos. That's a decrease of 75 percent over a period in which the population more than doubled. As much as people may love music, most of them apparently don't feel the need to make it for themselves. According to Census Bureau[3] statistics, only 7.3 percent of American adults have played a musical instrument in the past 12 months.

knitting for fun

3   Compare this with the 17.5 percent of adults who currently **engage** in what the Census Bureau calls "cooking for fun." Or consider that 41 percent of households have flower gardens, 25 percent raise vegetables, and 13 percent grow fruit trees—even though just 1 percent of Americans live on a farm today, down from 30 percent in 1920. On a more personal note: one of the authors of this column has a sister who runs a **thriving** yarn[4] store, while the other is married to a knitting devotee who might buy $40 worth of yarn for a single scarf and then spend ten hours knitting it. Even if her **labor** is valued at only $10 an hour, the scarf costs at least $140—or roughly $100 more than a similar machine-made scarf might cost.

Knitting: a way to relax

4   Isn't it puzzling that so many middle-aged Americans are spending so much of their time and money performing **menial** labor when they don't have to? Just as the radio and phonograph proved to be powerful substitutes for the piano, the forces of technology have greatly eased the burden of feeding and clothing ourselves. So what's with all the knitting, gardening, and "cooking for fun"? Why do some forms of menial labor survive as hobbies while others have been killed off? (For instance, we can't think of a single person who, since the invention of the washing machine, practices "laundry for fun.")

5   Economists have been trying for decades to measure how much **leisure** time people have and how they spend it, but there has been precious

---

[1] **player piano:** a piano that can play automatically
[2] **phonograph:** a record player (old-fashioned)
[3] **Census Bureau:** the U.S. government agency that collects information about the population

[4] **yarn:** thick thread (usually made of wool or cotton) that is used for knitting

little **consensus**. This is in part because it's hard to say what constitutes leisure and in part because measurements of leisure over the years have not been very consistent.

6   Economists typically separate our daily activities into three categories: market work (which produces income), home production (unpaid chores), and pure leisure. How, then, are we to categorize knitting, gardening, and cooking? While preparing meals at home can certainly be much cheaper than dining out and therefore viewed as home production, what about the "cooking for fun" factor?

7   In an attempt to address such **gray areas**, the economists Valerie A. Ramey and Neville Francis classified certain home activities as labor and others as leisure. In their recent paper "A Century of Work and Leisure," they employed a 1985 time-use survey in which people ranked their enjoyment of various activities on a scale of 0 to 10. Knitting, gardening, and cooking were in the middle of the scale, with a 7.7, 7.1, and 6.6, **respectively**. These ranked well behind some favorite activities—such as playing sports and fishing (which scored 9.2 and 9.1)—but firmly ahead of paying bills, cleaning the house and, yes, doing the laundry (5.2, 4.9, and 4.8).

8   But here's where it gets tricky. Ramey and Francis decided that anything at or above a 7.3 is leisure, while anything below is home production. (Knitting, therefore, makes the grade as leisure; gardening and cooking do not.) This leads them to calculate that we spend less time doing market work today than we did in 1900 but more time in home production. Men, it seems, have contributed mightily to this upsurge: in 1920, employed men spent only 2 or 3 hours a week on home production, but they averaged 11 hours by 1965 and 16 hours by 2004.

9   But how many of those home-production hours are in fact leisure hours? This, it seems, is the real question here: What makes a certain activity work for one person and leisure for another?

10   With no disrespect toward Ramey and Francis, how about this for an alternative definition: Whether or not you're getting paid, it's work if someone else tells you to do it and leisure if you choose to do it yourself. If you are the sort of person who likes to mow[5] your own lawn even though you can afford to pay someone to do it, consider how you'd react if your neighbor offered to pay you **the going rate** to mow his lawn. **The odds are** that you wouldn't accept his job offer.

11   And so a great many people who can afford not to perform menial labor choose to do so, because—well, why? An evolutionary biologist might say that embedded in our genes is a drive to feed and clothe ourselves and tame our surroundings. An economist, meanwhile, might argue that we respond to **incentives** that go well beyond the financial; and that, fortunately, we are left free to choose which tasks we want to do ourselves.

12   Of course, these choices may say something about who we are and where we come from. One of us, for instance (the economist, who lives in Chicago), grew up comfortably in a midwestern city

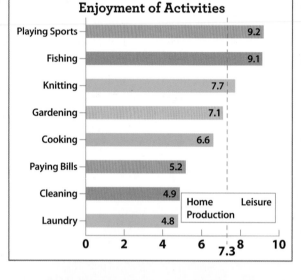

Enjoyment of Activities

Activity	Score
Playing Sports	9.2
Fishing	9.1
Knitting	7.7
Gardening	7.1
Cooking	6.6
Paying Bills	5.2
Cleaning	4.9
Laundry	4.8

Home Production · Leisure

0   2   4   6   7.3   8   10

---

[5] **mow**: to cut grass using a special machine or tool with a special blade or blades

and has fond memories of visiting his grandparents' small farm. This author recently bought an indoor hydroponic[6] plant grower. It cost about $150 and to date has produced approximately 14 tomatoes—which, once you factor in the cost of seeds, electricity, and even a small wage for the labor, puts the average price of a single tomato at roughly $20.

13 The other one of us (the journalist, who lives in New York) grew up on a small farm and was regularly engaged in all sorts of sowing, mucking, and reaping.[7] He, therefore, has little desire to grow his own food—but he is happy to spend hours shopping for and preparing a special dinner for family and friends. Such dinners, even if the labor were valued at only $10 an hour, are more expensive than a similar takeout meal.

14 Maybe someday the New York guy will get to cook a meal with some of the Chicago guy's cherry tomatoes. It might become one of the most expensive meals in recent memory—and, surely, worth every penny.

From "Laid-Back Labor: The $140 Homemade Scarf" by Stephen J. Dubner and Steven D. Levitt, *The New York Times*, May 6, 2007. © 2007 The New York Times. All rights reserved. Used by permission and protected by the Copyright Laws of the United States. The printing, copying, redistribution, or retransmission of the Material without express written permission is prohibited.

---

[6] **hydroponic:** growing in water or sand, rather than in soil

[7] **sowing, mucking, and reaping:** farm chores

MAIN IDEAS

Complete the summary of Reading 1 in your own words.

Some leisure activities that were popular in the past (such as playing the piano) are less popular today because of ___developments in technology___. On the other hand, some activities
1
that used to be considered _____ are now
2
popular as _____. Economists divide our time
3
into market work, _____, and pure leisure.
4
In one study, economists Valerie Ramey and Neville Francis found
that we do less _____ than in 1900 but more
5
_____. However, authors Stephen Dubner and Steven
6
Levitt suggest a different definition of work and leisure: an activity is work if
_____ and leisure if _____.
7   8
According to economists, people today do menial tasks when they don't need
to because _____.
9

DETAILS

Read the statements. Write *T* (true) or *F* (false). Then correct each false statement to make it true.

_____ 1. Fewer people buy pianos today because people don't like listening to music.

_____ 2. A homemade scarf costs more when you put a value on the time you take to make it.

_____ 3. An example of menial labor that is not popular today as a hobby is growing vegetables.

_____ 4. The difference between market work and household production is that market work happens outside the house.

_____ 5. Ramey and Francis classify knitting, gardening, and cooking as leisure activities.

_____ 6. According to Ramey and Francis, men do more chores today than in 1920.

_____ 7. If you mow your own lawn because you want to, you probably would not accept money to cut your neighbor's lawn.

_____ 8. Evolutionary biologists might say that we have a natural desire to do as little work as possible.

_____ 9. The author who likes growing tomatoes enjoyed visiting his grandparents' farm as a child.

_____ 10. The other author prefers cooking to growing vegetables because his parents owned a restaurant when he was a child.

WHAT DO YOU THINK?

Discuss the questions in a group. Then choose one question and write freely for five to ten minutes in response.

1. Think about the activities you do in your daily life. Which would you pay someone else to do for you if you could? Why?

2. The authors of this article both live in the United States, where it is possible for many people to buy food and clothes cheaply. Do you think their opinions would be different if they lived in another country? Why or why not?

3. The authors of "Laid-Back Labor" say that economists do not agree about the definition of leisure. After reading this article, how would you define work and leisure? Use your own examples to support your opinion.

Authors often present several different opinions in order to provide a balanced argument. They may also add their own opinion, which might differ from those of other experts. It is important to recognize whose opinion you are reading and to be aware of different opinions in a text. This will help you follow the authors' argument and main ideas. Here are some words and phrases you can look for to identify a new opinion or a different opinion.

Words that introduce an opinion	Words that show a different opinion
According to economists, . . .	. . . but / yet this is not always true.
In a recent study, Dubner found . . .	Some say . . . while/whereas others argue . . .
A critic might say . . .	However/On the other hand, . . .
Some people regard/see this as . . .	I disagree with Dubner about . . .
Francis argues/claims/states that . . .	Gardening is not work, but rather/instead . . .
We believe/think that . . .	A different/alternative/contrasting idea is . . .

A. Read the paragraph. Circle the words that introduce an opinion and underline the words that show a different opinion. Then compare your answers with a partner.

Do Americans have more leisure time than in the past? Economists cannot reach a consensus on this question. For example, Ramey and Francis (argue) that Americans have about the same amount of leisure time as they did in 1900 and slightly less than they did about 40 years ago. However, according to another study by Aguiar and Hurst, American adults actually have more leisure time than they did about 40 years ago. The differences result from disagreement over what constitutes work. Ramey and Francis consider the whole population, whereas Aguiar and Hurst only look at working-age adults, and they do not regard engaging in schoolwork and homework as labor. Rather than focusing on this difference, we believe that both studies support an alternative conclusion: Americans certainly do not have less leisure time than in the past.

Source: Adapted from Kristie M. Engemann and Michael T. Owyang (2007, January), "Working Hard or Hardly Working? The Evolution of Leisure in the United States." *The Regional Economist*, 10–11.

B. Complete the chart with the different opinions on the question *Do Americans have more leisure time now than in the past?* Use your answers from Activity A to help you.

Do Americans have more leisure time now than in the past?	
Ramey and Francis's opinion	
Aguiar and Hurst's opinion	
The authors' opinion	

C. Reread the article "Laid-Back Labor." Circle the words and phrases in Paragraphs 7–11 that introduce an opinion and a different opinion. Then compare your answers with a partner.

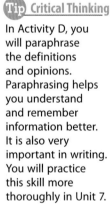 **Tip Critical Thinking**

In Activity D, you will paraphrase the definitions and opinions. Paraphrasing helps you understand and remember information better. It is also very important in writing. You will practice this skill more thoroughly in Unit 7.

D. Complete the charts. Use your own words to describe the definitions and opinions.

What is the definition of leisure?	
Levitt and Dubner	Leisure is something you choose to do; no one tells you to do it.
Ramey and Francis	

Why do people choose to do menial labor when they don't have to?	
Evolutionary biologists	
Economists (including the authors)	

READING 2 | Video Gamers

VOCABULARY

Here are some words and a phrase from Reading 2. Read the sentences. Then write each bold word or phrase next to the correct definition. You may need to change verbs to their base form and nouns to the singular form.

1. South Korea is one of the most **wired** nations on earth.

2. Fans often **idolize** their favorite sports stars, musicians, or other celebrities.

3. Chess is a game of **strategy** that requires players to think ahead to their next several moves.

4. **Commentators** describe sports events to TV viewers.

5. Modern video games are very **sophisticated**, which makes them much more interesting than earlier, simpler games.

6. In some games, players must act as soon as they see a **glimpse** of a new character on the screen.

7. Video game developers are looking for the next **emerging** market, where young people might start buying their products.

8. The graphics and action in the new video game were so much better that it left older games **playing catch-up**.

9. Video gaming **is regarded** as a waste of time by those who do not understand its benefits.

10. Some gamers **exaggerate** their skills when they talk about their best scores.

11. Researchers **estimate** that South Koreans spend $5 billion each year on video games.

12. When I play video games, I rely on my **reflexes** instead of thinking very much about my moves.

a. _____ (*v.*) to guess the approximate size of something

b. _____ (*n.*) an automatic reaction of nerves and muscles

c. _____ (*v.*) to adore, love, or admire a lot

d. _____ (*phr.*) to try to reach the same level of accomplishment as a competitor

e. _____ (*n.*) a very quick look

f. _____ (*n.*) a careful plan to reach a goal

g. _____ (*v.*) to consider (as); to see in a certain way

h. _____ (*adj.*) connected to telecommunications, especially the Internet

i. _____ (*adj.*) complicated or highly developed

j. _____ (*adj.*) rising or growing

k. _____ (*v.*) to describe as bigger or better than true

l. _____ (*n.*) a person who reports and discusses events or news

PREVIEW READING 2

You are going to read an article from the newspaper *The New York Times* that describes a new development in video-game playing in South Korea: professional competitions. Who do you think participates in these competitions? Do you think playing video games could be a sport? Why or why not?

CD 1
Track 10   **Read the article.**

Video Gamers

In Korea, video games at heart of **wired** nation; top players are treated like rock stars.

By Seth Schiesel

1   At first glance, the COEX mall here seemed like any other urban shopping destination on a recent late-summer day. But then there were the screams echoing down the corridors from one corner of this vast underground complex. Hundreds of young people, mostly women and girls, waved signs and sang slogans in the kind of fan frenzy[1] reserved for rock stars, movie stars, or sports stars.

a video game competition in South Korea

2   The objects of the throng's adoration were actually a dozen of South Korea's most famous celebrities: professional video gamers **idolized** for their mastery of the science-fiction **strategy** game "StarCraft."

[1] **frenzy:** a state of great activity and strong emotion that is often violent or frightening and not under control

3   On the other side of a glass wall from the throbbing crowd, players like Lim Yo-Hwan, Lee Yoon Yeol, and Suh Ji Hoon relaxed with a panel of **commentators**, their track suits covered with logos. With their easy confidence, they looked like athletes the world over. And they were not even competing. They were gathered to watch the draw[2] for a coming tournament season on MBC Game, one of the country's two full-time video game television networks.

4   In a country of almost 50 million people and home to the world's most advanced video game culture, more than 20,000 public PC gaming rooms, or "bangs," attract more than a million people a day. South Korea's roughly $5 billion annual game market comes to about $100 per resident, more than three times what Americans spend. As video games become more popular and **sophisticated**, Korea may provide a **glimpse** of where the rest of the world's popular culture is headed.

5   "Too often I hear people say 'South Korea' and '**emerging** market' in the same sentence," said Rich Wickham, the global head of Microsoft's Windows games business. "When it comes to gaming, Korea is the developed market, and it's the rest of the world that's **playing catch-up**."

6   South Korea is one of the most wired societies in the world. Yet despite widespread broadband Internet access at home, South Koreans still flock to the PC bangs.

7   "For us, playing with and against other people is much more interesting than just playing alone against a computer," said Woo Jong Sik, president of the Korea Game Development and Promotion Institute.

8   There are certainly concerns about gaming in South Korea. The government runs small treatment programs for gaming addicts, and there are reports every few years of young men keeling over[3] and dying after playing for days on end. But on the whole, gaming **is regarded** as good, clean fun.

9   In the Seoul district of Shinlim, Huh Hyeong Chan, a 42-year-old math tutor, seemed to be the respected elder at the Intercool PC bang, which covers two floors. "Among people in their 20s and 30s, I think there is no one who hasn't been to a PC bang because it's become a main trend in our society," he said from his prime seat at the head of a row of computers. "Most people think it's good for your mental health and it's a good way to get rid of stress. If you exercise your brain and your mind in addition to your body, that's healthy."

10   Lee Chung Gi, owner of the Intercool bang, said, "It's impossible for students in any country to study all the time, so they are looking for interesting things to do together. In America they have lots of fields and grass and outdoor space. They have lots of room to play soccer and baseball and other sports. We don't have that here. Here, there are very few places for young people to go and very little for them to do, so they found PC games, and it's their way to spend time together and relax."

11   But top pro gamers in South Korea do not get much chance to relax.

12   Lim Yo-Hwan, 27, the nation's most famous gamer, explained at the SK Telecom StarCraft team's well-guarded training house in Seoul that he usually gets up around 10 a.m. "After we wake up we have our breakfast, and then we play matches from 1 p.m. until 5. At 5 p.m. we have our lunch, and then at 5:30 for an hour and a half, I go to my gym, where I work out. Then I come home and play until 1 a.m. After 1, I can play more matches, or I can go to sleep if I want. But not many players sleep at 1."

13   Lim sat in what might be called the players' lounge: a spacious parlor of plush couches and flat-screen televisions. In an adjoining

[2] **draw:** the act of choosing something (competitors to be in a game)
[3] **keeling over:** falling over unexpectedly, especially because you feel ill or sick

apartment, the focus was on work. More than a half-dozen other members of the team sat at rows of PCs demolishing one another at "StarCraft." Outside, guards for the apartment complex kept an eye out for overzealous[4] fans.

14   "Without covering myself up in disguise, it's really difficult to go out in public," Lim said. "Because of the Internet penetration and with so many cameras around, I don't have privacy in my personal life. Anything I do will be on camera and will be spread throughout the Internet, and anything I say will be **exaggerated** and posted on many sites. It's hard because I can't maintain my relationships with friends. In terms of dating, the relationships just don't work out. So personally there are losses, but I don't regret it because it was my choice to become a pro gamer."

15   Woo, the president of the Korea Game Development and Promotion Institute, **estimated** that 10 million South Koreans regularly follow eSports, as they are known here, and said that some fan clubs of top gamers have 700,000 members or more.

16   "These fan clubs are actually bigger in size than the fan clubs of actors and singers in Korea," he said. In fact, Woo estimates that as many people watch professional gaming leagues as pro basketball, baseball, and soccer put together.

17   The celebrity of South Korea's top gamers is carefully managed by game-TV pioneers like Hyong Jun Hwang, general manager of Ongamenet, one of the country's full-time game networks.

18   "We realized that one of the things that keeps people coming back to television is the characters that the viewer gets to know and identify with, or maybe they begin to dislike," he said. "In other words, television needs stars. So we set out to make the top players into stars, promoting them and so on. And we also do a lot of education with the players, explaining that they have to try to look good, that they have to be ready for interviews."

19   For his part, Lim cultivates a relatively low-key image. He knows that at 27 he is nearing the end of his window as an elite player. There are 11 pro teams in the country, he said, and they are full of younger players who are trying to take his place. But, he said, experience could make up for a few milliseconds of lost **reflexes**.

20   "The faster you think, the faster you can move," he said. "And the faster you move, the more time you have to think."

[4] **overzealous:** showing too much energy or enthusiasm

MAIN IDEAS

Circle the answer to each question.

1. Which sentence expresses the main idea of the article?
    a. In South Korea, video games are only for professionals.
    b. Video games are both a hobby and a serious sport in South Korea.
    c. South Koreans do not take video games seriously as a sport.

2. Why are "bangs" so popular in South Korea, according to Woo Jong Sik?
   a. Few people have high-speed Internet connections at home.
   b. Professional video-game players go to the bangs.
   c. Many young people prefer to play video games with other people.

3. Why do many South Koreans play video games as a hobby, according to Huh Hyeong Chan?
   a. They consider it relaxing and good for mental health.
   b. They want to be professional video-game players.
   c. They can make a lot of money as amateur gamers.

4. What does the article say about the relationship between TV networks and professional video-game players?
   a. Video-game playing is popular because it is shown on TV.
   b. TV networks help find the best players in the country.
   c. TV networks help create celebrities out of the top video gamers.

5. Which statement best describes Lim Yo-Hwan's life as a professional video gamer?
   a. It's serious, hard work.
   b. It's fun all the time.
   c. It's a hobby that he gets paid to do.

DETAILS

Match each statement or opinion with the person who expressed it. You will use some people more than once.

a. the global head of Windows games for Microsoft

b. the president of the Korea Game Development and Promotion Institute

c. a top video-game player

d. the general manager of a TV network

____ 1. South Korea is ahead of the world in its video-game industry.

____ 2. Playing games at a PC "bang" is more interesting than playing by yourself at home.

____ 3. It's hard to have normal relationships when you're a video-game star.

____ 4. There are hundreds of thousands of members in some video-game players' fan clubs.

_____ 5. In South Korea, eSports are more popular than other professional sports.

_____ 6. Video-game professionals need to look good on TV.

_____ 7. Younger players try to take the places of older players on South Korea's professional teams.

_____ 8. Experience is sometimes more valuable than youth in professional gaming.

WHAT DO YOU THINK?

A. Discuss the questions in a group. Then choose one question and write one or two paragraphs in response.

1. Do you like playing video games? Why or why not?

2. After reading the article, do you think that video gaming can be considered a real sport?

3. If a hobby becomes a professional sport or job, do you think it is still fun? Why or why not?

B. Think about both Reading 1 and Reading 2 as you discuss the questions.

1. In Reading 1, the authors suggested these definitions of work and leisure: "Whether or not you're getting paid, it's work if someone else tells you to do it and leisure if you choose to do it yourself." According to these definitions, is professional video-game playing work or leisure?

2. Does the example of video gamers in Reading 2 change your opinion about the definitions of work and leisure presented in Reading 1? Why or why not?

When writing academic papers (research reports, essays, etc.), you often need to report information, ideas, or research by other authors. The choice of verb in the main clause can show your attitude toward the source. The verb can imply a supporting, distancing, or neutral attitude about the author's ideas or opinions. Use a dictionary to help you understand the exact meaning and use of different verbs so that you can accurately express your opinion and recognize other authors' attitudes.

Example	Type of verb	Explanation
The authors **prove** that leisure time has increased.	Supporting	**Prove** means to use facts or evidence to show that something is true; the authors have convinced you that leisure time has increased.
The authors **say** that leisure has increased.	Neutral	**Say** means to give information; you are reporting the information the authors gave without expressing your own opinion about it.
The authors **claim** that leisure time has increased.	Distancing	**Claim** means to say that something is true although it has not been proved and other people may not believe it; you do not accept the authors' conclusion that leisure time has increased.

Adverbs can also have a supporting or distancing effect on a sentence. For example, "The authors argue **convincingly** . . ." means you are persuaded by the argument, whereas "The authors **supposedly** prove that . . . " shows doubt about their conclusions.

A. Read the sentences. Do the words in bold have a supporting, neutral, or distancing effect? Circle the correct answer.

1. Although most people would prefer to have more leisure time, a minority of experts **unconvincingly argue** that people don't need any leisure time at all.
   a. supporting   b. neutral   c. distancing

2. Research **unfailingly demonstrates** that people are more productive after they've had a vacation.
   a. supporting   b. neutral   c. distancing

3. The author's analysis and the scientific evidence **validate** the position that individuals do not need the same amount of leisure time to be satisfied.

   a. supporting   b. neutral   c. distancing

4. A United Nations report **states** that a certain amount of unemployment is inevitable in all economies.

   a. supporting   b. neutral   c. distancing

5. The authors **incorrectly contend** that people value their leisure time more than their time at work.

   a. supporting   b. neutral   c. distancing

6. Some economists **tell** politicians how to present employment data in different ways to support their position.

   a. supporting   b. neutral   c. distancing

B. Choose five ideas, opinions, facts, or statistics about sports, work, or leisure. Write sentences that show your attitude. Use a dictionary or thesaurus to find other reporting verbs or adverbs.

1. _____

_____

2. _____

_____

3. _____

_____

4. _____

_____

5. _____

_____

C. Exchange your sentences from Activity B with a partner. Read each sentence. Identify your partner's attitude.

WRITING

Most academic writing requires you to make an argument and try to persuade the reader that your opinion is correct. Writers use evidence (examples, quotations, statistics, explanations, etc.) to make their arguments more convincing. All evidence must be relevant (connected to the topic and meaningful), or it will confuse and not convince the reader.

The authors of Reading 1, for example, used several types of evidence to support their argument. They argued that activities that were once considered work are now considered hobbies by using:

- **statistics** (Twenty-five percent of Americans grow vegetables.)
- **comparisons** (Only 1 percent of Americans live on farms now, compared with 30 percent in 1920.)
- **personal examples** (The sister of one of the writers runs a yarn store.)
- **analysis/mathematical calculations** (If we calculate labor at $10/hour, the actual cost of a homemade scarf is $140.)

Tip for Success

Different academic subjects have different rules for good evidence, so always find out what kind of evidence your reader will accept. Ask your teacher or look closely at your readings for examples.

A. **Read each section of this draft outline of an essay. The essay will argue that playing video games is a sport. Answer the question after each section.**

> ### Video Games Are a Real Sport
>
> The gaming industry has seen a boom in recent years. Video games have developed from childhood hobbies into a massive, worldwide industry. As with other leisure activities, this has resulted in "professional amateurs" and finally full-time professional video gamers. As a result, video-game playing can now be called a real sport.

1. What evidence could the writer add to this section of the essay? Check (✓) all the appropriate answers.

   ☐ a. Dubner and Levitt define sport as "an activity that you do for pleasure and that needs physical effort or skill, usually done in a special area and according to fixed rules."

   ☐ b. Video games are similar to rugby, which began as a game at an English school and became an international professional sport.

   ☐ c. The video-game industry is worth roughly $5 billion in South Korea.

   ☐ d. My friend plays video games all the time, and she even won a prize at a regional competition last year.

> Video games are a sport because they are played by amateurs and professionals for both pleasure and profit.

2. What evidence could the writer add to this section of the essay? Check (✔) all the appropriate evidence.

☐ a. I conducted an informal survey of students in my class, and 85 percent said that they sometimes or often played video games.

☐ b. I think that about 85 percent of teenagers play video games.

☐ c. National and international professional gaming leagues exist. This makes video games similar to baseball, which is played in community parks and also in major leagues.

☐ d. Some video games are expensive, so some young people cannot afford them.

> Critics of professional video-game leagues suggest that gaming does not qualify as a sport because it is not a physical activity and it is a game of chance more than skill and strategy. However, these objections are not valid.

3. What evidence could the writer add to this section of the essay? Check (✔) all the appropriate evidence.

☐ a. Good video-game players need excellent motor control and reflexes in the arms, hands, and fingers.

☐ b. Not all sports involve movement; shooting is an Olympic sport, for example.

☐ c. Some people argue that card games should be a sport because they also take skill and practice to master.

☐ d. More sophisticated video games clearly require strategy; for example, players may have to control a character, solve puzzles, and shoot at monsters.

When writers include other people's speech, thoughts, questions, or results in their writing, they often use **noun clauses**. A noun clause is a dependent clause that can replace a noun or pronoun as a subject or object.

> main clause / noun clause
>
> Some economists say that we have less free time now than in the past.

There are three types of noun clauses:

- Noun clauses formed from statements

> noun clause
>
> Many Americans say (**that**) they cook for fun.

- Noun clauses formed from *wh-* questions

> noun clause
>
> We asked the man **why** he plays video games.

- Noun clauses formed from *yes/no* questions

> noun clause
>
> TV networks wonder **if/whether** people will watch video-game competitions.

Noun clauses formed from questions always have sentence word order (subject-verb). They do not have the inverted word order typically used in questions, and they omit the form of *do* that is needed to form questions.

> ✗ We asked the man why does he play video games.

Remember that you can use different verbs in the main clause to show your attitude toward the information in the noun clause. (See page 73.)

Tip for Success

The word *that* may be deleted in a noun clause, but it is usually kept in academic writing.

Tip for Success

In academic writing, you should try to present a balance of opinions. One way to do this is by using noun clauses; for example, *Professional gamers argue that video games are a real sport. However, many traditional athletes insist that a sport requires special skill and intense physical training.*

A. Complete the paragraph with words from the box. Use each word once.

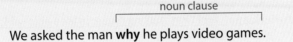

if	how	that	which	who	why

Although most people would say _____ gardening is
                                      1
a hobby, for a few enthusiastic gardeners, it is almost a sport. If you've

ever wondered _____ anyone would grow a one-meter-long
                  2
cucumber or a 770-kilogram pumpkin, here's your answer. Amateur

gardeners bring their produce to competitions where judges measure

them to determine _____ fruits and vegetables are the
                              3

largest. Every year, pumpkin growers gather near San Francisco to see

_____ has grown the heaviest orange gourd. After the results
            4

are announced, all the gardeners want to know _____ the
                                                          5

winners will share their secrets. But few champion growers will reveal

_____ they turned ordinary vegetables into giants.
            6

B. Complete each sentence using a noun clause with an appropriate
reporting verb from the box. Use each verb once.

argue	discuss	~~feel~~	study	wonder

1. Making music is less enjoyable than listening to it.

   Most Americans _feel that making music is less enjoyable than listening to it._

2. How much time do we spend doing work?

   Ramey and Francis _____

3. What makes an activity work for one person and leisure for another?

   The authors _____

4. Something is leisure if you choose to do it yourself.

   Dubner and Levitt _____

5. Are video games as popular in rural places as in urban areas?

   Some readers _____

Unit Assignment | Write a persuasive essay

Q In this assignment, you will choose a leisure activity and write a persuasive
essay arguing why it should or should not be considered work. As you
prepare your essay, think about the Unit Question, "What is the difference
between work and fun?" and refer to the Self-Assessment checklist on
page 80. Use information from Readings 1 and 2 and your work in this unit
to support your ideas.

For alternative unit assignments, see the *Q: Skills for Success Teacher's Handbook*.

PLAN AND WRITE

 Your Writing Process

For this activity, you could also use Stage 1A, *Freewriting* or *Clustering* in Q Online Practice.

A. **BRAINSTORM** Think of an activity that you enjoy and do not get paid to do. You can choose one of the examples from the chapter (such as cooking, gardening, or video-game playing) or something else (such as photography or another leisure activity). Complete the chart.

Activity:

It should/shouldn't be regarded as work because:

_____

_____

_____

_____

_____

B. **PLAN** Write your best ideas from Activity A that support your position.

1. _____

_____

2. _____

_____

3. _____

_____

C. **WRITE** Write a first draft of your essay. Support each main idea with evidence from your knowledge, experience, and reading. Look at the Self-Assessment checklist on page 80 to guide your writing.

REVISE AND EDIT

A. **PEER REVIEW** Read a partner's essay. Answer the questions and discuss them with your partner.

1. Is the essay persuasive? Why or why not?

2. Should anything be added? If yes, what?

3. Should anything be deleted? If yes, what?

4. Should anything else be changed? If yes, what?

5. Should any part of the essay be reorganized? If so, which part and how?

B. **REWRITE** Review the answers to the questions in Activity A. You may want to revise and rewrite your essay.

C. **EDIT** Complete the Self-Assessment checklist as you prepare to write the final draft of your essay. Be prepared to hand in your work or discuss it in class.

Yes	No	SELF-ASSESSMENT
☐	☐	Does the essay build a convincing argument using main ideas supported with good evidence?
☐	☐	Are contrasting ideas introduced clearly?
☐	☐	Did you use noun clauses?
☐	☐	Are there a variety of reporting verbs?
☐	☐	Does the essay include vocabulary from the unit?
☐	☐	Did you check the essay for punctuation, spelling, and grammar?

Track Your Success

Circle the words you learned in this unit.

Nouns
boom
commentator AWL
consensus AWL
glimpse
gray area
incentive AWL
labor 🔑 AWL
leisure
reflex
strategy 🔑 AWL

Verbs
estimate 🔑
exaggerate 🔑
idolize
regard 🔑

Phrasal Verb
engage in

Adjectives
emerging AWL
menial

sophisticated
thriving
wired

Adverb
respectively

Phrases
play catch-up
the going rate
the odds are

🔑 Oxford 3000™ words
AWL Academic Word List

Check (✓) the skills you learned. If you need more work on a skill, refer to the page(s) in parentheses.

READING	○	I can identify contrasting ideas. (p. 65)
VOCABULARY	○	I can recognize and use reporting verbs. (p. 73)
WRITING	○	I can use evidence to support an argument. (p. 75)
GRAMMAR	○	I can recognize and use noun clauses. (p. 77)
LEARNING OUTCOME	●	I can develop a persuasive essay arguing why a particular leisure activity should or should not be considered work.

UNIT

4

Deception

READING ● previewing a text
VOCABULARY ● Latin and Greek roots
WRITING ● writing with unity
GRAMMAR ● quantifiers

LEARNING OUTCOME ●

Create an advertising proposal describing your idea for a print or Web advertisement.

Q?

Unit QUESTION

How well does a picture illustrate the truth?

PREVIEW THE UNIT

A Discuss these questions with your classmates.

Do you like taking photographs? Why or why not?

How would you define *honesty* and *lying*?

Look at the photo. What tricks is the man using to make the scene look real?

B Discuss the Unit Question above with your classmates.

Listen to *The Q Classroom*, Track 11 on CD 1, to hear other answers.

83

C Work with a partner. This chart lists several different types of images and graphics. In what kinds of texts can you find these images and graphics? Why would this type of image or graphic be used in this type of text? Complete the chart with your answers.

Image or graphic		What kind of text?	Why?
Photograph		newspaper	to show people and events in the article
Map			
Graph			
Cartoon			
Diagram			
Artist's drawing			

D Number the types of images and graphics from 1 (most objective, or realistic) to 6 (most subjective, or influenced by personal feelings). Explain your decisions to your partner.

E Have you ever seen images or graphics that were deceptive? Where?

READING 1 | How to Lie with Maps

Vocabulary

Here are some words and a phrase from Reading 1. Read their definitions.
Then complete each sentence.

> **campaign** (*n.*) a series of planned activities that are intended to achieve a particular social, commercial, or political aim
>
> **competitor** (*n.*) a person or an organization that competes against others, especially in business
>
> **distort** (*v.*) to twist or change facts, ideas, etc., so that they are no longer correct or true
>
> **justify** (*v.*) to give an explanation or excuse for something
>
> **omit** (*v.*) to not include something
>
> **paradox** (*n.*) a person, thing, or situation that has two opposite features and therefore seems strange
>
> **portray** (*v.*) to show somebody or something in a picture
>
> **precision** (*n.*) the quality of being exact, accurate, and careful
>
> **principal** (*adj.*) most important; main
>
> **prominent** (*adj.*) easily seen
>
> **scale** (*n.*) the relation between the actual size of something and its size on a map
>
> **white lie** (*n.*) a harmless or small lie, especially one that you tell to avoid hurting somebody

1. An advertiser often hopes to sell more products than a _____ in the same business sells.

2. I told a(n) _____ and said that I loved his drawing, even though I really didn't, so that he would not feel bad.

3. There are many reasons to advertise, but the _____ one is to attract new customers.

4. I wanted to take a photo that would accurately _____ life in a small town.

5. I checked to make sure my ad did not _____ important information, such as the address of my store.

6. I tried not to _____ the facts by sharing too many of my own opinions when I told the story.

7. The photograph was in a(n) _____ position on the opening page of the website.

8. Mapmakers face a(n) _____; in order to give accurate information, they must leave out some features of the real world.

9. Our last advertising _____ was successful; a week's worth of ads increased sales by 20 percent.

10. Drawing a map requires great _____ to ensure that every tiny detail is correct.

11. People often attempt to _____ lies by claiming they told them in order to help someone else.

12. The _____ of the map made it seem like a short distance, but it took all day to drive between the two cities.

Reading Skill | Previewing a text

Before you read a text, it is helpful to make guesses about its content. **Preview a text** by following these steps:

- Look at the text without reading it: What type of text is it? Who wrote it? Who is it written for?
- Read the title and subtitles: What is the topic of each section?
- Look at the images or graphics and read the captions: What do you expect to read about in the text?

Previewing a text helps you:

- predict the content of the reading using your existing knowledge about the topic.
- read faster because you have already thought about the ideas.
- make connections between the text and the graphics.
- recognize main ideas and details or examples.

A. Preview Reading 1. Circle the answer that best completes each statement.

1. This reading is probably from ____.
    a. a magazine
    b. an academic book
    c. a student essay

2. The first paragraph probably ___.
   a. explains some history
   b. gives an example
   c. introduces the main idea

3. The first section ("Maps That Advertise") probably says that ___.
   a. maps are useful as ads
   b. maps and ads are completely different
   c. maps are always commercial

4. The second section ("Transport Ads: Gentle Lines and Well-Connected Cities") contains ___.
   a. one example of a map for an ad
   b. two examples of maps for ads
   c. a new idea about maps

5. The third section ("Accessibility: Ad Maps with a Single-Place Focus") is probably about ___.
   a. ads for one business or organization
   b. ads that will appear in only one physical place
   c. ads that will appear in only one medium

Tip Critical Thinking

Activity B asks you to transfer information you receive from visual sources such as maps and apply it to textual information in the reading. This helps you understand more about a topic, and can help you remember information better.

B. **Look closely at the figures and captions in Reading 1. Read the statements. Then write *T* (true) or *F* (false) for each statement.**

___ 1. Figures 1 and 2 portray the same railway lines.

___ 2. Figure 2 is more accurate than Figure 1.

___ 3. Figure 3 implies that Rudy's customers come from many different towns.

___ 4. Rudy's store must be very tall (Figure 3).

PREVIEW READING 1

Dr. Mark Monmonier is a professor of geography and a cartographer (a person who makes or studies maps). In his book *How to Lie with Maps*, Monmonier shows the ways in which different maps can show the world differently. You are going to read an excerpt from his book in which Monmonier discusses how maps can be used in the service of advertising.

Based on the preview you have just done, write your prediction of the main idea of the reading.

_____

_____

How to Lie with Maps

1   Not only is it easy to lie with maps, it's essential. A map must **distort** reality in order to **portray** a complex, three-dimensional world on a flat sheet of paper. To take a simple example, a map is a scale model, but the symbols it uses for parks, restaurants, and other places are not drawn to the same **scale**, which—if taken literally—would make them much bigger or smaller in reality. Furthermore, a map cannot show everything, or it will hide critical information in a fog of detail. The map, therefore, must offer a selective, incomplete view of reality. There's no escape from the cartographic **paradox**: to present a useful and truthful picture, an accurate map must tell **white lies**.

Maps That Advertise

2   What do advertising and map-making have in common? The best answer is that both ads and maps need to communicate a limited version of the truth. An advertisement must create an image that's appealing, and a map must present an image that's clear. However, neither can meet its goal by telling or showing everything. Ads will suppress, or play down, negative aspects of the company or service they advertise. In this way, they can promote a favorable comparison with similar products or differentiate a product from its **competitors**. Likewise, the map must **omit** details that would confuse or distract.

3   When a company's physical location is important for customers to know, its ads often include a map. There are two reasons for this. First, since maps are necessarily simplified and selective, they serve the advertiser's need to leave out certain features and exaggerate others. Second, ads must attract attention, and maps are proven attention getters. In fact, some maps are used more for decoration than information.

Transport Ads: Gentle Lines and Well-Connected Cities

4   Imagine you are the president of the new Springfield & Northern Railway, and you need to advertise your route. Your engineering department's map (Figure 1) does not seem quite suitable. It draws too much attention to your **principal** competitor—the Fairview & Springfield Railway—whose more direct route actually reaches downtown Springfield. Your railway terminates in the smaller town of West Springfield, three miles from

Springfield's town center. You also want to **justify** the word *Northern* in your name by showing that future routes north of Springfield are planned. Furthermore, the overall shape of the map is inappropriate: you want your railway line clearly in the center, not your competitor's.

5   You explain your needs to a cartographer, who proudly delivers the map in Figure 2. Its dominant feature is a nearly straight line connecting Springfield with Fairview. It ignores West Springfield, instead suggesting a direct link with other rail lines in Springfield. An equally **prominent** dashed line running off the map to the north suggests the future development of your railway. In contrast, a thin, graphically weak line portrays your principal competitor. The Fairview & Springfield Railway now appears to take a less direct route than the Springfield & Northern. Thanks to the map, the Springfield and Northern Railway has become an attractive option for travelers and investors.

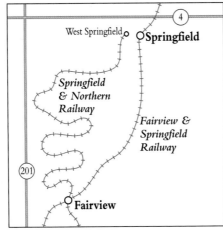

Figure 1 Engineering department's map of the Springfield & Northern Railway

Figure 2 Advertising map of the Springfield & Northern Railway

Accessibility: Ad Maps with a Single-Place Focus

6   In an ad promoting a store, hotel, or other business, a map might not only offer travel directions but also stimulate demand. For many goods and services, the trip itself is an important part of the purchase. If the trip is difficult (bad roads, unsafe neighborhoods, heavy traffic), the customer might consider travel an added cost and look for an easier alternative. Thus, the map needs not only to suggest straightforward routes for getting there but also to present an image of convenient accessibility. And if an attractive image requires distorted distances, the advertising map will indeed distort. Accuracy and **precision**, after all, are seldom prime goals in advertising.

7   Accessibility is particularly important for products needed in a hurry. Thus when Rudy Swenson stops by your advertising firm to discuss a **campaign** for his plumbing[1] supplies company, you suggest a map as the ideal display ad. The map needs to convince local customers that Rudy's store is both popular and convenient. You decide to use a reliable advertising trick: mention other place names. Your design (Figure 3) mentions many other neighboring towns,

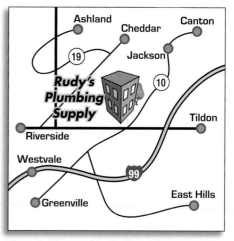

Figure 3 Map used in display ad for Rudy's Plumbing Supply

some of which have their own plumbing supplies stores. By showing how to get to Rudy's from other towns, the map now wrongly implies that customers ignore their local stores, preferring to make the trip to Rudy's instead. Rudy hopes that local homeowners will be impressed by this thought and thus choose his shop.

8   A map used in commercial advertising can be clever or deceptive. In most cases, though, the consumer is not deceived but recognizes the map as playful, like any other artwork in an ad, and enjoys the humor of the distorted map. In the next chapter, however, we will see how maps can be used to trick people. Maps *must* be white lies but may *sometimes* become real lies.

---

[1] **plumbing:** anything that uses water in your house: sinks, baths, showers, toilets, etc.

MAIN IDEAS

Answer these questions. Discuss your answers with a partner.

1. "To present a useful and truthful picture, an accurate map must tell white lies." (Paragraph 1) Why is this paradox true?

   _____

   _____

2. "What do advertising and map-making have in common?" (Paragraph 2)

_____

_____

3. Why do ads for some products and services "often include a map"?
   (Paragraph 3)

_____

_____

4. How can a map help "in an ad promoting a store, hotel, or other business"?
   (Paragraph 6)

_____

_____

5. Why would consumers like "the humor" of a distorted or inaccurate map?
   (Paragraph 8)

_____

_____

DETAILS

A. These are techniques that cartographers might use when making maps.
Write *R* if the technique was used in the railway example, *P* if it was used
in the plumbing store example, or *X* if the technique was not mentioned.
More than one answer may be correct.

R, P **1.** Distort distances to make the product or service look more convenient.

_____ **2.** Omit negative features of the product or service.

_____ **3.** Leave out towns.

_____ **4.** Make travel connections appear more convenient than they are.

_____ **5.** Center the map on the advertiser, not competitors.

_____ **6.** Include towns where people might not actually use the product
or service.

_____ **7.** Draw scale models of buildings.

B. Discuss with a partner any technique in Activity A that was not in Reading 1 (any technique that you marked *X*). Do you think it would be effective?

Q WHAT DO YOU THINK?

Discuss the questions in a group. Then choose one question and write freely for five to ten minutes in response.

1. When a company uses a distorted map in its ad, do you think the company is being dishonest? Why or why not?

2. Do you think advertising is always deceptive? Can you ever trust an ad?

3. What sorts of information and/or graphics do you find persuasive in an advertisement?

READING 2 | Phototruth or Photofiction?

VOCABULARY

Here are some words and a phrase from Reading 2. Read the paragraph. Then write each bold word or phrase next to the correct definition. You may need to change verbs to their base form and nouns to the singular form.

Newspaper articles can never tell the entire truth: some element of lying is **inherent** in all journalism because it is impossible for one article to include all the details of the story. Journalists may also **manipulate** the order in which they present information to achieve more drama or other effects in their writing. Choosing details and the order to describe them is considered proper and **ethical** behavior for journalists. Editors can even reflect their paper's political **bias** when writing opinion pieces about elections and politics.

In book publishing, many companies do not always **scrutinize** the information authors write. A best-selling book can make a lot of money, so some authors find it **tempting** to make up lies. In one famous case, a writer **concocted** a completely fictitious history about himself. The writing seemed **credible**, so most readers believed his story. However, the writer later was unable to **document** the facts in the book, and he was revealed as a fake. Although the writer's tale was not **legitimate**, many people still found it meaningful. Even these readers agree that they would rather not be **left in the dark**, wondering whether or not a story is true. They would rather be aware of any major **alteration** of facts that could turn a good true story into just a good story.

1. _____ (v.) to control or use in a skillful way

2. _____ (phr.) prevented from learning something

3. _____ (v.) to invent a story, an excuse, etc.

4. _____ (n.) a strong feeling in favor of or against one group of people or one side in an argument, often not based on fair judgment

5. _____ (n.) a change to something

6. _____ (v.) to look at or examine somebody or something carefully

7. _____ (adj.) can be believed or trusted

8. _____ (adj.) morally correct or acceptable

9. _____ (adj.) valid; fair

10. _____ (adj.) existing as a basic or permanent part of somebody or something

11. _____ (v.) to prove or support something with evidence

12. _____ (adj.) attractive, making people want to have it or do it

PREVIEW READING 2

You are going to read an excerpt from the college textbook *Phototruth or Photofiction? Ethics and Media Imagery in the Digital Age* by Thomas H. Wheeler. It asks how far journalists can go when manipulating photographs.

Think about the title and look at the picture. What do you predict the author will say about manipulating photographs in journalism?

☐ It is always acceptable.

☐ It is sometimes acceptable.

☐ It is never acceptable.

Phototruth or Photofiction?

1   Any discussion of "**manipulated**" photography must begin with the recognition that photography itself is an **inherent** manipulation—a manipulation of light, a process with many steps and stages, all subject to the **biases** and interpretations of the photographer, printer, editor, or viewer. Photography is not absolute "reality." It is not unqualified "truth." It is not purely "objective." It was never any of those things, and it has always been subject to distortion. Indeed, many of its earliest practitioners were more concerned with **concocting** fantasy than **documenting** reality. They were artists, not journalists.

2   Still, one branch of photography—called "photojournalism"—has acquired a special standing in the public mind. Newspaper and magazine readers generally believe that a photo can *reflect* reality in a **credible** way.

3   But why? Why has photography seemed so inherently realistic for so long? Much of the trust in photojournalism comes from average citizens' everyday experiences with personal photography. We point our cameras at our families, friends, and vacation sights and view the prints as **legitimate** documents that "capture" the events and scenes in meaningful ways. Countless millions of us collect our photos in albums and pass them on to future generations, not only for entertainment or curiosity value but as evidence of the way we once looked and the way the world once worked. As Dartmouth College professor Marianne Hirsch has said, "People say if there was a fire, the first thing they would save is their photo albums. We almost fear we'll lose our memories if we lose our albums."

4   This credibility has survived despite photography's history of occasional duplicity[1]. However, digital manipulation may challenge this trust more than a century and a half of other methods of fakery. Commentators have observed, "There's nothing new about faking photos," but that is not quite right. There is something new. Computer technology has made photo doctoring much easier to do and accessible to many more people.

5   It seems that with each new graphics software program, the opportunities for fictionalizing images become ever more numerous and **tempting**. One result is that "the objective 'truth' of photographs has become something of a quaint[2] concept" (*American Photo*). Michael Morse of the National Press Photographers Association agrees: "People have no idea how much **alteration** is going on." This raises thorny **ethical** challenges for professionals, educators, and students alike.

6   For decades, photojournalists and editors have opposed misleading alterations, particularly in "hard news" photos (images of war, crime scenes, political events, natural disasters, etc.). As computer manipulations have become more common, however, adherence to photojournalistic norms has given way to the temptations of commerce, even in respected newspapers and news magazines.

7   For example, during the processing of *National Geographic's* February 1982 photo of the Great Pyramids of Giza, a pyramid was digitally shifted to make the image fit the cover. The alteration provoked much

---

[1] **duplicity:** dishonest behavior that is intended to make people believe something that is not true
[2] **quaint:** attractive in an unusual or old-fashioned way

controversy, not so much because it was drastic (it was relatively insignificant) but because it appeared in a magazine long respected for its authenticity.

National Geographic's February 1982 photo of the Great Pyramids of Giza

8   In 1998, *National Geographic* editor Bill Allen said, "Nearly two decades ago we moved one pyramid to get the same effect as if the photographer had walked perhaps fifty yards to the left before taking the photograph. And yet after all that time, one of the most common questions I'm asked is, 'Do you guys still move pyramids?' This reminds all of us of just how fragile our credibility is. If you lose it, it's almost impossible to ever get it back. It's why we're such fanatics about disclosure[3] now at *National Geographic*."

9   Kenneth Brower's article in the May 1998 *Atlantic Monthly* listed a number of faked nature photos and sequences, including a polar bear in Antarctica that appeared in a full-page ad for *National Geographic Online* (there are no polar bears in Antarctica; there are polar bears in the Arctic—and also in the Ohio zoo where this particular animal was photographed)!

10   The following are just some of the many other examples of "photomanipulation" that have appeared in print:

- The September 8, 2000, edition of the *New York Daily News* carried a picture of U.S. President Bill Clinton shaking hands with Cuban President Fidel Castro. In fact, the handshake was not photographed. The picture was a computerized composite[4] labeled "photo illustration."

- The winner of a spelling bee[5] sponsored by the *New York Daily News* was photographed for a story in the *New York Post*, which removed the name of its rival newspaper from the image of the winner's identification card.

- One person was deleted from the center of a news photo appearing in the *Asbury Park Press* in New Jersey. The space was filled with cloned portions of a background object.

- In all of their outdoor photos of the 1984 Summer Olympic Games, editors at the *Orange County Register* changed the color of the Los Angeles sky (notorious for its smog) to clear blue.

11   Some professionals might consider a few of this chapter's examples to be relatively innocuous[6], but in most cases readers were **left in the dark**. In these images, photography's presumed relationship to reality was disrupted. Readers might have a simpler description: They might call the photos lies.

12   The inherent trustworthiness once attributed to photography is withering[7], at least in the opinion of many observers. Whether it will vanish altogether is an open question. In any case, from now on, assumptions once taken for granted will be **scrutinized**—for good reason. Visual journalists will have to accommodate these shifts and re-examine their own practices and ethics if they are to successfully separate their work from art, cartoons, fantasy, and fiction.

---

[3] **disclosure:** the act of making information public

[4] **composite:** two or more pictures edited together
[5] **spelling bee:** a competition in which participants have to spell difficult words correctly
[6] **innocuous:** not harmful or dangerous
[7] **withering:** growing weaker before disappearing completely

MAIN IDEAS

Answer these questions. Write the number of the paragraph where you found each answer. Then compare your answers with a partner.

1. Why are photographs always manipulated in some way? **Paragraph** ____

   _____

   _____

2. Why do most people trust the photographs they see in the news media? **Paragraph** ____

   _____

   _____

3. How is digital fakery different from earlier forms of photographic manipulation? **Paragraph** ____

   _____

   _____

4. What does the example of the pyramid in *National Geographic* say about the credibility of photojournalism? **Paragraph** ____

   _____

   _____

5. Why are the examples in this reading important even though many of them are relatively minor changes? **Paragraph** ____

   _____

   _____

DETAILS

Match each sentence with the correct person or publication.

____ 1. Photographs have such great value for many people that they are almost afraid of losing their memories if their photo albums are lost.

____ 2. It is old-fashioned to believe that photographs are inherently objective.

____ 3. Most magazine readers do not realize how much photographs have been manipulated.

_____ 4. When people stop believing in your honesty, it is very hard to convince them otherwise.

_____ 5. Many nature photographs in magazines have been faked (for example, showing a polar bear in Antarctica).

a. Bill Allen of *National Geographic*

b. *Atlantic Monthly* article by Kenneth Brower

c. *American Photo* magazine

d. Professor Marianne Hirsch of Dartmouth College

e. Michael Morse of the National Press Photographers Association

 **WHAT DO YOU THINK?**

A. Discuss the questions in a group. Then choose one question and write one or two paragraphs in response.

1. Are photographs important to you? Why or why not?

2. Do you think of photography as more a form of art or journalism? Please explain.

3. Do you care if a photograph in a magazine or newspaper has been manipulated? Why or why not?

B. Think about both Reading 1 and Reading 2 as you discuss the questions.

1. How might an advertiser manipulate a photograph to improve an ad?

2. If maps and photographs always lie in some ways, how can we learn the truth?

Identifying **Greek and Latin roots** (or **stems**) will help you recognize and understand new words. Words with these roots are especially common in formal written English, so using these words will aid in reading comprehension and add sophistication to your writing.

Common roots

Root	Meaning	Examples
mot-/mov-/mob-	move	promote, immobile
just-/jur-	right, legal	justify, jury
her-/hes-	stick	coherent, cohesive
vid-/vis-	see, notice	evidence, visible

You should also watch for other roots when you recognize groups of words with similar meanings.

A. Read each sentence. Using your knowledge of roots, circle the word or phrase that best matches the meaning of each bold word.

1. The patient reported reduced **mobility**.
   a. ability to speak
   b. ability to read
   c. ability to move

2. You need to choose an **adhesive** that works on wood.
   a. paint
   b. pencil
   c. glue

3. I don't **envisage** any problem with this plan.
   a. remember
   b. create
   c. expect

4. She was angry at the **injustice** of the professor's decision.
   a. humor
   b. unfairness
   c. danger

5. The student was **motivated** to study hard by her teacher.
   a. moved
   b. told
   c. warned

6. There is an **inherent** problem with this type of car.
   a. unusual
   b. unavoidable
   c. annoying

7. She was unable to provide a **justification** for her behavior.
   a. plan
   b. wish
   c. good explanation

8. Successful companies are often led by great **visionaries**.
   a. people with a lot of money
   b. people with a lot of power
   c. people with a lot of imagination

 Tip for Success

Learning Greek and Latin roots can improve your English spelling. For example, if you know *millimeter* comes from *milli-*, you will remember to write it with a double *l*.

B. Look at the sets of words below the box. The common root is bold. Choose the answer in the box that best defines each bold root. Then explain your choices to a partner.

break	follow	life	thousand
circle/round	law	other/different	write

1. hemi**sphere**, **spher**ical, blogo**sphere**   sphere   = _____

2. **alter**native, **alter**ation, **alter**   alter-   = _____

3. **sequ**ence, **sec**ond, **sequ**el   sequ-/sec-   = _____

4. sur**viv**e, **viv**id, re**viv**e   viv-   = _____

5. de**scrip**tion, post**script**, **scrib**ble   scrip-/scrib-   = _____

6. **leg**itimate, **leg**al, **leg**islation   leg-   = _____

7. **mill**ennium, **milli**meter, **milli**pede   milli-   = _____

8. **frag**ile, **frag**ment, **fract**ion   frag-/fract-   = _____

Writing Skill	Writing with unity

In good writing, each paragraph has **unity**: it explores one idea. This helps readers to understand all the main ideas in a text. If you mix different ideas in a paragraph, your readers may become confused, and your writing will not be effective. Sometimes, one idea needs several paragraphs, in which case each paragraph should describe one part of the idea. This keeps the reader focused on one point at a time.

The complete piece of writing (essay, article, report, etc.) also needs unity. All the points and ideas in the paragraphs should support one topic, argument, thesis, or purpose. This will keep your writing clear, interesting, and persuasive.

A. A cartographer working for an advertising agency is writing a proposal for an ad campaign for Rudy's Plumbing Supply. Look at the writer's notes, and then follow the instructions below.

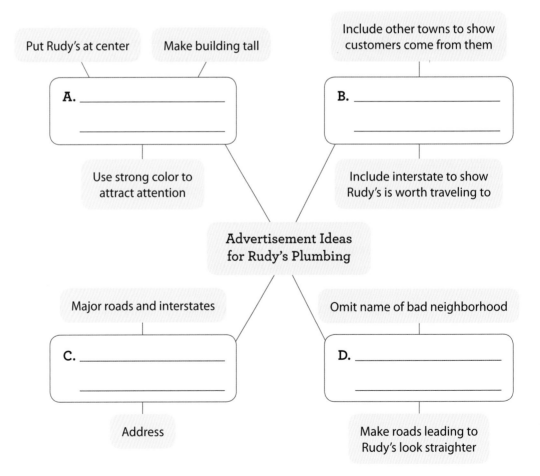

1. Label each cluster with an idea. You will not use one idea.

> Basic features of the map | Make Rudy's look more accessible
> Information about other businesses | Stimulate demand
> Make Rudy's look impressive

2. Check (✓) each idea that the writer could include without affecting the unity of the proposal. Write *X* if an idea does not fit anywhere.

_____ a. Add this line of copy (text): "Just around the corner!"

_____ b. Give Rudy's website.

_____ c. Print a customer's review of Rudy's service.

_____ d. Suggest that people don't mind traveling a long way to go to Rudy's.

_____ e. Put a photograph of Rudy at the top to add personal appeal.

Tip for Success

Notice the format of this business proposal. A proposal is a common form of real-world writing. Proposals always include the company's name and address as well as the date.

B. Read this draft of the agency's proposal and answer the questions below.

Tildon Advertising
290 West Main, Tildon, PA

From: Liz Madison, Account Executive
To: Mr. Rudy Swenson, Manager, Rudy's Plumbing Supply
Date: March 14
Re: Ad Proposal
Dear Mr. Swenson,

1   Thank you for asking us to design an advertisement for your store. Please find below a description of the ad we are proposing.

2   The centerpiece of the ad is a map. Maps are excellent attention-getters. The map will contain all the practical information customers need to find your business: the address, the major roads, and the nearby interstates. Obviously, most of your customers are local, and few of them need the interstate to get to your store. However, we want to show them that your store is so good that a number of customers might also come from far away. In this way, we can stimulate a great deal of demand for your business.

3   In addition to including the interstate, we will mention the names of several neighboring towns. You might attract a few customers from other towns, but mainly we will show that your business is popular and known throughout the region.

4   In our meeting, you asked us to stress the accessibility of your business, and our ad will make customers feel comfortable about visiting you. You told us you were concerned that your business is not located in the best

---

part of town. Therefore, we recommend omitting the name of your neighborhood and some road names. The ad will encourage new customers to visit you and judge the quality of your service, not the neighborhood.

5   A good impression is also achieved by using strong colors in the ad and drawing your building from an angle that increases the scale of the building. The building will be at the center of the ad, and its prominent position and size will bring in plenty of new business.

6   We hope you approve of this proposal. We feel that it tells a truthful and persuasive story about Rudy's Plumbing Supply. Please do not hesitate to contact me if you have any questions.

1. Write the purpose or main idea of each paragraph. Use the cluster map in Activity A to help you.

Paragraph 1: _____

Paragraph 2: _____

Paragraph 3: _____

Paragraph 4: _____

Paragraph 5: _____

Paragraph 6: _____

2. What idea does the writer use to give unity through the entire proposal?

_____

Grammar   Quantifiers   web

Quantifiers are words that modify nouns and noun phrases and talk about amounts. They give information about *how much* (for a non-count noun) and *how many* (for a plural count noun). Quantifiers generally come before the noun.

Noncount nouns

little   much   a large amount of   too much
    a little   a great deal of   so much

Plural count nouns

few   several   a large number of   too many

    a few   many   so many

Both count and noncount nouns

no   hardly any   plenty of   most (of)   all

    none of   any/some   a lot/lots of   almost all

Be especially careful with these quantifiers:

A few / a little have positive meanings: the quantity is small but still important.

☐ There is **a little** demand for the product, so we will keep selling it.

Few / little have negative meanings: the quantity is almost zero.

☐ There is **little** demand for the product, so we will stop selling it.

Use *a lot of* instead of *much* in affirmative sentences.

✓ We did **a lot of** advertising this year.
✗ We did much advertising this year.

Any is used in negative sentences and questions to mean *some*.

☐ Do you have **any** questions? Yes, I have **some** questions

However, *any* can also mean "it doesn't matter which" in affirmative sentences with a singular count or non-count noun.

☐ Look in **any** book for an example at **any** time.

Almost all means nearly 100 percent.

Note: Do not use *almost* by itself; it is an adverb, not a quantifier.

✓ **Almost all** people take photographs.
✗ Almost people take photographs.

A. Circle the correct quantifier to complete each sentence.

1. *Some / Any* magazine photographs are manipulated.

2. Your ad should not contain *too much / too many* details.

3. *Almost / Almost all* our trust in photography comes from our experience with it.

4. Anyone can fake a photograph with the right software and *little / a little* experience.

5. *Few / A few* readers are using our map, so we must improve it.

6. I will draw attention to your business by using *a lot of / much* color.

B. Circle the correct sentence to complete each conversation.

1. I don't like this book. There's too much text, and there aren't enough pictures.
   a. You're right. There are some photographs.
   b. You're right. There are few photographs.

2. Is this a popular magazine?
   a. No, few people read it.
   b. No, a few people read it.

3. Why do you think this ad uses a map?
   a. Because it has so much good information.
   b. Because it has hardly any good information.

4. Can you finish the proposal by tomorrow?
   a. I don't think so. I need little more time.
   b. I don't think so. I need a little more time.

5. The survey found that 45 percent of people expect magazines to manipulate photographs.
   a. OK, but plenty of people still trust photojournalists!
   b. OK, but almost all people still trust photojournalists!

C. Look back at the model proposal in Activity B of the Writing Skill on page 101. Circle the quantifiers in the proposal.

In this assignment, you will pretend that you work for an advertising agency that designs print or Web advertisements. You will write a proposal for a client describing your idea for an ad. As you prepare your proposal, think about the Unit Question, "How well does a picture illustrate the truth?" and refer to the Self-Assessment checklist on page 106. Use information from Readings 1 and 2 and your work in this unit to support your ideas.

For alternative unit assignments, see the *Q: Skills for Success Teacher's Handbook*.

PLAN AND WRITE

A. BRAINSTORM Complete the following tasks.

1. Work with a partner. Choose a product or service for another pair of students to advertise: for example, your school, a business you know, a product you use, or something that does not exist yet. Imagine you represent that product or service. In your notebook, write a paragraph describing it and the type of advertisement you want to create, such as a poster or a newspaper ad.

2. Exchange paragraphs with another pair. Read and discuss the paragraphs. Ask for clarification as necessary. You are going to write a proposal to convince the other pair to hire you to design an ad for their product or service.

3. With your partner, answer these questions.
   a. What type of graphic will you use in the ad? Draw or describe in words the map, photograph, drawing, or other graphic you will use.

   _____

   _____

   _____

   b. How will the graphic make the ad persuasive?

   _____

   _____

   c. How will the graphic help promote the product or service?

   _____

   _____

   _____

B. PLAN Draw a cluster diagram to help you plan and organize your proposal. Write each main idea in a circle. Then connect supporting details, explanations, and examples outside each circle. See the Writing Skill on page 100 for help.

C. WRITE Write a draft of the proposal. Use your cluster diagram and any other ideas from your discussions. Think about the unity of each paragraph and of the whole proposal. Be sure to vary your vocabulary. Look at the Self-Assessment checklist below to guide your writing.

REVISE AND EDIT

A. PEER REVIEW Exchange proposals with the same pair of students you worked with in the Brainstorm activity. Read their proposal. As you read, write key words for the main ideas in your notebook. Look at the key words as you answer the questions, and discuss them with your partner.

1. Are the ideas in a logical order?

2. Does each paragraph have unity?

3. Is the proposal persuasive?

4. Does the proposal need more details or explanations?

5. Would you hire this pair to create an ad for your product or service? Explain why or why not.

B. REWRITE Review the answers to the questions in Activity A. You may want to revise and rewrite your proposal.

C. EDIT Complete the Self-Assessment checklist as you prepare to write the final draft of your proposal. Be prepared to hand in your work or discuss it in class.

Yes	No	SELF-ASSESSMENT
☐	☐	Is each paragraph written with unity?
☐	☐	Does the entire proposal have unity?
☐	☐	Are quantifiers varied and used correctly?
☐	☐	Does the proposal include vocabulary from the unit?
☐	☐	Did you check the proposal for punctuation, spelling, and grammar?

Track Your Success

Circle the words you learned in this unit.

Nouns	Verbs	Adjectives
alteration AWL	concoct	credible
bias AWL	distort AWL	ethical AWL
campaign 🔑	document 🔑 AWL	inherent AWL
competitor	justify 🔑 AWL	legitimate
paradox	manipulate AWL	principal 🔑 AWL
precision AWL	omit	prominent
scale 🔑	portray	tempting
white lie	scrutinize	

Phrase
left in the dark

🔑 Oxford 3000™ words

AWL Academic Word List

Check (✓) the skills you learned. If you need more work on a skill, refer to the page(s) in parentheses.

READING	⬤	I can preview a text. (p. 86)
VOCABULARY	⬤	I can use Latin and Greeks roots to understand words. (p. 98)
WRITING	⬤	I can write with unity. (p. 100)
GRAMMAR	⬤	I can use quantifiers correctly. (pp. 102–103)
LEARNING OUTCOME	⬤	I can create an advertising proposal describing my idea for a print or Web advertisement.

UNIT 5

Global Citizenship

READING ●	making inferences
VOCABULARY ●	prefixes
WRITING ●	organizing supporting ideas
GRAMMAR ●	parallel structure and ellipsis

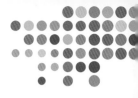

LEARNING OUTCOME ●

Prepare an essay describing the
importance of global cooperation.

Unit QUESTION

Why is global cooperation important?

PREVIEW THE UNIT

A Discuss these questions with your classmates.

Have you ever worked with someone from another country?
What were the benefits of cooperating with this person?

What issues or problems in your country do other countries
also have? How do they affect you personally? Would
cooperating with other countries help solve these problems?

Look at the photo. Why do you think all of these people
from different countries are working together?

B Discuss the Unit Question above with your classmates.

Listen to *The Q Classroom*, Track 2 on CD 2, to hear other answers.

109

C Complete the survey. Compare your rankings with a partner.

Global Cooperation Survey

Rank the success of global cooperation in the following fields from 1 (highest) to 8 (lowest).

____ Stopping the spread of disease

____ Preventing hunger

____ Maintaining peace

____ Developing new technology

____ Advancing science and medicine

____ Protecting the environment

____ Exploring space

____ Improving education

D Choose a successful example of global cooperation from a field in the survey. Write three reasons why you think it was successful.

_____

_____

_____

E Discuss these questions with your partner.

1. Would the different countries in your examples have achieved the same results working alone? Why was it important that the different countries in your examples worked together?

2. Choose one of the fields in the survey for which you gave a low ranking. How might countries better cooperate in this field?

3. In your opinion, are there any fields in which it is impossible for countries to work together successfully? Why?

READING 1 | In Norway, Global Seed Vault Guards Genetic Resources

VOCABULARY

Here are some words and a phrase from Reading 1. Read the sentences. Circle the answer that best matches the meaning of each bold word or phrase.

1. The seeds of each plant carry all of the **genetic** information necessary to transfer characteristics from a parent plant to a new plant.
   a. related to nutrition or ingredients
   b. related to development or origin

2. There are so few members of some plant species left that they are in danger of becoming **extinct**.
   a. gone forever
   b. overgrown

3. The Global Seed Vault in Norway is trying to **consolidate** many smaller collections of rare plant seeds and shoots from all over the world.
   a. bring together in a single place
   b. sell for a large amount of money

4. Some scientists worry that the loss of plants and animals all around the world is **inevitable** because of global warming and human activity.
   a. faster
   b. unavoidable

5. Fears of rapid climate change gives many scientists a sense of **urgency** about gathering rare seeds and shoots while there is still time.
   a. immediate importance
   b. value

6. Natural disasters, as well as the effects of **erosion** over time, can lead to the loss of a plant's natural habitat.
   a. human activities
   b. destruction and wearing away

7. The Global Seed Vault will play a **crucial** role in protecting the world's food crops from weather disasters and climate change.
   a. small
   b. very important

8. Plants have even more **vulnerability** to climate change and natural disasters than animals do because plants cannot move.

   a. ability to protect oneself

   b. openness to attack or damage

9. Seeds are stored in many different locations, but the Global Seed Vault is a **Plan B** in case of disasters at other storage sites.

   a. an alternative solution in case the first idea or arrangement does not succeed

   b. a single, obvious best solution to a problem

10. Food crops are always in danger from **devastating** diseases and natural disasters.

   a. extremely destructive and damaging

   b. minor and easy to stop

11. It is important to **conserve** seeds and shoots so that future generations can enjoy and use the same plants we have today.

   a. plant

   b. look after and save

12. Many of the challenges **confronting** the world can be solved only through global cooperation.

   a. facing or threatening

   b. hiding from or tricking

PREVIEW READING 1

Tip for Success

As you are reading, ask yourself questions about the text, such as "What is the main idea of this paragraph?" or "How do I feel about this?"

You are going to read an article from the newspaper *International Herald Tribune* that reports on the world's response to the dangers threatening the genetic diversity of the world's food supply.

What do you think might cause plants to become extinct? Write three possible reasons.

1. _____

2. _____

3. _____

In Norway, Global Seed Vault Guards Genetic Resources

By Elisabeth Rosenthal

1   LONGYEARBYEN, Norway: With plant species disappearing at an alarming rate, scientists and governments are creating a global network of plant banks to store seeds and sprouts[1]— precious **genetic** resources that may be needed for man to adapt the world's food supply to climate change.

Global Seed Vault

2   This week, the flagship of that effort, the Global Seed Vault, received its first seeds here—millions of them. Bored[2] into the middle of a snow-topped Arctic mountain, the seed vault has as its goal the storing of every kind of seed from every collection on the planet. While the original seeds will remain in ordinary seed banks, the seed vault's stacked gray boxes will form a backup in case natural disaster or human error erases the seeds from the outside world.

3   The seed vault is part of a far broader effort to gather and classify information about plants and their genes. In Leuven, Belgium, scientists are scouring[3] the world for banana samples and cryo-preserving their shoots[4] in liquid nitrogen before they become **extinct**. A similar effort is under way in France on coffee plants. A number of plants, most from the tropics, do not produce seeds that can be stored.

cryo-preserved garlic shoot

4   For years, a hodgepodge network of seed banks has been amassing[5] seed and shoot collections. Labs in Mexico banked corn species. Those in Nigeria banked cassava. These scattershot efforts are being **consolidated** and systematized, in part because of better technology to preserve plant genes and in part because of rising alarm about the trajectory of climate change and its impact on world food production.

5   "We started thinking about this post-9/11 and on the heels of Hurricane Katrina," said Cary Fowler, president of the Global Crop Diversity

---

[1] **sprout:** a new part growing on a plant
[2] **bore:** to make a long, deep hole with a tool or by digging

[3] **scour:** to search very carefully because you are looking for something
[4] **shoot:** the part that grows up from the ground when a plant starts to grow
[5] **amass:** to collect something, especially in large quantities

Trust, the nonprofit group that runs the vault. "Everyone was saying, 'Why didn't anyone prepare for a hurricane before?'

6 "Well, we are losing biodiversity every day—it's a kind of drip, drip, drip. It's also **inevitable**. We need to do something about it."

7 This week, the **urgency** of the problem was underscored as wheat prices reached record highs and wheat stores dropped to the lowest level in 35 years. Droughts[6] and new diseases cut wheat production in many parts of the world.

8 "The **erosion** of plants' genetic resources is really going fast," said Rony Swennen, head of crop biotechnics at the Catholic University of Leuven, who has cryo-preserved half of the world's 1,200 banana varieties. "We're at a critical moment, and if we don't act fast we're going to lose a lot of plants that we may need."

banana varieties

9 The United Nations International Treaty on Plant Genetic Resources, ratified in 2004, created a formal global network for banking and sharing seeds, as well as studying their genetic traits. Last year, its database received thousands of new seed varieties.

10 A well-organized system of plant banks could be **crucial** in responding to climate crises because it could identify genetic material and plant strains that are better able to cope with a changed environment. At the Global Seed Vault, hundreds of grey boxes containing seeds from Syria to Mexico were being moved this week into a freezing vault to be placed in suspended animation. Collectively they harbor[7] a vast range of characteristics, including the ability to withstand drier, warmer climate.

11 Climate change is expected to bring new weather stresses as well as new plant pests into agricultural regions. Heat-trapping carbon dioxide emissions will produce not only global warming but also an increase in extreme weather events, like floods and droughts, the Intergovernmental Panel on Climate Change concluded.

12 Already, three-quarters of biodiversity in crops has been lost in the last century, according to the UN Food and Agriculture Organization. Eighty percent of corn varieties that existed in the 1930s no longer exist today, for example. In the United States, 94 percent of peas are no longer grown.

13 Seed banks have operated for decades, but many are based in agricultural areas and few are as technologically advanced or secure as the Global Seed Vault. Earlier efforts had been regarded as resources for gardeners, scientists, farmers, and food aficionados rather than a tool for human survival.

14 The importance and **vulnerability** of seed banks have become apparent in recent years. Centers in Afghanistan and Iraq were destroyed during conflicts by looters who were after the plastic containers that held the seeds. In the Philippines, a typhoon demolished the wall of a seed bank, destroying many samples.

15 In reviewing seed bank policies a few years ago, experts looked at the banks in a new light, said Fowler of the Global Crop Diversity Trust. "We said, 'We may have some of the best seed banks in the world, but look at where they are: Peru, Colombia, Syria, India, Ethiopia, and the Philippines.' So a lot of us were asking, 'What's **Plan B**?'"

---

[6] **drought:** a long period of time when there is little or no rain   [7] **harbor:** to contain something and allow it to develop

16 The goal of the new global plant bank system is to protect the precious stored plant genes from the vagaries[8] of climate, politics, and human error. Many banks are now "in countries where the political situation is not stable and it is difficult to rely on refrigeration," said Swennen, the biotechnics expert. Seeds must be stored at minus 20 degrees Celsius (minus 4 Fahrenheit), and plant sprouts that rely on cryo-preservation must be far colder.

17 "We are inside a mountain in the Arctic because we wanted a really, really safe place that operates by itself," Fowler said.

18 Underground in Longyearbyen, just 1,000 kilometers, or 600 miles, from the North Pole, the seeds will stay frozen regardless of power failures. The Global Crop Diversity Trust is also funding research into methods for storing genetic material from plants like bananas and coconuts that cannot be stored as seed.

19 The vault was built by Norway, and its operations are financed by government and private donations, including $20 million from the United Kingdom, $12 million from Australia, $11 million from Germany, and $6.5 million from the United States.

20 The effort to preserve a wide variety of plant genes in banks is particularly urgent because many farms now grow just one or two crops. They are particularly vulnerable to pests, disease, and climate change.

21 Just as efforts to preserve biodiversity increase, economics encourages farmers to focus on fewer crops. But those seeds may contain traits that will prove advantageous in another place or another time. Scientists at Cornell University recently borrowed a gene from a South American potato to make potatoes that resist late blight, a **devastating** disease that caused the Irish potato famine[9] in the 19th century.

22 "You need a system to **conserve** the variety so it doesn't go extinct," Fowler said. "A farmer may make a bowl of porridge with the last seeds of a strain that is of no use to him, and then it's gone. And potentially those are exactly the genes we will need a decade later."

23 Scientists are also working to learn more about the genetic characteristics of each banked seed—crucial knowledge that is often not recorded. Ultimately, plant breeders will be able to consult a global database to find seeds with genes suitable for the particular challenge **confronting** a region, like corn with a stalk that is strong enough to resist high winds or wheat that needs less water.

24 "The seed vault is adding a new dimension to an evolving global system," Swennen said. "We should have done it sooner. But the technology and the global interest weren't available."

---

[8] **vagaries:** changes that are difficult to predict or control   [9] **famine:** a lack of food during a long period of time in a region

Main Ideas

Each main idea contains an error. Cross out the incorrect information and correct it.

1. Plant species are disappearing quickly, but scientists and governments are not doing much to save them.

2. The Global Seed Vault has the goal of storing seeds from North America and Europe in case an emergency destroys any of them.

3. The United Nations International Treaty on Plant Genetic Resources created a global network for banking and sharing seeds, but it ignored the need to study their genetic traits.

4. The Intergovernmental Panel on Climate Change decided that plants will be affected by global warming, but not by extreme weather events.

5. The Global Seed Vault is located in a dangerous place that is too cold to protect seeds and plant sprouts.

6. Preserving a variety of plant genes in the Global Seed Vault isn't going to help protect the world's food supply from changing climate conditions or new plant diseases.

DETAILS

Match each detail with the country it is associated with.

Countries

___ 1. Norway   ___ 6. the United States

___ 2. Belgium   ___ 7. Afghanistan

___ 3. France   ___ 8. the Philippines

___ 4. Mexico   ___ 9. the United Kingdom

___ 5. Nigeria   ___ 10. Ireland

Details

a. This country is the location of the Global Seed Vault.

b. This country was the location of a potato famine in the 19th century.

c. This nation donated $20 million to the Global Seed Vault.

d. Ninety-four percent of peas are no longer grown here.

e. Scientists in this country are searching the world for banana samples and preserving their shoots.

f. A typhoon hit a seed bank here, destroying many samples.

g. Scientists in this country are searching for and preserving coffee plant samples.

h. Labs here banked cassava.

i. Seed banks in this country were destroyed in conflicts.

j. Labs here banked corn species.

Q WHAT DO YOU THINK?

Discuss the questions in a group. Then choose one question and write freely for five to ten minutes in response.

1. Will the global partnerships being formed while working on the Global Seed Vault help the world in other ways? Why or why not?

2. Do you think the scientists and governments in the article on the Global Seed Vault will be successful in preserving seeds and shoots from around the world? What are the consequences for humanity if the Global Seed Vault project is not successful?

3. Does your home country have any unique plants or crops that aren't found anywhere else? Do you feel they should be preserved in the Global Seed Vault? Why or why not?

Reading Skill   Making inferences   web+

Writers often use facts and opinions to suggest ideas rather than giving the ideas to the reader directly. The reader has to determine, or **infer**, what the writer is saying. Making an inference is making a logical conclusion about something based on the information that is given. Making inferences while reading a text can improve your overall comprehension and can help you become a more critical reader.

This excerpt is taken from Reading 1:

☐   Bored into the middle of a snow-topped Arctic mountain, the seed vault . . .

The text doesn't need to say exactly what kind of place is best for preserving the world's seeds and shoots. From the information in the excerpt, you can determine that it is a place that needs to be safe and secure, as well as cold and far away. You come to this conclusion because of clues such as *bored, snow-topped, Arctic*, and *middle of a . . . mountain*.

Tip Critical Thinking

When you infer ideas from a text, you are using separate pieces of information as clues or evidence to support a conclusion. This is an analytical process and shows a deeper understanding of the material.

A. Match each excerpt from Reading 1 with the correct inference.

Excerpts

_____ 1. With plant species disappearing at an alarming rate, scientists and governments are creating a global network of plant banks to store seeds and sprouts—precious genetic resources that may be needed for man to adapt the world's food supply to climate change. (Paragraph 1)

_____ 2. In Leuven, Belgium, scientists are scouring the world for banana samples and cryo-preserving their shoots in liquid nitrogen before they become extinct. (Paragraph 3)

_____ 3. Those [seed banks] in Nigeria banked cassava. (Paragraph 4)

_____ 4. Collectively they [seeds from many different countries] harbor a vast range of characteristics, including the ability to withstand drier, warmer climate. (Paragraph 10)

_____ 5. Eighty percent of corn varieties that existed in the 1930s no longer exist today, for example. In the United States, 94 percent of peas are no longer grown. (Paragraph 12)

_____ 6. Seeds must be stored at minus 20 degrees Celsius (minus 4 Fahrenheit), and plant sprouts that rely on cryo-preservation must be far colder. (Paragraph 16)

Inferences

a. These seeds are important because the genetic information they contain will help grow food despite climate change and global warming.

b. Some food crops are more important in certain countries than others.

c. The world's food supply is in danger.

d. Some rare varieties of important food crops are hard to find, and they are in danger of disappearing soon.

e. Cold areas of the globe, such as the Arctic, are excellent locations for seed banks.

f. Farmers are growing fewer varieties of crops compared to the past.

B. Read each statement. What can you infer from the information in the statement? Write your inferences. Then compare your inferences with a partner.

1. **Statement:** Bored into the middle of a snow-topped Arctic mountain, the seed vault has as its goal the storing of every kind of seed from every collection on the planet.

   Inference: _As many of the world's seeds as possible need to be stored in a safe place that is cold and far away._

2. **Statement:** Mexico is the perfect place for corn seeds to be banked.

   Inference: _____

   _____

   _____

3. **Statement:** Scientists cheered when the United Nations International Treaty on Plant Genetic Resources finally created a formal global network for banking seeds and studying their genetic traits.

   Inference: _____

   _____

   _____

4. **Statement:** In the Philippines, a typhoon demolished the wall of a seed bank, destroying many valuable samples.

   Inference: _____

   _____

   _____

READING 2 | The Long Countdown: For U.S. Astronauts, a Russian Second Home

VOCABULARY

Here are some words and phrases from Reading 1. Read their definitions. Then complete each sentence.

---

a bump in the road (*phr.*) a minor problem that is easily solved

approach (*n.*) a way of dealing with somebody or something

collaboration (*n.*) the act of working together to create or produce something

counterpart (*n.*) a person who has a position or function similar to somebody else's

dedication (*n.*) a willingness to devote your time and energy to something that you believe to be important

dependable (*adj.*) able to be trusted to do what it (they, he, or she) is supposed to do

eliminate (*v.*) to remove something that is not wanted or needed

orbiting (*adj.*) moving around something in space in a circular motion

playing hardball (*phr.*) doing anything in order to win, especially by acting tough and aggressive

robust (*adj.*) strong

scarcity (*n.*) a situation in which something does not exist in large quantities and is very hard to find

wariness (*n.*) an attitude of care and uncertainty because you think there may be a problem

---

1. During the negotiations, the Americans were _____, so they refused to compromise on any of their demands.

2. Difficulties between two governments can sometimes cause _____ for joint projects between the two nations, but the delay is usually ended quickly.

3. The American astronaut and her Russian _____ are cooperating closely in the International Space Station together.

4. The International Space Station is the result of years of _____ among the many different countries who contributed their efforts.

5. The International Space Station is a(n) _____ laboratory that circles Earth.

6. There was certainly no _____ of food when the Russian astronauts threw a party for the Americans; everybody had plenty to eat.

7. Before they came to trust each other, there was _____ between the Russian and Americans astronauts who were training together.

8. The Americans and Russians sometimes have a different _____ to problems, but the problems are usually solved in the end.

9. Astronauts will always face some risks because is impossible to _____ all of the dangers in outer space.

10. Astronauts must be _____ because they have to follow the same steps in the same way each time they encounter an emergency.

11. A spacecraft must be _____ to stand the stress of launching and the extreme cold once it reaches space.

12. Scientists from around the world have shown a great deal of _____; some have spent years trying solve the problems of extended space travel.

This article from the newspaper *The New York Times* looks at the relationship between Americans and Russians working on the International Space Station. Look at the title and subtitle of the article. Do you think that this example of countries working together will be a success?

CD 2
Track 4   **Read the article.**

The Long Countdown

For U.S. astronauts, a Russian second home

By John Schwartz

1   STAR CITY, Russia — Garrett Reisman was on his way to this formerly secret military base for several weeks of training, making his way through Kennedy Airport, when his cell phone rang. It was his boss, Steven W. Lindsey, the head of NASA's[1] astronaut office.

2   "Come back to Houston. They've canceled your training—they're **playing hardball**," Mr. Reisman recalled his boss saying. He was caught in a momentarily important dispute between NASA and the Russian space agency, Roscosmos.

3   Ultimately, Mr. Reisman's aborted trip was just **a bump in the road** on the way to space: he spent three months aboard the International Space Station earlier this year, performed a spacewalk, and even traded jokes over a video link with the TV host Stephen Colbert.

4   Everyone who works with the Russian space program has similar stories. And many of those stories are played out here in Star City, where cosmonauts and, now, astronauts from all over the world train to fly on Russian Soyuz spacecraft to go to the $100 billion International Space Station.

5   Star City has become an important second home for Americans working with their Russian **counterparts**, and it is about to become more important still. During the five-year gap after NASA shuts down the space shuttle program in 2010 and the next generation of spacecraft makes its debut by 2015, Russia will have the only ride for humans to the station.

American astronaut and Russian cosmonaut

6   Those who work side by side with their Russian counterparts say that strong relationships and mutual respect have resulted from the many years of **collaboration**. And they say that whatever the broader geopolitical concerns about relying on Russia for space transportation during the five years when the United States cannot get to the space station on its own rockets, they believe that the multinational partnership that built the station will hold.

[1] **NASA:** the National Aeronautics and Space Administration, the department of the U.S. government that is responsible for space exploration

7   "It's an amazing political achievement," Mr. Reisman said. "We've gone through so many different administrations[2]," not just in the United States and Russia, but in the dozen other nations that have taken part in building the **orbiting** laboratory. "It survived all of that," he said. "It's held together, and it's only strengthened over time as we've learned to work together."

8   To understand why people like Mr. Reisman believe the next 7 years can work, it is important to understand the previous 15, when the United States and Russia joined forces, first putting Americans aboard the Russian Mir space station and then building the International Space Station together. That joining of forces occurred here, at Star City. And in some ways, it did not have an auspicious[3] start.

9   In the earliest days of the partnership, in the mid-1990s, after the Soviet Union had crumbled and the new Russia was struggling to be born, **scarcity** of supplies meant real hunger. "There was no food on the shelves at all," said Dr. Michael Barratt, who worked among the first crews to prepare astronauts who would serve aboard the Mir. "Five nights out of seven, we had rice and beans."

10   Those early days were also marked by **wariness** and distrust. Energia, the spacecraft manufacturing company near the Mission Control Center in Korolev, near Moscow, would not let the Americans enter its facilities. Instead, Energia rented part of a nearby engineering college to prepare American hardware for the station. "The heat didn't work," said Mark Bowman, an early contract employee in Russia who is now the deputy director of NASA's human space flight program in Russia. The winter of 1994–95 was particularly bitter, he said, with temperatures that reached minus-30 degrees. The workers wore gloves and parkas indoors.

Delicate biological experiments designed for use inside the climate-controlled station froze and had to be replaced.

11   The next seven years look brighter, and warmer. "Things have improved so much since then," Mr. Bowman said. The Russian system has become more open, and the level of personal comfort and convenience has improved greatly.

12   Many of the Americans live in a set of duplexes at Star City that look a little like suburban condominiums that have been dropped, seemingly, from space into this Soviet landscape of brick buildings, fences, and barriers. They were designed and built to United States standards so that visitors could, for example, plug their laptops into the wall without having to dig around for an adapter.

13   Working side by side with the Russians, the Americans say, has helped them understand the nations' **approaches** to safety. Dr. Barratt said that when he first walked the grounds of Star City, he was surprised by how uneven the sidewalks were. At NASA, he said, "there'd be big red placards" warning people to watch their step. And if someone did fall, a lawsuit would soon follow. In Russia, he said, people simply watch their step.

14   The underlying point, said Mark Thiessen, the deputy to the current director of American operations at Star City, is that "Russians accept risk." Americans try "to **eliminate** risk instead of minimize it." The American approach is laudable[4], he said, but not always possible, and Americans end up more cautious than Russians. "No one is willing to say, 'I accept this risk,'" he said.

15   Many who write about the Russian space program focus on the impression of creaky age that the program can give—the abandoned buildings and rust at the launching site in

---

[2] **administration:** in the U.S., the president and the people and departments working with the president; the government of a country

[3] **auspicious:** showing signs that something is likely to be successful in the future

[4] **laudable:** deserving to be praised or admired

Baikonur, Kazakhstan, and the fact that the basic design of the Soyuz spacecraft has not changed in some 40 years.

16   But American experts suggest that the Russians' disregard for cosmetic perfection and development is immaterial, and that the age of the design shows a conservative approach to the risks of space travel that has served them well. "They spend their money where they have to," said Philip Cleary, a former director of NASA's human space flight program in Russia. "They're not so much worried about splashing a new coat of paint on a building if it's not required."

17   The Americans insist that, appearances aside, the Russians take safety every bit as seriously as they do. The result, several astronauts said, is that they have confidence in the Soyuz, which is as sturdy and **dependable** as a Kalashnikov rifle.

18   "Its inherent design is very **robust**," said Edward T. Lu, an astronaut who lived aboard the station in 2003 and now works for Google. He has flown to the space station and returned on a Soyuz, and he brought up two recent Soyuz re-entries, in which the capsule malfunctioned and tumbled back to Earth in a steep "ballistic[5]" path that subjected those inside to G-forces higher than usual. The astronauts were safe, however, because of the simplicity and strength of the Soyuz design.

19   The Americans say they have learned a great deal about getting things done in Russia. They know that the first answer to any request is likely to be no, but that negotiations can often bring things around to yes. Getting to know the people you deal with is more important than the rules. "No agreement is better than your relationship," Dr. Barratt said.

20   And none of them questions the **dedication** of their Russian counterparts. At the worst of the Soviet economic crisis, Dr. Barratt said, workers "were told to go on vacation" for a couple of months so they would not have to be paid. "They showed up at work the next day," he recalled.

21   The American workers at Star City say that on a personal level, geopolitics simply do not matter. Mr. Thiessen said that when such issues came up in conversation with his Russian counterparts, they would say: "That's politics. Let the government worry about the government. We're engineers. Let's solve this problem."

[5] **ballistic:** shot or fired through the air

MAIN IDEAS

Number the main ideas in the order they were presented in Reading 2.

____ a.   The history of U.S.-Russian collaboration in space shows why some people believe the next seven years will be successful.

____ b.   The Americans have learned a lot about getting things done in Russia.

__1__ c.   Star City in Russia is an important second home for Americans in the space program.

____ d.   The Russians and the Americans have different approaches to safety.

_____ e. The Americans and the Russians have a strong relationship and mutual respect for each other.

_____ f. The Russian space program can give the impression of being old and out of date, but it is quite good.

DETAILS

Match each detail with the main idea (a through f above) that it supports. There are two supporting details for each main idea.

_d_ 1. Russians accept risk.

_____ 2. NASA is shutting down its space shuttle program in 2010.

_____ 3. The Americans believe the Russians are very dedicated.

_____ 4. The basic design of the Soyuz spacecraft has not changed in 40 years, but it is sturdy and dependable.

_____ 5. Mr. Reisman considers the partnership "an amazing political achievement" because both countries have had many different administrations over the years.

_____ 6. Personal comfort and convenience have improved greatly since the days of eating rice and beans during training for nearly every meal.

_____ 7. Americans who have worked with the Russians believe that the multinational partnership that built the International Space Station will hold.

_____ 8. The Russian system has become more open since the early days, when Energia barred Americans from its facilities.

_____ 9. There are no signs warning people about the uneven sidewalks on the grounds of Star City, as there would be in the U.S.

_____ 10. The Soyuz capsule recently malfunctioned twice, but the astronauts were safe because of its simple and strong design.

_____ 11. Russia will have the only ride to the International Space Station from 2010 to 2015.

_____ 12. It is important to get to know the people you are dealing with.

Q WHAT DO YOU THINK?

A. Discuss the questions in a group. Then choose one question and write one or two paragraphs in response.

1. What kinds of challenges do you think you would face if you were working on a collaborative global project like the International Space Station? Would you be successful working on a project like this?

2. Could the resources being used for the International Space Station be put to better use? In your opinion, what projects are more important than the International Space Station? Why?

3. Is global cooperation necessary for a project like the International Space Station to be successful? Why or why not?

B. Think about both Reading 1 and Reading 2 as you discuss the questions.

1. Is the Global Seed Vault or the International Space Station a better example of global cooperation? Why?

2. Do you think there will be more of these sorts of global initiatives in the future? Why or why not?

Understanding the meanings of the different parts of a word is an important way to build vocabulary. A **prefix** can be added to the beginning of a word to change or add meaning, or create an entirely new word. For instance, the *un-* in *unhappy* changes the root word, *happy*, to mean its opposite. Another example is *tele-* (over a long distance; far) and the word *vision* (the ability to see). They combine to create the word for a piece of electronic equipment with a screen to watch moving pictures (*television*). Use a dictionary to learn more about various prefixes. For example, in this dictionary entry for *co-*, you learn that it can be used with a variety of root words and in different parts of speech. It adds the meaning of *together with* to the root word.

> **co-** /kou/ *prefix* (used in adjectives, adverbs, nouns, and verbs) together with: *co-produced* ♦ *cooperatively* ♦ *co-author* ♦ *coexist*

In this dictionary entry for *mal-*, you learn that it can also be used with a variety of root words and in different parts of speech.

> **mal-** /mæl/ *combining form* (in nouns, verbs, and adjectives) bad or badly; not correct or correctly: *malpractice* ♦ *malodorous* ♦ *malfunction*

All dictionary entries are from the *Oxford Advanced American Dictionary for learners of English* © Oxford University Press 2011.

A. Write the correct prefix from the box next to its definition on page 127. Then write as many words as you know that can use each prefix along with their parts of speech. When you are finished, check your answers in the dictionary and add to the chart if possible.

bio-	dis-	im-	mal-	non-
cryo-	geo-	inter-	multi-	re-

Prefix	Definition	Possible words	Possible parts of speech
1. multi-	more than one; many	multicolored, multimillionaire	nouns, adjectives
2.	not		
3.	involving the use of very low temperatures		
4.	(also il- /in- / ir-) not; the opposite of		
5.	of the earth		
6.	again		
7.	between; from one to another		
8.	bad or badly; not correct or correctly		
9.	not; the opposite of		
10.	connected with living things or human life		

 **Tip for Success**

Whenever you
encounter new
vocabulary words you
want to remember,
try writing sentences
with them in your
own words. This will
help you practice
using them correctly.

B. **Complete each sentence with the correct prefix from the chart.**

1. When parts of the Soyuz spacecraft break down, they need to be

    __*re*__placed before it can be used to travel to the International

    Space Station.

2. Some scientists are using _____-preservation to store shoots from

    banana plants.

3. The design of the Soyuz spacecraft is so strong that even if there are a

    couple of _____functions, the crew is most likely going to land safely

    on Earth.

4. One of the main goals of the Global Seed Vault is to preserve the

    _____diversity of the world's edible plant species.

5. The scientists working on the International Space Station don't worry

    about _____politics because it's their job to solve engineering problems.

6. The Global Seed Vault is run by a(n) _____profit group called the

    Global Crop Diversity Trust.

7. The space station was built by a(n) _____national partnership that has

    become stronger over time.

8. The _____governmental panel came to the conclusion that extreme

    weather events were going to increase in the future.

9. The age of the Soyuz spacecraft is _____material because its design

    is robust.

10. Plant species are _____appearing at a very fast rate all around the world.

WRITING

Tip for Success

Expository writing fully explains and describes an author's ideas on a subject. *Classification writing* puts people, things, or ideas into groups.

A piece of writing is **coherent** when the ideas are organized in a logical way so that the reader can easily follow them and understand what the writer wants to communicate. The order of ideas and supporting ideas depends on the writer's subject and purpose. Three of the most common methods of organization are explained below.

Specificity

Specificity works well with descriptive essays, expository writing, and classification essays.

- Organize your ideas from the more general to the more specific.
- Give one or more general ideas with increasingly specific supporting ideas, facts, and examples.

Emphasis

This form of organization works well with persuasive essays, comparison and contrast essays, and business letters.

- Organize your ideas from the least to the most important. Readers tend to remember best what they read last. This organization strengthens your argument by building up to the strongest ideas.

Time

Time organization works well with process essays, narrative essays, cause and effect essays, case studies, biographies, book reports, and short stories.

- Follow a chronological order.
- Organize your information from the past to the present or from the present to the past.
- Organize a process from the beginning to the end or from the end to the beginning.

A. Look at the brief outlines for short paragraphs answering the question "What is a good example of global cooperation?" Decide if the ideas have been organized according to specificity, emphasis, or time.

1. Type of organization: _____
   Global Polio Eradication Initiative
   a. In 1988, the World Health Assembly passed a resolution to eradicate polio.
   b. Nelson Mandela started the Kick Polio Out of Africa campaign in 1996.

c. The service club *Rotary International* had raised $500 million in the fight against polio by 2003.

d. In 2004, 23 countries in west and central Africa immunized more than 80 million children.

2. Type of organization: _____
The World Health Organization (WHO)

a. The WHO works towards the highest possible levels of health for people around the world.

b. It supports the development and strengthening of health systems in every country.

c. It sets health standards for health systems to follow.

d. It carries out worldwide campaigns for people to eat healthier food and stop smoking.

3. Type of organization: _____
International Migratory Bird Day

a. International Migratory Bird Day is celebrated in Canada, the United States, Mexico, Central and South America, and the Caribbean.

b. This day can involve bird walks, presentations, and music.

c. People learn about threats to migratory birds on this day.

d. By raising public awareness of migratory birds, people can save them from danger and extinction.

B. Read this response to an essay question on a political science test. Then answer the questions in a group or with a partner.

What is a good example of global cooperation?

International peace parks are a good example of global cooperation. An increasing number of peace parks can be found all over the world. International peace parks are protected areas that are located on the borders of two or more countries. There are no fences between the countries in the parks, and animals are free to move wherever they want in the park. Three peace parks in particular illustrate how these sorts of global initiatives can bring different countries closer together.

The first peace park in the world, Waterton-Glacier International Peace Park, was established in 1932. It lies on the border between the United States and Canada, and it was created as a symbol of friendship and peace between these two countries. The United Nations Educational, Scientific and Cultural Organization (UNESCO) recognizes this park as a biosphere reserve and a World Heritage Site.

Another peace park that is also a UNESCO World Heritage Site is located in Central America. La Amistad International Park is shared by Costa Rica and Panama, and it was created in 1988. It is very remote, and Costa Rica and Panama work together to manage the park and maintain its fragile tropical environment.

Finally, the first peace park in Africa, Kgalagadi Transfrontier Park, was founded on May 12, 2000, between Botswana and South Africa. These two countries currently work together to manage the park as a single ecological unit. Kgalagadi is a large wildlife reserve in which people are also able to move freely across the international borders.

International peace parks such as Waterton-Glacer, La Amistad, and Kgalagadi show that global cooperation is possible. Because of these successful examples, the number of international peace parks is sure to increase in the future. It is hoped that people and organizations around the world will continue to promote the collaboration of different governments in the creation of more transfrontier parks like these.

1. What is the main idea of this essay?

2. What are the supporting ideas for the main idea?

3. How are the supporting ideas organized?

4. Is the organization of the supporting ideas effective? Why or why not?

5. Is there another way the supporting ideas could have been organized? If so, what is it?

 **Tip for Success**

When answering an essay question on a test, write out your thesis statement first, before you start writing your essay. This will help you organize your ideas and ensure you are happy with the most important sentence of your essay.

C. Complete these steps to write a brief outline for a paragraph on the topic *What is a good example of global cooperation?*

1. Decide on a good example of global cooperation that you are familiar with.

2. Brainstorm a list of five to six ideas that support your choice as a good example of global cooperation.

3. Check (✔) the three or four ideas that you are going to use in your outline.

4. Decide if you are going to organize your ideas according to specificity, emphasis, or time.

5. Number your ideas in the order that you want to include them in your outline.

When words, phrases, and clauses are used in a series in the same sentence, they should have **parallel structure**. That is, they should have the same grammatical form. Using parallel structure makes it easier for the reader to understand a text, especially when a sentence is more complex or contains several supporting points.

> **Noun**
> Dedication and tolerance are two things people need if they want to cooperate.
>
> **Adjective + noun**
> Those who work side by side with their Russian counterparts say that strong relationships and mutual respect have resulted from the many years of collaboration.

When you use parallel structure, you often omit words that are repeated in a phrase or sentence. This is called **ellipsis**. You can use ellipsis with modals or verb forms that have auxiliary verbs, such as the present continuous or present perfect. In parallel structure, the auxiliary verbs are usually omitted.

> **Modal** *could*
> A collaborative space program could build greater understanding, promote world peace, and improve scientific knowledge.
>
> **Present perfect auxiliary verb** *have*
> Scientists have identified and solved several problems related to the Global Seed Vault.

A. Read each sentence. Underline the error in parallel structure. Then correct it.

1. The French scientists are taking part in an expedition to the Amazon rain forest, a conference in Rio de Janeiro, and discussing with Brazilian coffee farmers.   *a discussion*

2. Russian cosmonauts and American astronauts are working on experiments, build new space station modules, and learning together.

3. The scientists cataloged the seeds, cryo-preserved the shoots, and have sent them to the Global Seed Vault.

4. Global warming has many people worried, feeling concerned, and frustrated about the future.

5. The rusty launch site, abandoned buildings, and uneven sidewalks are surprising to Americans because of the dependability, famous, and prestige of the Russian space program.

B. Complete the sentences with your own ideas. Use parallel structure.

1. The Global Seed Vault is an important resource that could save many plants,

   _____.

2. Future global collaborations should focus on promoting peace,

   _____.

3. Peace parks encourage global cooperation,

   _____.

4. The World Health Organization has monitored health problems,

   _____.

5. Global cooperation is important in order to fight poverty,

   _____.

Unit Assignment | Write an essay

Q In this assignment, you will write an essay that answers the Unit Question, "Why is global cooperation important?" As you prepare your essay, refer to the Self-Assessment checklist on page 135. Use information from Readings 1 and 2 and your work in this unit to support your ideas.

For alternative unit assignments, see the *Q: Skills for Success Teacher's Handbook*.

PLAN AND WRITE

Your Writing Process
For this activity, you could also use Stage 1A, *Listing* or *Charting* in *Q Online Practice*.

A. BRAINSTORM Based on the readings and your own personal knowledge, think about why global cooperation is important or why international cooperation is not important. In your notebook, record your best two or three main ideas. Provide two or three supporting ideas or details for each main idea.

B. PLAN Review Activity A and decide which information you want to include in your answer. Then complete these tasks to organize your ideas.

1. Check (✓) the method of organizing your ideas that fits best with the information you plan to include in your essay.

   ☐ specificity   ☐ emphasis   ☐ time

2. In your notebook, write an outline of your essay based on the method you've chosen. Plan a four- or five-paragraph essay, depending on the number of main ideas you have to support your thesis statement.

Introduction
- Introductory information
- Thesis statement

Paragraph 1 (Continue with as many paragraphs as you need.)
- Topic statement
- Two or three supporting ideas or details

Conclusion
- Concluding statement
- Concluding thoughts and comments

C. **WRITE** Write an essay answering the Unit Question, "Why is global cooperation important?" Look at the Self-Assessment checklist on page 135 to guide your writing.

REVISE AND EDIT

A. **PEER REVIEW** Read a partner's essay. Answer the questions and discuss them with your partner.

1. Is the essay convincing?

2. What method of organization did the writer choose? Is it consistent?

3. Is there a logical order to the main ideas? If not, do you have any suggestions to make the order of the main ideas more logical?

4. Are there enough supporting ideas or details for each main idea?

5. Is there a logical order to the supporting ideas or details for each main idea? If not, do you have any suggestions to make the order of the supporting ideas or details more logical?

6. Are prefixes, parallel structure, and ellipsis used correctly?

B. **REWRITE** Review the answers to the questions in Activity A. You may want to revise and rewrite your essay.

C. **EDIT** Complete the Self-Assessment checklist as you prepare to write the final draft of your essay. Be prepared to hand in your work or discuss it in class.

Yes	No	SELF-ASSESSMENT
☐	☐	Is there a logical order to the main ideas?
☐	☐	Is there a logical order to the supporting ideas?
☐	☐	Are parallel structure and ellipsis used correctly?
☐	☐	Are there words with prefixes?
☐	☐	Does the essay include vocabulary from the unit?
☐	☐	Did you check the essay for punctuation, spelling, and grammar?

Track Your Success

Circle the words you learned in this unit.

Nouns
approach 🔑 AWL
collaboration
counterpart
dedication
erosion AWL
Plan B
scarcity
urgency
vulnerability
wariness

Verbs
confront 🔑
conserve
consolidate
eliminate 🔑 AWL

Adjectives
crucial 🔑 AWL
dependable
devastating
extinct

genetic
inevitable 🔑 AWL
orbiting
robust

Phrases
a bump in the road
play hardball

🔑 Oxford 3000™ words
AWL Academic Word List

Check (✓) the skills you learned. If you need more work on a skill, refer to the page(s) in parentheses.

READING	○	I can make inferences. (p. 117)
VOCABULARY	○	I can use prefixes. (pp. 125–126)
WRITING	○	I can organize supporting ideas. (p. 129)
GRAMMAR	○	I can use parallel structure and ellipsis. (p. 132)
LEARNING OUTCOME	○	I can prepare an essay describing the importance of global cooperation.

UNIT **6**

Public Space

READING ● following ideas
VOCABULARY ● using the dictionary: verb complements
GRAMMAR ● passive voice to focus information
WRITING ● connecting information

LEARNING OUTCOME ●

Develop an analytical essay depicting a public place and ways to make it more appealing.

Unit QUESTION

What makes a public place appealing?

PREVIEW THE UNIT

(A) Discuss these questions with your classmates.

What public places do you spend time in (for example, parks, libraries, banks, or malls)?

Does your hometown have many public places you can walk to? What are they?

Look at the photo. Is this public place appealing to you?

(B) Discuss the Unit Question above with your classmates.

🔊 Listen to *The Q Classroom*, Track 5 on CD 2, to hear other answers.

C If you were designing a new library for your town or school, how important would each feature be? Complete the questionnaire. Circle the number that best corresponds to your opinion, from 1 (Not at All Important) to 5 (Very Important).

What do you want in your new library?

Feature	Not at All Important (1) →				Very Important (5)
1. Wireless Internet access	1	2	3	4	5
2. Lots of windows and views	1	2	3	4	5
3. Places to sit alone	1	2	3	4	5
4. Places to sit in a group	1	2	3	4	5
5. Coffee shop	1	2	3	4	5
6. Access to public transportation	1	2	3	4	5
7. Bright colors	1	2	3	4	5
8. Your idea:	1	2	3	4	5

_____

Write your three most important features:

_____

_____

_____

D In a group, discuss your answers for Activity C and explain the reasons for your choices. As a group, agree on the three most important features. Present your group's top three features to the class.

READING 1 | The New Oases

VOCABULARY

Here are some words and phrases from Reading 1. Read the sentences. Circle the answer that best matches the meaning of each bold word or phrase.

1. Frank Gehry likes to create **controversy**, to get people discussing his challenging, modern style of architecture.
   a. fun
   b. disagreement
   c. harmony

2. College students lead a **nomadic** lifestyle; every day they move among dormitories, classroom buildings, and libraries.
   a. traveling often
   b. being busy
   c. working hard

3. The new building is a **hybrid** space suitable for both work and play.
   a. different
   b. mixed-use
   c. beautiful

4. The building's design is not **specialized**, so it can easily be adapted to different purposes.
   a. made for a particular use
   b. unusual
   c. finished

5. City officials **intentionally** created a place where people could sit and work during their lunch hour in order to create a sense of community.
   a. then
   b. accidentally
   c. deliberately

6. A good public space should be safe, **neutral**, and informal.
   a. brightly colored
   b. open only for some people
   c. open for all people

7. The city needs to spend more money downtown because many older buildings are **in decline**.
   a. being offered for sale
   b. getting worse
   c. being used

8. A community is stronger when people care about each other and **form bonds**.
   a. work together
   b. play musical instruments
   c. make connections

9. Customers in many coffee shops never talk to other people there, so they feel **isolated**.
   a. alone
   b. intelligent
   c. private

10. In good public places, people can **mingle**, getting to know new people if they want.
   a. sit together   b. make noise   c. mix and chat

11. If possible, architects should design places so that visitors **encounter** a welcoming atmosphere in any public space.
   a. meet with   b. hope for   c. appreciate

12. New public places **pop up** all the time in growing cities.
   a. get larger   b. appear suddenly   c. fail

Reading Skill | Following ideas

When you read longer texts from newspapers, magazines, and books, you often have to follow complicated ideas and understand how the ideas develop. It is important not just to recognize these ideas, but also to understand how they connect to present a story or argument. Here are some tips that can help you follow ideas through a text:

When you see a pronoun (*it, they, them, her, who, which,* etc.), make sure you know the **referent** (the noun that the pronoun replaces). Find the referent by scanning back in the text.

The new library is a beautiful building. **It** is light, open, and welcoming.

Demonstrative pronouns such as *this* and *these* usually refer to the last idea, not just the last noun (for example, the last sentence or the entire last paragraph). Stop and ask yourself this question: What was the idea?

Many students rely on their laptops. This means that they can work anywhere.

A sentence or paragraph might begin with a word or phrase that acts as a summary of the previous idea. Often, the word is a different part of speech (for example, a noun instead of a verb).

When you see a summary word or phrase, check that you understood the last idea and expect examples, supporting details, or a new topic to come next. In this example, "This shift" refers to the change in the design of public buildings, and details regarding the change follow.

The design of public buildings **has changed. This shift** can be seen everywhere, from university libraries to public parks.

Tip Critical Thinking

Activity A asks you to recognize the referent for each pronoun. This kind of recognition requires you to understand prior information, and apply your knowledge of grammar to follow the ideas. This kind of analysis is critical to your understanding of complicated texts.

A. Read the paragraph about an urban designer named Ray Oldenburg. Write the referent below each bold word or phrase.

Ray Oldenburg is an urban sociologist from Florida **who** writes about the
1
_____Oldenburg_____

importance of informal public gathering places. In **his** book *The Great Good*
2
_____

Place, Oldenburg demonstrates why **these places** are essential to community
3
_____

and public life. **The book** argues that bars, coffee shops, general stores,
4
_____

and other "third places" (in contrast to the first and second places of

home and work) are central to improving communities. By exploring how

these places work and what roles **they** serve, Oldenburg offers tools and
5   6
_____   _____

insight for individuals and communities everywhere.

Source: Adapted from Ray Oldenburg. Project for Public Spaces. Retrieved October 12, 2010, from http://www.pps.org/roldenburg.

B. Complete each second sentence with a noun from the box. Your choices should reflect the meaning of the phrases in bold in the first sentence.

concept	spaces	problem	shift	term

1. In recent years, more effort has gone into the design of **public places**. These
   _____ function as an alternative to the home and the office.

2. Today, more people **are turning to wireless Internet and cell phones for business**. This _____ makes the traditional office seem old-fashioned.

3. It has been nearly two decades since Oldenburg first used **the expression "third places."** Since then, many companies have used the _____ to describe their stores and restaurants.

4. Oldenburg believes that **third places could strengthen a community**. This

_____ has been a powerful motivation for many urban planners.

5. However, sometimes **people in third places interact with just their computers, not other human beings**. Some café owners are trying to solve this _____.

PREVIEW READING 1

You are going to read a special report from the magazine *The Economist* that describes a change in the design of public places to fit new "nomadic lifestyles."

Look at the photograph in the article. It shows the Stata Center at the Massachusetts Institute of Technology (MIT), a university in the U.S. What do you think people do in this building? Write three predictions.

1. _____

2. _____

3. _____

CD 2
Track 6   **Read the article.**

The New Oases

1   Frank Gehry, a celebrity architect, likes to cause aesthetic **controversy**, and his Stata Center at the Massachusetts Institute of Technology (MIT) did the trick. Opened in 2004 and housing MIT's computer-science and philosophy departments behind its façade[1] of bizarre angles and windows, it has become a new landmark. But the building's most radical innovation is on the inside. The entire structure was conceived with the **nomadic** lifestyles of modern students and faculty in mind. Stata, says William Mitchell, a professor of architecture and computer science at MIT who worked with Mr. Gehry on the center's design, was conceived as a new kind of "**hybrid** space."

2   This is best seen in the building's "student street," an interior passage that twists and meanders through the complex and is open to the public 24 hours a day. It is dotted with nooks and crannies[2]. Cafés and lounges are interspersed with work desks and whiteboards, and there is free Wi-Fi[3] everywhere. Students, teachers, and visitors are cramming for exams, napping, instant-messaging, researching, reading, and discussing. No part of the student street is physically **specialized** for

---

[1] **façade:** the front of a building

[2] **nooks and crannies:** small, quiet places that are sheltered or hidden from other people

[3] **Wi-Fi:** wireless Internet access

any of these activities. Instead, every bit of it can instantaneously become the venue for a seminar, a snack, or relaxation.

3 The fact that people are no longer tied to specific places for functions such as studying or learning, says Mr. Mitchell, means that there is "a huge drop in demand for traditional, private, enclosed spaces" such as offices or classrooms, and simultaneously "a huge rise in demand for semi-public spaces that can be informally appropriated to ad-hoc[4] workspaces." This shift, he thinks, amounts to the biggest change in architecture in this century. In the 20th century, architecture was about specialized structures— offices for working, cafeterias for eating, and so forth. This was necessary because workers needed to be near things such as landline phones, fax machines, and filing cabinets.

4 The new architecture, says Mr. Mitchell, will "make spaces **intentionally** multifunctional." Architects are thinking about light, air, trees, and gardens, all in the service of human connections. Buildings will have much more varied shapes than before. For instance, people working on laptops find it comforting to have their backs to a wall, so hybrid spaces may become curvier, with more nooks, in order to maximize the surface area of their inner walls.

interior "student street" of the Stata Center of MIT

> " Flexibility is what separates successful spaces and cities from unsuccessful ones. "

5 This "flexibility is what separates successful spaces and cities from unsuccessful ones," says Anthony Townsend, an urban planner at the Institute for the Future. Almost any public space can assume some of these features. For example, a not-for-profit organization in New York has turned Bryant Park, a once-derelict[5] but charming garden in front of the city's public library, into a hybrid space popular with office workers. The park's managers noticed that a lot of visitors were using mobile phones and laptops in the park, so they installed Wi-Fi and added some chairs with foldable lecture desks. The idea was not to distract people from the flowers but to let them customize their little bit of the park.

6 The academic name for such spaces is "third places," a term originally coined by the sociologist Ray Oldenburg in his 1989 book *The Great Good Place*. At the time, long before mobile technologies became widespread, Mr. Oldenburg wanted to distinguish between the sociological functions of people's first places (their homes), their second places (offices), and the public spaces that serve as safe, **neutral**, and informal meeting points. As Mr. Oldenburg saw it, a good third place makes admission free or cheap—the price of a cup of coffee, say—offers creature comforts[6], is within walking distance for a particular neighborhood, and draws a group of regulars.

---

[4] **ad hoc:** arranged or happening when necessary and not planned in advance

[5] **derelict:** not used or cared for and in bad condition
[6] **creature comforts:** things that make life, or a particular place, comfortable, such as good food, comfortable furniture, or modern equipment

7   Mr. Oldenburg's thesis was that third places were **in** general **decline**. More and more people, especially in suburban societies such as America's, were moving only between their first and second places, making extra stops only at alienating[7] and anonymous locations such as malls, which in Mr. Oldenburg's opinion fail as third places. Society, Mr. Oldenburg feared, was at risk of coming unstuck without these venues for spreading ideas and **forming bonds**.

8   No sooner was the term coined than big business queued up to claim that it was building new third places. The most prominent was Starbucks, a chain of coffee houses that started in Seattle and is now hard to avoid anywhere. Starbucks admits that as it went global, it lost its ambiance[8] of a "home away from home." However, it has also spotted a new opportunity in catering to nomads. Its branches offer not only sofas but also desks with convenient electricity sockets. Bookshops are also offering "more coffee and crumbs," as Mr. Oldenburg puts it, as are churches, YMCAs,[9] and public libraries.

9   But do these oases for nomads actually play the social role of third places? James Katz at Rutgers University fears that cyber-nomads are "hollowing them out." It is becoming commonplace for a café to be full of people with headphones on, speaking on their mobile phones or laptops and hacking away at their keyboards, more engaged with their e-mail in-box than with the people touching their elbows. These places are "physically inhabited but psychologically evacuated," says Mr. Katz, which leaves people feeling "more **isolated** than they would be if the café were merely empty."

A Third Place . . .

- is not expensive, or is free;
- usually offers food or drink;
- is easily accessible to many people;
- has "regulars" (people who go there often);
- has a friendly atmosphere; and
- is a good place to meet old friends and new people.

---

10   Many café owners are trying to deal with this problem. Christopher Waters, the owner of the Nomad Café in Oakland, regularly hosts live jazz and poetry readings, and he actually turns off the Wi-Fi at those times so that people **mingle** more. He is also planning to turn his café into an online social network so that patrons opening their browsers to connect **encounter** a welcome page that asks them to fill out a short profile and then see information about the people at the other tables.

11   As more third places **pop up** and spread, they also change entire cities. Just as buildings during the 20th century were specialized by function, towns were as well, says Mr. Mitchell. Suburbs were for living, downtowns for working, and other areas for playing. But urban nomads make districts, like buildings, multifunctional. Parts of town that were monocultures, he says, gradually become "fine-grained mixed-use neighborhoods" more akin[10] in human terms to pre-industrial villages than to modern suburbs.

---

[7] **alienating:** making you feel as if you do not belong
[8] **ambiance:** the character and atmosphere of a place (also *ambience*)
[9] **YMCA:** Young Men's Christian Association; an association-run community and sports center

[10] **akin:** similar to

Main Ideas

Complete this outline of the main ideas in the article. Use the Reading Skill ("Following ideas") to help you.

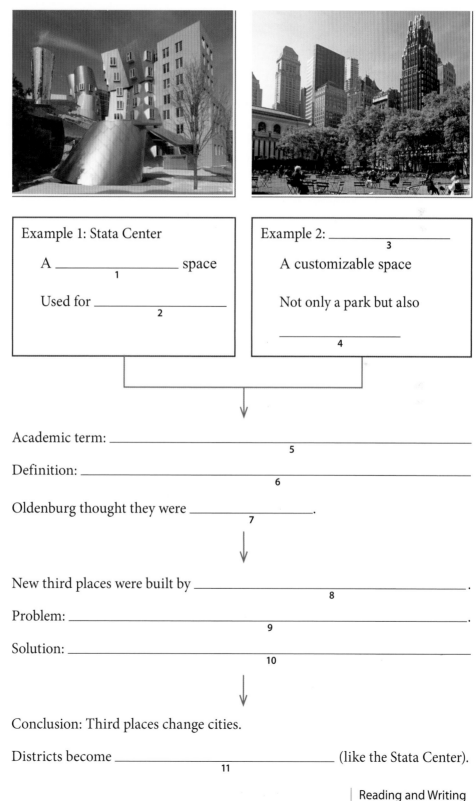

Example 1: Stata Center

A _____ space
        1

Used for _____
              2

Example 2: _____
                        3

A customizable space

Not only a park but also

_____
        4

Academic term: _____
                              5

Definition: _____
                      6

Oldenburg thought they were _____.
                                      7

New third places were built by _____.
                                              8

Problem: _____.
                  9

Solution: _____
                  10

Conclusion: Third places change cities.

Districts become _____ (like the Stata Center).
                          11

DETAILS

A. The article describes three reactions to three modern problems. Complete the chart with details from the article.

	Problem	Solution
1. Classrooms and office buildings	Spaces were specialized because workers needed access to landline phones and other equipment.	
2. Bryant Park		
3. Starbucks		

B. Circle the correct answers.

1. Why does the "student street" in the Stata Center have twists and curves?
   a. only for artistic value
   b. because there are no landline telephones
   c. to create controversy and something to discuss
   d. to create space that is comfortable for different uses

2. According to Oldenburg's definition, which is a third place?
   a. a bookstore that holds free weekly discussion groups for local residents
   b. a coffee shop with Internet access
   c. a suburban shopping mall
   d. a museum that charges people to attend public lectures

3. What can you infer from Reading 1 about people who live in the suburbs?
   a. They work longer hours than other people.
   b. They don't have much contact with other people outside work.
   c. They dislike shopping in urban centers.
   d. They do not have access to coffee shops.

4. What is causing the shift to multifunctional districts, according to the last paragraph of Reading 1?
   a. third places   c. modern architecture
   b. the Internet   d. changes in lifestyle

WHAT DO YOU THINK?

Discuss the questions in a group. Then choose one question and write freely for five to ten minutes in response.

1. Do you know any third places? What features make them third places? Describe them and explain whether they are appealing.

2. Do you accept the idea in Reading 1 that technology can have an alienating effect? Do you like the ideas that the café owner had to encourage people to mingle more? Explain the reasons for your opinion.

3. Do you think third places differ from country to country? What are some examples of third places in your country that might not exist elsewhere?

READING 2 | A Path to Road Safety with No Signposts

VOCABULARY

Here are some words from Reading 2. Read the sentences. Then write each bold word next to the correct list of synonyms.

1. In most countries, driving is a **regulated** activity.

2. Drivers learn traffic laws when they get their licenses, but signs **reinforce** the laws, in case drivers forget.

3. Urban planners try to **anticipate** conflict between cars and pedestrians when they design streets.

4. Most street planners try to create a strict **division** between the road and the sidewalk.

5. Whenever possible, roads are built to **accommodate** all the vehicles that are likely to use them.

6. Streets can be hard to **negotiate** if rules are complicated or there is a lot of traffic.

7. Despite many safety measures, there are still sometimes **fatal** accidents on the roads.

8. Many home buyers think houses on large, busy streets are less **appealing** than those on small, quiet streets.

9. One street designer is a **proponent** of a planned shared-space movement and is trying to convince other people of the plan's value.

10. The shared-space approach is **counterintuitive** to traditional street design because it removes the traditional traffic signs and signals.

11. Shared-space designers **concede** that the idea does not work everywhere.

12. There are several **criteria** for a successful shared space; only streets that meet these guidelines are likely to succeed.

a. _____ (*v.*) admit • acknowledge • recognize

b. _____ (*v.*) expect • await • look for

c. _____ (*v.*) clear • get around • get past • pass

d. _____ (*v.*) adapt • fit • suit • receive • shelter • work with

e. _____ (*v.*) strengthen • cement • make stronger • repeat

f. _____ (*adj.*) surprising • unexpected • contrary to usual thinking

g. _____ (*adj.*) deadly • lethal

h. _____ (*adj.*) popular • attractive • desirable

i. _____ (*n.*) standards • measures • guides

j. _____ (*adj.*) overseen • policed • supervised • governed

k. _____ (*n.*) separation • split • partition

l. _____ (*n.*) advocate • champion • supporter • promoter

PREVIEW READING 2

Tip for Success

Newspaper and magazine articles often have many short paragraphs. They allow the writer to create rhythm and emphasis. However, in academic writing, you should write longer paragraphs.

You are going to read an article from _The New York Times_, which is a profile of Dutch traffic engineer Hans Monderman. Although he died in 2008, Monderman's ideas about cars, pedestrians, and bicyclists sharing roads have become very popular, especially in Europe.

Read the title, subheadings, and caption. What do you think Monderman did in order to make roads safer?

_____

_____

A Path to Road Safety with No Signposts

By Sarah Lyall

1 DRACHTEN, The Netherlands. "I want to take you on a walk," said Hans Monderman, abruptly stopping his car and striding—hatless, and nearly hairless—into the freezing rain.

an intersection in Drachten, The Netherlands

2 Like a naturalist conducting a tour of the jungle, he led the way to a busy intersection in the center of town, where several odd things immediately became clear. Not only was it virtually naked, stripped of all lights, signs, and road markings, but there was no **division** between road and sidewalk. It was, basically, a bare brick square.

3 But in spite of the apparently anarchical[1] layout, the traffic, a steady stream of trucks, cars, buses, motorcycles, bicycles, and pedestrians, moved along fluidly and easily, as if directed by an invisible conductor. When Mr. Monderman, a traffic engineer and the intersection's proud designer, deliberately failed to check for oncoming traffic before crossing the street, the drivers slowed for him. No one honked or shouted rude words out of the window.

4 "Who has the right of way?" he asked rhetorically. "I don't care. People here have to find their own way, **negotiate** for themselves, use their own brains."

5 Used by some 20,000 drivers a day, the intersection is part of a road-design revolution pioneered by the 59-year-old Mr. Monderman. His work in Friesland, the district in northern Holland that takes in Drachten, is increasingly seen as the way of the future in Europe.

6 His philosophy is simple, if **counterintuitive**.

7 To make communities safer and more **appealing**, Mr. Monderman argues, you should first remove the traditional paraphernalia[2] of their roads—the traffic lights and road signs; the center lines separating lanes from one another; even the speed bumps, speed-limit signs, bicycle lanes, and pedestrian crossings. In his view, it is only when the road is made more dangerous, when drivers stop looking at signs and start looking at other people, that driving becomes safer.

8 "All those signs are saying to cars, 'This is your space, and we have organized your behavior so that as long as you behave this way, nothing can happen to you,'" Mr. Monderman said. "That is the wrong story."

9 The Drachten intersection is an example of the concept of "shared space," a street where cars and pedestrians are equal, and the design tells the driver what to do.

10 "It's a moving away from **regulated** traffic toward space which, by the way it's designed and configured, makes it clear what sort of behavior is **anticipated**," said Ben Hamilton-

---

[1] **anarchical:** without order

[2] **paraphernalia:** a large number of different objects or personal possessions, especially the equipment that you need for a particular activity

Baillie, a British specialist in urban design and movement and a **proponent** of many of the same concepts.

11 Highways, where the car is naturally king, are part of the "traffic world" and another matter altogether. In Mr. Monderman's view, shared-space schemes thrive only in conjunction with well-organized, well-regulated highway systems.

Social Space

12 Mr. Monderman is a man on a mission. On a daylong automotive tour of Friesland, he pointed out places he had improved, including a town where he ripped out the sidewalks, signs, and crossings and put in brick paving on the central shopping street. An elderly woman crossed slowly in front of him.

13 "This is social space, so when Grandma is coming, you stop, because that's what normal, courteous human beings do," he said.

14 Planners and curious journalists are increasingly making pilgrimages[3] to meet Mr. Monderman, considered one of the field's great innovators, although until a few years ago he was virtually unknown outside Holland. Mr. Hamilton-Baillie, whose writings have helped bring Mr. Monderman's work to wider attention, remembers with fondness his own first visit.

15 Mr. Monderman drove him to a small country road with cows in every direction. Their presence was unnecessarily **reinforced** by a large traffic sign with a picture of a cow on it.

16 "He said: 'What do you expect to find here? Wallabies[4]?'" Mr. Hamilton-Baillie recalled. "'They're treating you like you're a complete idiot, and if people treat you like a complete idiot, you'll act like one.' Essentially, what it means is a transfer of responsibility to the individual and the community."

17 Dressed in a beige jacket and patterned shirt, with scruffy facial hair and a stocky build, Mr. Monderman has the appearance of a football hooligan but the temperament of an engineer, which indeed he trained to be. He was working as a civil engineer building highways in the 1970s when the Dutch government, alarmed at a sharp increase in traffic accidents, set up a network of traffic safety offices. Mr. Monderman was appointed Friesland's traffic safety officer.

18 In residential communities, Mr. Monderman began narrowing the roads and putting in design features like trees and flowers, red brick paving stones, and even fountains to discourage people from speeding. This principle is now known as psychological traffic calming, where behavior follows design.

19 He made his first nervous foray into[5] shared space in a small village whose residents were upset at its being used as a daily thoroughfare for 6,000 speeding cars. When he took away the signs, lights, and sidewalks, people drove more carefully. Within two weeks, speeds on the road had dropped by more than half.

20 In fact, he said, there has never been a **fatal** accident on any of his roads.

Limits of Shared Space

21 Mr. Monderman **concedes** that road design can do only so much. It does not change the behavior, for instance, of the 15 percent of drivers who will behave badly no matter what the rules are. Nor are shared-space designs appropriate everywhere, like major urban centers, but only in neighborhoods that meet particular **criteria**.

22 Recently a group of well-to-do parents asked him to widen the two-lane road leading to their children's school, saying it was too small to

---

[3] **pilgrimage:** a journey to a place that is connected with someone or something that you admire

[4] **wallaby:** an Australian animal like a small kangaroo

[5] **make a foray into:** to attempt to become involved in (a new activity)

accommodate what he derisively calls "their huge cars."

23   He refused, saying the fault was not with the road, but with the cars. "They can't wait for each other to pass?" he asked.

MAIN IDEAS

A. **Which techniques did Hans Monderman use in his intersections? Check (✓) all the correct answers.**

☐ 1. adding more road signs
☐ 2. forcing cars, bikes, and pedestrians to share the same space
☐ 3. removing lane divisions
☐ 4. making roads wider
☐ 5. reducing the speed limit on highways
☐ 6. letting people negotiate their own behavior
☐ 7. prohibiting large cars

B. **Why did Hans Monderman use these techniques? Check (✓) all the correct answers.**

☐ 1. to make drivers share the road with other users
☐ 2. to regulate traffic more carefully
☐ 3. to help drivers be able to go faster
☐ 4. to force drivers to look at other people, not at the signs and markings
☐ 5. to encourage drivers to think, be more responsible, and use common courtesy

DETAILS

Answer these questions. Then circle and number information in the article that supports your answers.

1. Why are intersections like the one in Drachten safe?

_____

_____

2. In Monderman's view, why are roads with road signs, speed limits, and lane markings more dangerous?

_____

_____

3. Why do shared-space ideas not apply to highways?

_____

_____

4. How are the principles of psychological traffic calming different from those of the shared-space movement?

_____

_____

5. Why did Monderman refuse to widen a road leading to a school?

_____

_____

 WHAT DO YOU THINK?

A. Discuss the questions in a group. Then choose one question and write one or two paragraphs in response.

1. Could Monderman's ideas work in your home country or in the place you live now? Give reasons to support your opinion.

2. In some cities, cars are not allowed or are heavily restricted in the downtown area. What do you think about this idea?

B. Think about both Reading 1 and Reading 2 as you discuss the questions.

1. Do you believe the design of public spaces should change to better suit our behavior (as in the buildings in Reading 1) or should we change our behavior to meet the expectations of the design (as in the intersections in Reading 2)? Give reasons to support your opinion.

2. Do you agree with the assumption in both readings that few public spaces today are really pleasant to live and interact in? Why or why not?

| Vocabulary Skill | Using the dictionary | web |

The main verb controls the pattern of a clause or sentence. Knowing the **verb complements**, or the types of words and phrases allowed with the verb, is important in improving your writing and speaking. For example, some verbs can be followed by a direct object (transitive verbs), but others cannot (intransitive verbs). The dictionary can help you write better sentences by telling you which complements are possible or required with each verb: objects, prepositional phrases, noun clauses, infinitives, or gerunds.

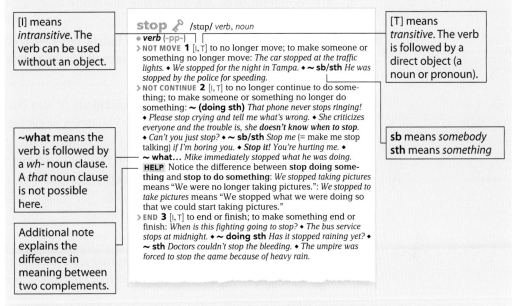

[I] means *intransitive*. The verb can be used without an object.

~**what** means the verb is followed by a *wh-* noun clause. A *that* noun clause is not possible here.

Additional note explains the difference in meaning between two complements.

stop /stap/ *verb, noun*
● **verb** (-pp-)
> **NOT MOVE** **1** [I, T] to no longer move; to make someone or something no longer move: *The car stopped at the traffic lights.* ◆ *We stopped for the night in Tampa.* ◆ *~ sb/sth He was stopped by the police for speeding.*
> **NOT CONTINUE** **2** [I, T] to no longer continue to do something; to make someone or something no longer do something: *~ (doing sth) That phone never stops ringing!* ◆ *Please stop crying and tell me what's wrong.* ◆ *She criticizes everyone and the trouble is, she doesn't know when to stop.* ◆ *Can't you just stop?* ◆ *~ sb/sth Stop me* (= make me stop talking) *if I'm boring you.* ◆ *Stop it! You're hurting me.* ◆ *~ what... Mike immediately stopped what he was doing.*
HELP Notice the difference between **stop doing something** and **stop to do something**: *We stopped taking pictures* means "We were no longer taking pictures.": *We stopped to take pictures* means "We stopped what we were doing so that we could start taking pictures."
> **END** **3** [I, T] to end or finish; to make something end or finish: *When is this fighting going to stop?* ◆ *The bus service stops at midnight.* ◆ *~ doing sth Has it stopped raining yet?* ◆ *~ sth Doctors couldn't stop the bleeding.* ◆ *The umpire was forced to stop the game because of heavy rain.*

[T] means *transitive*. The verb is followed by a direct object (a noun or pronoun).

sb means *somebody*
sth means *something*

When a verb can be followed by a prepositional phrase, it is especially important to use a dictionary because it is very difficult to guess the correct preposition.

~**(with sb):** This use of *negotiate* is intransitive, so it does not take a direct object. Use *with* to add the person you are negotiating with.

ne·go·ti·ate /nɪˈgoʊʃiˌeɪt/ *verb* **1** [I] ~ **(with sb) (for/about sth)** to try to reach an agreement by formal discussion: *The government will not negotiate with terrorists.* ◆ *We have been negotiating for more pay.* ◆ *a strong negotiating position* ◆ *negotiating skills* **2** [T] ~ **sth** to arrange or agree to something by formal discussion: *to negotiate a deal/contract/treaty/settlement* ◆ *We successfully negotiated the*

(for/about sth): Use *for* or *about* to say what you are negotiating.

All dictionary entries are from the *Oxford Advanced American Dictionary for learners of English* © Oxford University Press 2011.

A. Are the bold verbs transitive or intransitive? Write *T* (transitive) or *I* (intransitive). Check your answers in a learners' dictionary.

_____ 1. This is best seen in the building's "student street," which twists and **meanders** through the complex.

_____ 2. Architects **are thinking about** light, air, trees, and gardens.

_____ 3. Bookshops **are** also **offering** "more coffee and crumbs."

_____ 4. He **led** the way to a busy intersection.

_____ 5. The drivers **slowed** for him.

_____ 6. Mr. Hamilton-Baillie's writings **have helped** bring Mr. Monderman's work to wider attention.

_____ 7. It does not change the behavior, for instance, of the 15 percent of drivers who **will behave** badly no matter what the rules are.

_____ 8. Mr. Monderman **began** narrowing the roads.

B. Five of the bold words in the paragraph below have verb complement errors. Read the paragraph. Then complete the tasks below.

> The design of my high school did not **appeal** me. It was built to **accommodate** 1,000 students. However, more than 1,500 students **occupied** the building. The designers did not **anticipate**. Every day, we had to **negotiate** with the crowded corridors and staircases to **go** to class. The principal **told** that they could not **improve** the situation. However, he **conceded** that a better system was necessary. Consequently, some staircases were **called** as "up" stairs. When you wanted to go down a level, you **looked** for the "down" stairs.

1. Look up each bold verb in a learner's dictionary. Find the meaning that fits the context of the paragraph. Write the correct complement in the chart.

Verb	Complement	Correct in paragraph? Yes	No
1. appeal	verb + to somebody	☐	☐
2. accommodate		☐	☐
3. occupy		☐	☐
4. anticipate		☐	☐
5. negotiate		☐	☐
6. go		☐	☐
7. tell		☐	☐
8. improve		☐	☐
9. concede		☐	☐
10. call		☐	☐
11. look		☐	☐

2. Is the complement of each verb correct in the paragraph? Check (✓) _Yes_ or _No_ in the chart.

3. For each complement that is incorrect, write the correct sentence in your notebook.

WRITING

Grammar Passive voice to focus information *Part 1*

Forming the passive

In most **active** sentences, the subject of the verb is also the **agent**: that is, it does the action of the verb.

> active sentence
> The architect **designed** the new library in a modern style.
> subject/agent

In a **passive** sentence, the agent of the verb is not the subject. The passive voice is formed with *be* + the past participle of a transitive verb.

> passive sentence
> The new library **was designed** in a modern style (by some architect).
> subject   agent

The *by* phrase containing the agent is often omitted in academic writing.

Focusing information

The passive is used when you want to focus on the result or receiver of the action instead of the agent of the action.

> The entire structure **was conceived** with the nomadic lifestyles of modern students and faculty in mind.

The focus is on *The entire structure*, not the architect who conceived it.

The passive also allows writers to report opinions without saying whose they are.

> His work in Friesland . . . **is** increasingly **seen** as the way of the future in Europe.

The focus is on Monderman's work, and the sentence emphasizes his reputation; it is not important who specifically has this opinion.

Active voice is more common than passive voice. The passive should not be used in contexts where active sentences are more direct and easier to understand. However, the passive voice can be useful in academic and other formal writing.

A. Read each sentence. Circle the best sentence to follow it. Then explain your choice.

1. Monderman distinguished the "social world" of the town from the "traffic world" of the highway.
   a. Engineers design the traffic world for cars.
   b. The traffic world is designed for cars.

   Why? _The first sentence ends with "the traffic world," so the traffic world_

   should be the focus of the next sentence. The engineers are not important.

2. Small towns and villages are examples of the social world.
   a. There, we decide how to behave based on politeness and human contact.
   b. There, behavior is determined by politeness and human contact.

   Why? _____

   _____

3. Many drivers do not notice the schools, shops, and people that they pass.
   a. Road signs distract them from the social world.
   b. They are distracted from the social world by road signs.

   Why? _____

   _____

4. Thanks to road signs, villages often appear to be part of the traffic world.
   a. Therefore, drivers often speed through them.
   b. Therefore, they are often driven through too fast.

   Why? _____

   _____

5. Traditional traffic-calming techniques, such as stop signs, are ineffective.
   a. Drivers simply speed up between the stop signs.
   b. Cars are simply driven faster between the stop signs.

   Why? _____

   _____

Source: Activity text adapted from Vanderbilt, Tom. *Traffic: Why We Drive the Way We Do (and What It Says About Us)* (2008). New York: Knopf, 189–190.

B. Read the paragraph. Complete each sentence with the correct passive or active form of the verb. Use your dictionary if you are not sure whether a verb is intransitive or transitive in this context.

Some social networking websites _____ are considered _____ third
₁

places. Some experts believe that these websites _____
₂

(need) because they fit our nomadic lifestyle better than traditional third

places. For example, websites can _____ (access)
₃

from any computer and many cell phones anywhere in the world. However,

some users _____ (encounter) unexpected
₄

problems. One study found that family time _____
₅

(decrease) because of increased use of social networking sites. Ironically,

we _____ (isolate) by technology that
₆

_____ (design) to connect us. Proponents of
₇

social networking sites _____ (concede) that they
₈

should be used responsibly. Children's use of such sites, for example, should

_____ (regulate) by their parents.
₉

Grammar   Passive voice to focus information *Part 2*   web⁺

Focus information with passive infinitives and passive gerunds

Two other forms of the passive are the *passive infinitive* and the *passive gerund*. These structures, which both require complements, can help make sentences more logical and focused because they avoid introducing a new grammatical subject into the sentence. If you don't know whether a verb takes a gerund or an infinitive complement, look it up in a learner's dictionary. A few verbs allow both types of complement.

> **?** The road **needs** someone to widen it.
> **✓** The road **needs to be widened**.

> **?** Customers **like** coffee shop owners treating them as members of a community
> **✓** Customers **like being treated** as members of a community.

Remember that only transitive verbs can be used in the passive voice. Intransitive verbs do not have a passive form. However, many verbs have both transitive and intransitive meanings. (See the Vocabulary Skill on page 152.)

C. Complete each sentence with a passive infinitive or a passive gerund. Use your dictionary if you are not sure which is the correct complement.

1. The architect agreed _____to be interviewed_____ (interview) for this story.

2. The building seems _____ (design) for modern student life.

3. I appreciate _____ (tell) about the problem, and I will try to find a solution.

4. Cyclists keep _____ (hit) by drivers at this intersection.

5. The Internet has started _____ (see) as an obstacle to human interaction.

Writing Skill   **Connecting information** *Part 1*   web

Good paragraphs have unity and are written in a logical order (see the Writing Skill in Unit 4, page 100 and Unit 5, page 129). They contain clues to help readers follow the main ideas (see the Reading Skill in this unit, page 140). To achieve this, most clauses and sentences follow a regular pattern of information: old information followed by new information. Often, the new information in one sentence becomes the old information—and, therefore, the beginning—of the next sentence.

The old-new pattern allows writers to connect sentences logically while developing ideas.

old (third place)   new

No sooner was **the term** coined than big business queued up to claim that it was building new third places.

old   new

The most prominent **was** Starbucks.

old   new

Starbucks admits that as it went global, it lost its ambiance.

This is called **linear information structure** because the logic flows in a straight line. The new information in one sentence becomes the old information in the next. You can use this pattern to create smooth, logical connections between the sentences in your paragraphs when you are developing an idea or argument.

A. Read the first two paragraphs in a description of another third place. Then complete the tasks below.

"The Third Place" Coffeehouse

"The Third Place" is the name of a coffeehouse in Raleigh, North Carolina. (Raleigh) is the home of the state capitol and many businesses. However, many workers have not had options for spending their time in locations other than their first places (downtown offices) and second places (homes in the suburbs). The Third Place is a friendly café that fills this gap.

When you walk into the Third Place, you first see the cozy, inviting chairs. Behind them, on the walls, are colorful rugs, suggesting an international theme. Between the rugs, you will see original works by local artists. The artwork is changed monthly and really helps to develop a sense of community. This feeling of community is enhanced by the customers, who represent the range of Raleigh's inhabitants. Businesspeople, students, and families can be found at the Third Place on any day of the week.

1. If a sentence contains old information, circle the old information.

2. Connect each circled phrase to the new information in the previous sentence.

3. Explain how the last sentence in paragraph 1 is linked to the previous sentence.

_____

_____

4. Compare your answers to 1–3 with a partner.

5. Underline the three passive verbs in the second paragraph. Why is the passive voice used in each case?

a. _____

b. _____

c. _____

In Activity A, you saw an example of linear information structure, in which the new information in one sentence becomes the old information at the start of the next. An alternative organization is **constant information structure**. In this pattern, the same old information is used at the start of several sentences, and each sentence adds new information on the topic. Use constant information structure to define or explain a complex topic.

> The new architecture . . . will make spaces intentionally multifunctional.
> Architects are thinking about light, air, trees, and gardens, all in the service of human connections.
> Buildings will have much more varied shapes than before.

Synonyms and pronouns help you to avoid repetition and make a smooth flow of information.

B. Read the next paragraph in the description of the Third Place coffeehouse. Then complete the tasks below.

(1) The menu at the Third Place is varied. (2) It is available from 11 a.m. to 7 p.m. (3) Much of the food is homemade and includes creative sandwiches, delicious soups, and fresh salads. (4) All the meals are vegetarian and use local ingredients. (5) Weekly specials offer something new even to regular customers. (6) And of course, good coffee is served all day and evening! (7) _____ will keep you coming back.

1. Explain how the first words in sentences 2–6 are related to *The menu* in sentence 1.

   Sentence 2: _____

   Sentence 3: _____

   Sentence 4: _____

   Sentence 5: _____

   Sentence 6: _____

2. Complete Sentence 7 with the appropriate information. Explain your answer to a partner.

In this assignment, you will write an analytical essay about a particular public place and suggest ways to make it more appealing. As you prepare your essay, think about the Unit Question, "What makes a public place appealing?" and refer to the Self-Assessment checklist on page 162. Use information from Readings 1 and 2 and your work in this unit to support your ideas.

For alternative unit assignments, see the *Q: Skills for Success Teacher's Handbook*.

PLAN AND WRITE

A. **BRAINSTORM** Choose a public place that you know well to write about. Some examples of public places are cafés, restaurants, parks, sports stadiums, public buildings at a college or university, bus or train stations, or the downtown area of your city. Follow the steps below to brainstorm ideas.

1. In your notebook, list descriptions of the place, its design, the people who use it, and the activities that happen there.

 **for Success**

When comparing and contrasting, it is important to develop strong criteria to support your conclusions.

2. Make a chart to evaluate the place. Write a list of criteria that make a public place appealing in the first column. Explain why your place does (not) meet those criteria in the second column.

Criteria	Evaluation + Reasons
easy to meet with others	yes: well-maintained tables with three or four comfortable chairs

3. Make a list of suggestions for improving the public place based on your negative evaluations. Use ideas from Readings 1 and 2 to help you.

B. **PLAN** In your notebook, write an outline of your essay using these headings.

1. **Description** (Give general information about the place any main ideas for your report.)

2. **Evaluation** (Describe what meets your criteria and what doesn't.)

3. **Suggestions** (Make recommendations to improve the place.)

C. **WRITE** Write your essay. Look at the Self-Assessment checklist below to guide your writing.

REVISE AND EDIT

A. **PEER REVIEW** Read a partner's essay. Answer the questions and discuss them with your partner.

1. What else would you like to know about the place?

2. What is the writer's evaluation of the place?

3. Do you agree with the writer's suggestions for improvement? Why?

4. How could the writer improve the information structure of the essay?

5. What other advice do you have for the writer?

Your Writing Process

For this activity, you could also use Stage 2B, *Rewrite* in *Q Online Practice.*

B. **REWRITE** Review the answers to the questions in Activity A. You may want to revise and rewrite your essay.

C. **EDIT** Complete the Self-Assessment checklist as you prepare to write the final draft of your essay. Be prepared to hand in your work or discuss it in class.

SELF-ASSESSMENT		
Yes	No	
☐	☐	Did you use linear or constant information structure clearly?
☐	☐	Is the writing correctly formatted?
☐	☐	Is the passive voice used appropriately?
☐	☐	Did you use the correct verb complements?
☐	☐	Does the essay include vocabulary from the unit?
☐	☐	Did you check the essay for punctuation, spelling, and grammar?

Track Your Success

Circle the words you learned in this unit.

Nouns
controversy AWL
criteria 🔑 AWL
division 🔑
proponent

Verbs
accommodate AWL
anticipate 🔑 AWL
concede
encounter 🔑 AWL
mingle
negotiate
reinforce AWL

Adjectives
appealing
counterintuitive
fatal
hybrid
isolated AWL
neutral AWL
nomadic
regulated AWL
specialized

Adverb
intentionally

Phrasal Verb
pop up

Phrases
in decline
form bonds

🔑 Oxford 3000™ words

AWL Academic Word List

Check (✓) the skills you learned. If you need more work on a skill, refer to the page(s) in parentheses.

READING	○	I can follow ideas. (p. 140)
VOCABULARY	○	I can use the dictionary. (pp. 152–153)
GRAMMAR	○	I can use passive voice to focus information. (pp. 155 and 157)
WRITING	○	I can connect information. (pp. 158 and 160)
LEARNING OUTCOME	○	I can develop an analytical essay depicting a public place and ways to make it more appealing.

UNIT 7

Alternative Thinking

READING	●	anticipating content through questions
VOCABULARY	●	suffixes
WRITING	●	paraphrasing
GRAMMAR	●	modals of possibility

LEARNING OUTCOME

Prepare a business plan that describes an innovative new garbage recycling company to potential investors.

Unit QUESTION

How can we turn trash into treasure?

PREVIEW THE UNIT

(A) Discuss these questions with your classmates.

What do you do with things you no longer use? What do you throw away? What do you recycle?

Do you think society is wasteful? How could people decrease the amount of garbage they throw away?

Look at the photo. What material was reused to make this art? Do you think this is a good way to reuse trash?

(B) Discuss the Unit Question above with your classmates.

Listen to *The Q Classroom*, Track 8 on CD 2, to hear other answers.

C Take the quiz on waste disposal. Write the letter of each definition next to the correct location. Then write two examples of things that can go in each location.

WHERE DO THINGS GO WHEN YOU DON'T WANT THEM ANYMORE?

a. a place for decaying organic waste that can eventually be mixed with soil to grow plants

b. a place where waste is sorted before it is used to make new products

c. a container or machine for burning garbage

d. a place where large amounts of garbage are put into the ground and covered with earth

LOCATION	DEFINITION	THINGS THAT CAN GO HERE
1. landfill		
2. incinerator		
3. composter		
4. recycling depot		

D What is the alternative to throwing away your garbage? Think about the five items in the chart. What else could you do with them? Write your ideas.

Garbage	What else can you do with these items?
old cell phone	
plastic drink bottles	
old music CDs	
a TV	
bicycle wheels	

READING 1 | Garbage of Eden

VOCABULARY

Here are some words from Reading 1. Read the sentences. Then match each bold word with its definition.

_____ 1. Many people are interested in the **conservation** of Earth's resources so that future generations will benefit from them.

_____ 2. Some countries **incinerate** their garbage before it is put into a landfill. However, this often contributes to pollution in the atmosphere.

_____ 3. The safe **disposal** of garbage is very important in order to protect the environment.

_____ 4. The government **anticipates** that local landfills will become full in the next five years.

a. expects and is preparing for the fact

b. burn

c. the protection of the natural world

d. throwing away and removing

_____ 5. The local water supply became **contaminated** because someone dumped toxic waste into the river.

_____ 6. The **elimination** of recyclable materials from people's garbage reduces the amount of trash that goes to landfills.

_____ 7. Environmental activists hope that one day everything will be recycled and landfills will become **obsolete**.

_____ 8. The **habitat** of this area is in danger because pollution has made it difficult for birds and animals to live here.

e. dirty and unsafe

f. no longer used because they are out of date

g. natural home or environment

h. taking away

_____ 9. Although there are only a few trees on the island, they can **thrive** because they have enough sunshine and fresh water.

_____ 10. Fish are **abundant** in this lake. They are everywhere you look!

_____ 11. Many countries want long-term, **sustainable** economic growth that preserves their resources.

_____ 12. Putting **constraints** on the amount of garbage we can throw away stops us from making more trash than the environment can handle.

i. plentiful and existing in large numbers

j. limits

k. continued and environmentally friendly

l. grow and develop well

Reading Skill | Anticipating content through questions

Being an active reader is the key to becoming a better reader. One way to be an active reader is to think about the topic of a text and form questions before you begin reading. Base your questions on the information or content you think will be in the reading. Use question words (*who, what, where, when, why,* and *how*). Then, while you read, keep your questions in mind and look for the answers.

For example, this title, subtitle, and photo are from a newspaper article.

Stop! I'm Full
No more room in local landfill; it will close at the end of this year.

These are possible questions to ask before reading the article:

Who is in charge of this landfill?
What kinds of garbage are in this landfill?
Where is this landfill?
When was the landfill opened?
Why is the landfill full?
How are they going to clean up this landfill so it doesn't harm the environment?

While reading the article, note any answers to your questions. After you finish reading, use the answers to your questions to help you identify the main ideas of the text.

A. Read the title and subtitle of Reading 1 on page 170. You may also look ahead at the photos and landfill plan that accompany the article. Use the *wh*-word question chart to write six questions that you think the reading should answer.

Question	Answer
Who	
What	
Where	
When	
Why	
How	

B. As you read the article "Garbage of Eden," look for the answers to your questions. Annotate your text to remind you where you found the answers. Do not complete the chart yet.

PREVIEW READING 1

You are going to read an article from *NewScientist* magazine that examines the unique and environmentally friendly way that Singapore is dealing with its garbage.

What do you think is the environmentally friendly way Singapore is using to get rid of waste?

Garbage of Eden

Want to be at one with nature? Take a stroll around Singapore's island of trash.
By Eric Bland

1   SINGAPORE'S only landfill is a 20-minute ferry ride south from the main island. On Pulau Semakau, coconut trees and banyan bushes line an asphalt road. Wide-bladed grass, short and soft, forms a threadbare carpet. The only visible trash is a bit of driftwood on the rocky shore, marking high tide in an artificial bay. Water rushes out of the bay through a small opening, making waves in the Singapore Strait. The smell of rain is in the air.

ecotourists on Pulau Semakau

2   You would never know that all the trash from Singapore's 4.4 million residents is being dumped here 24 hours a day, seven days a week—as it will be for the next 40 years. This is no ordinary landfill: the island doubles as a biodiversity hotspot, of all things, attracting rare species of plants and animals. It even attracts ecotourists on specially arranged guided tours. Eight years in the making, the artificial island is setting an example for the future of **conservation** and urban planning.

3   Pulau Semakau, which is Malay for Mangrove[1] Island, is not the first isle of trash to rise from the sea. That dubious honor goes to a dump belonging to another island nation, the Maldives, off the southern coast of India. In 1992, the Maldives began dumping its trash wholesale into a lagoon on one of its small islands. As the island grew, it was named Thilafushi; its industries include a concrete manufacturing plant, a shipyard, and a methane bottler.

4   What distinguishes Semakau from Thilafushi—and most any other landfill—is that its trash has been **incinerated** and sealed off from its surroundings. Singapore burns more than 90 percent of its garbage, for reasons of space. Since its independence from Malaysia in 1965, Singapore has grown to become one of the world's 50 wealthiest nations. Not bad for a city-state little more than one-quarter the size of the smallest U.S. state, Rhode Island. Its rapid rise, however, created a huge waste problem. In the early 1990s, the government began to heavily promote a national recycling program and to campaign for industry and residents to produce less waste.

---

[1] **mangrove:** a tropical tree that grows in mud or at the edge of rivers

From trash to ash

5   Since 1999 garbage **disposal** companies have been recycling what they can—glass, plastic, electronics, even concrete—and incinerating the rest. The Tuas South incineration plant[2], the largest and newest of four plants run by the Singapore government, is tucked away in the southwest part of the main island. A recent visit by *New Scientist* found it surprisingly clean and fresh. The incinerator creates a weak vacuum that sucks the foul air from the trash-receiving room into the combustion[3] chamber.

6   Not that incineration is problem-free. When Singapore began burning garbage, its carbon emissions into the atmosphere rose sharply while its solid carbon deposits dropped, according to data gathered by the Oak Ridge National Laboratory in Tennessee. During the last couple of years, however, its emissions have stabilized. "Our recycling program has been more effective than we **anticipated**," says Poh Soon Hoong, general manager of the Tuas South plant.

7   Once they started burning trash, the big question was where to put the ash. In 1998 the government built a seven-kilometer-long rock bund[4] to connect two offshore islands, Semakau and Sekang, and named the new island Pulau Semakau. The complex cost about 610 million Singapore dollars (U.S.$400 million). The first trash was dumped there in April 1999, the day after the last landfill on the main island closed. "We weren't trying to design an island that would attract tourists," says Semakau's manager, Loo Eng Por. "Disposing of the waste was a matter of survival."

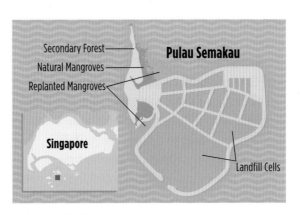

Semakau Island Plan

8   How they do that is key to the island's success. At the receiving station, cranes unload the ash from barges into dumptrucks, which drive out to one of 11 interconnected bays, called cells, where they dump their debris (see Plan). The seawater is first pumped out of a cell, which is then lined with a layer of thick plastic to seal in the trash and prevent any leakage. Materials that can't be burned or recycled, such as asbestos, are wrapped in plastic and buried with dirt. Each month, samples are tested from the water surrounding a working cell, and so far there is no sign of any **contaminated** water seeping into the ocean. Four of the 11 cells have been filled to about two meters above sea level, then topped off with dirt and seeded with grass. A few trees dot the landscape. "Gifts from the birds," says Loo. "We plant the grass, but not the trees." Once all the cells are filled, which will be in 2030 or so, workers will start over again, dumping burnt trash onto the plots and covering it with earth, gradually forming taller hills. The government predicts that by 2045 its recycling and waste **elimination** programs will make its landfills **obsolete**.

---

[2] **plant:** a factory
[3] **combustion:** the process of burning
[4] **bund:** embankment or wall

9   One complaint about Pulau Semakau was that it called for the destruction of mangroves on part of the original island. Singapore's National Environmental Agency saw to it that the mangroves were replanted in areas adjoining the landfill. "We expected some of the new mangroves to die off," says Poh. "But they all survived. Now we have to trim them back." The island now has more than 13 hectares[5] of mangroves, which serve as a **habitat** for numerous species.

10   "Pulau Semakau is quite a success," says Wang Luan Keng of the Raffles Museum of Biodiversity Research at the National University of Singapore, and by all accounts the ecosystem is **thriving**—so much so that since July 2005, the island has been open for guided tours. "Visitors are stunned and amazed to see the rich biodiversity," says Ria Tan, an expert in ecology who runs wildsingapore.com, a website on nature-related activities in the area. At low tide, nature groups walk the intertidal zone, where they can see starfish, snails, and flatworms. Coral reefs are **abundant** off the western shore, and dolphins, otters, and green turtles have been spotted. Fishing groups come to catch and release grouper,

barracuda, and queenfish. Birdwatchers look for the island's most famous resident, a great billed heron named Jimmy, as well as brahminy kites and mangrove whistlers[6]. In 2006 the island logged more than 6,000 visitors, and that number is expected to rise.

11   The island is crucial to Singapore's future. "People may say the Semakau landfill is bad," Tan says. "What is the alternative? Toss it to some other country? Kill off some other habitat on the mainland? The garbage has to go somewhere. I see the Semakau landfill as an example of one aspect of successful, **sustainable** urbanization." Tan shares the concerns of city planners. "The resource **constraints** that Singapore faces today will be those the rest of the world will face eventually," she says.

12   That is why the rest of the world should be watching: time will tell whether Semakau is a useful model for conservation. Meanwhile, the island's managers would like to see it become a permanent nature reserve where people can come to hike, relax, and learn about nature, without a guide. As Loo says, "It's a great place to get away from the boss."

---

[5] **hectare:** a measurement equal to 10,000 square meters; 2,471 acres

[6] **heron, kite, and whistler:** types of birds that live near water

MAIN IDEAS

A. Look at the questions you wrote in the Reading Skill activity on page 169. Complete the chart with the answers you were able to find in the reading.

B. Write short answers to these questions. Then tell a partner or group which of your questions from the chart on page 169 helped you.

1. What kind of landfill does Singapore have?

   _____

2. What does Singapore do with its trash?

   _____

3. How is trash disposed of in Singapore's landfill?

   _____

4. What is the state of the environment on and around the island?

   _____

5. What can the rest of the world learn from the Semakau landfill?

   _____

DETAILS

A. Read the statements. Write *T* (true) or *F* (false). Then correct each false statement to make it true.

_____ 1. The landfill is located 20 minutes by car from the main island.

_____ 2. The landfill took eight years to make.

_____ 3. Singapore incinerates less than 20 percent of its garbage.

_____ 4. Garbage disposal companies incinerate glass, plastic, electronics, and concrete.

_____ 5. Singapore has four incineration plants.

_____ 6. The rock wall that created the artificial island is 17 kilometers long.

_____ 7. The landfill is made up of 11 cells, which are being filled with waste.

_____ 8. Four of the eleven cells have been filled to about two meters above sea level.

_____ 9. The Government of Singapore plants trees on each filled cell.

_____ 10. Singapore's National Environmental Agency destroyed all of the mangroves on the original island.

B. Write the number of each true and corrected statement from Activity A next to the main idea it supports.

Main ideas of Reading 1	Supporting details
1. Singapore has an environmentally friendly and unique landfill.	
2. Singapore is able to reduce a large amount of the waste going into its landfill.	
3. Singapore has carefully planned the building of its island landfill.	
4. Singapore has done a lot to maintain the natural environment on and around its landfill.	

 WHAT DO YOU THINK?

Discuss the questions in a group. Then choose one question and write freely for five to ten minutes in response.

1. How did Singapore turn its trash into treasure? Is this project worth 610 million in Singapore dollars (about $400 million in U.S. dollars)? Why or why not?

2. Would Singapore's solution to its garbage problem work in other countries? Why or why not?

Pulau Semakau: no ordinary landfill

READING 2 | Trash Talker: Garbage Mogul Makes Millions from Trash

VOCABULARY

Here are some words from Reading 2. Read their definitions. Then complete each sentence. You may need to change the form of the word to make the sentence grammatically correct.

> **bankruptcy** (*n.*) the state of being without enough money to pay what you owe
>
> **commit** (*v.*) be willing to work hard and give time and energy to something
>
> **consultant** (*n.*) a person who knows a lot about a particular subject and is employed to give advice about it to other people
>
> **corporation** (*n.*) a large business company
>
> **deficit** (*n.*) the amount by which money spent or owed is greater than money earned in a particular period of time
>
> **desperation** (*n.*) the feeling of needing or wanting something very much
>
> **entrepreneur** (*n.*) a person who makes money by starting or running businesses, especially when this involves taking financial risks
>
> **fertilizer** (*n.*) a substance added to soil to make plants grow more successfully
>
> **founder** (*n.*) the person who starts an organization, institution, etc.
>
> **investor** (*n.*) a person or organization that invests money in something in hopes of making money
>
> **retailer** (*n.*) a person or business that sells goods to the public
>
> **revenue** (*n.*) the money that a government receives from taxes or that an organization receives from its business

1. The company's _____ was down last year because it did not sell very much of its product.

2. Starting up my own business will be financially difficult, but I prefer to be a poor _____ instead of working for others.

3. In poor economic times, many companies have to declare _____ when they do not make enough money to cover all of their expenses.

4. The _____ of the environmental group started the club when he was only 12 years old.

5. When people are in great need, their _____ can force them to do things they would rather not do.

6. Worms can eat garbage and make a natural _____ that helps plants grow well.

7. She is _____ to protecting the environment; she has pledged to recycle as much of her garbage as possible.

8. Large _____ employ so many people that these companies generate huge amounts of trash.

9. It is becoming profitable for a _____ to sell environmentally friendly products in his or her store.

10. Because that company sold its products for less money than it cost to make them, it had a $3.5 million _____ last year.

11. She is a green-business _____ who gives companies advice to help them lower their negative impact on the environment.

12. Environmentally conscious _____ can buy stocks in many green businesses.

PREVIEW READING 2

Tip for Success

Read articles on related topics. This will give you a greater chance of seeing new vocabulary again and will help you to remember and understand new words.

You are going to read an article from *Fortune Small Business* magazine that looks at the rise of a new type of business: one that recycles trash into products people want.

Look at the title and subtitle of this reading. Then think of three or four questions that may be answered by this article and write them below.

1. _____

2. _____

3. _____

4. _____

Trash Talker

Garbage Mogul Makes Millions from Trash

With a brilliant business model built around recycling, TerraCycle will either go big or go broke.

By Loren Feldman

1   In a sprawling former suitcase factory in New Jersey, a camera crew is filming **entrepreneur** Tom Szaky and his company, TerraCycle, for a new reality TV show. Ten of the recycling firm's 46 employees sit around a table awaiting Szaky's next challenge. "So, guys," says Szaky, reaching into the pocket of his corduroy jacket and tossing a used toothbrush onto the table. "What are we going to do with this?"

Tom Szaky, founder of TerraCycle

2   You could ask the same question about every piece of trash in this 250,000-square-foot warehouse. Those boxes of Capri Sun juice pouches will become pencil cases. Circuit boards will be reincarnated as picture frames and clocks. Oreo wrappers will morph into kites. "We want to be the Wal-Mart of garbage," says Szaky, 26. Today's order of business: Toothbrush manufacturer Colgate-Palmolive is

prepared to ink a recycling deal if Szaky's team can dream up the right product. Their ideas include bending the toothbrushes into bracelets, purse handles, and toothbrush holders.

3   Creative recycling like this has helped double TerraCycle's **revenue** every year since 2004. Sales are likely to hit $15 million this year. Meanwhile, *Garbage Moguls*, the reality-show pilot, will air on the National Geographic Channel on Earth Day, April 22, and may be turned into a series. Szaky's TerraCycle memoir, *Revolution in a Bottle*, was published by Penguin in February. And he can boast new agreements to make tote bags out of cloth scraps from Brooks Brothers, coffee sacks from Starbucks, and film from Warner Bros.

4   Yet all is not well in the land of garbage. Despite its brilliant business model—shipping free junk in by the truckload, then spinning it into gold—TerraCycle is low on cash. In 2008 the company lost $3.5 million. TerraCycle's capital levels are always trailing behind Szaky's restless ambition, and the company's short history is filled with crises.

5   As the cameras roll, Szaky strikes a dire[1] note. "We are not stable," he tells his team. "We're on the edge of **bankruptcy** and of being a huge success at the same time." Right now, he estimates, the company has six weeks before it runs out of cash.

6   Both Szaky and TerraCycle reached this point via circuitous routes. Born in Hungary under the Communist regime, Szaky fled with his parents to Toronto in 1986. They were both doctors, but Szaky had entrepreneurship in his blood. At the age of 14, he started a business designing

---

[1] **dire:** very serious

websites. One of his clients, serial entrepreneur Robin Tator, would later co-found TerraCycle.

7   In 2002 Szaky was a freshman at Princeton when he heard about a friend's discovery: If you fed organic waste to earthworms, they produced **fertilizer** that plants seemed to love. Szaky smelled a strong business model. . . .

8   From that point on, Szaky was a man obsessed. He paid a Florida inventor $20,000 for a contraption that housed millions of worms and fed waste to them on conveyor belts. He won business plan competitions, found investors, dropped out of school, and ramped up production. Only then did Szaky realize he had no money left to design and make packaging for his precious worm poop.

9   That led to his second breakthrough. Out of **desperation**—and not knowing it was illegal—Szaky started raiding recycling bins for soda bottles. The bottles came in four standard sizes, which meant he could run them through a bottling machine. To build up a surplus of bottles, he persuaded church and school groups to form "bottle brigades," which would collect bottles in their neighborhoods—legally—in return for small donations.

10   The unusual recycled packaging—worm poop in Coke bottles!—helped TerraCycle's fertilizer stand out from the crowd. By 2007 it was being sold at Home Depot, Target, and Whole Foods. But Szaky had decided that worm fertilizer was a niche product that would never grow faster than 20 percent a year—not bad, but not the explosive growth for which he had dropped out of Princeton.

11   That's when Seth Goldman, the **founder** and CEO of Honest Tea, came along. Goldman had recently launched Honest Kids, a new line of organic juice in pouches, but feared that the nonrecyclable packaging would end up in landfills. "You guys are the trash people," he told Szaky. "Can you help me?"

12   Szaky bought some pouches and a sewing machine and got to work designing tote bags and pencil cases. Goldman loved them and agreed to fund "juice pouch brigades" at a penny per pouch. Szaky convinced Safeway, Target, and Walgreens to place orders for the bags and cases. The only problem: He had **committed** to manufacturing so many of them that he would need 10 million used pouches. The brigades were then delivering just 1,000 pouches a day.

13   After a few weeks of panic, co-founder Tator discovered the solution in British Columbia. The province, which required **retailers** to pay consumers who returned used juice pouches, was storing 20 million of them, pressed into sticky, smelly blocks. Tator persuaded the Canadian officials to let him take every last one to the U.S. in a fleet of rented trucks. . . .

14   Two years after that first call from Honest Tea, TerraCycle sells 50 different products and is bringing more out at the rate of one a week. Szaky has agreements with nearly all of the 50 **corporations** that produce most of the world's nonrecyclable trash. (No other company holds the rights to reuse Coke and Pepsi bottles, for example.) The contracts are nonexclusive, and the original manufacturers reserve the right to nix products, especially when their branding is visible. But TerraCycle doesn't have to give them any kind of share in sales. . . .

15   From the outside, it looks as if TerraCycle can do no wrong. "I think this is one of those rare instances where what seems too good to be true is actually that good," says Joel Makower, a green business **consultant** in Oakland. But insiders know from experience that Szaky's frenetic dealmaking can lead to costly gambles. In 2008 Szaky reached an agreement with Target to collect its plastic bags and fuse them into a superstrong carrying bag, the ReTote, which Target is now selling for $5.99.

16   The ReTote was TerraCycle's highest-grossing product last year, but all 142,000 units were sold at a loss. Szaky decided that the only way to produce the ReTote in time was to outsource it to a domestic manufacturer that charged him $20 a bag. That accounted for much of the company's $3.5 million **deficit** in 2008. Szaky has since shifted ReTote production

to Mexico, and he projects a $1 million profit for 2009—assuming that TerraCycle can survive until the end of the year.

17 One brisk January evening, soon after the reality show wrapped, the cash-strapped Szaky made a presentation to a group of angel **investors** at an exclusive Manhattan club. He was looking to raise $3 million, which in turn would trigger the release of $2 million from other investors. "If this meeting goes south[2]," he fretted beforehand, "I'm in a boatload of trouble." Szaky screened a rough cut of *Garbage Moguls* and delivered a treatise on the economics of garbage. Targus

CEO Brett Johnson, the group's head and a new TerraCycle board member, told the group Szaky was "the most unique entrepreneur I've ever known." Afterward, Szaky slumped against a wall, drained. "Let's see if they ante up," he said quietly. It would be almost a week before the call came: The group would kick in up to $4 million. For now, the Tom Szaky reality show will go on.

[2] **go south:** go bad; fail

MAIN IDEAS

A. Match each subheading with the paragraph(s) it best describes.

Paragraphs		Subheading
1. Paragraphs 1–3	____	a. Unstable Success
2. Paragraphs 4–5	____	b. Corporate Agreements
3. Paragraphs 7–10	____	c. Environmentally Friendly Fertilizer
4. Paragraphs 11–13	____	d. Problems with the ReTote
5. Paragraph 14	____	e. Juice Pouch Solutions
6. Paragraphs 15–16	____	f. Creative Recycling

B. Write the main idea of each subtitled section from Activity A.

1. _____

2. _____

3. _____

4. _____

5. _____

6. _____

DETAILS

Circle the answer that best completes each statement.

1. TerraCycle makes picture frames and clocks out of ____.
   a. plastic bottles
   b. old circuit boards
   c. juice pouches
   d. old kites and toys

2. TerraCycle's ideas to recycle used toothbrushes include making ____.
   a. jewelry
   b. packaging
   c. fertilizer
   d. tote bags

3. TerraCycle generally does not have enough ____.
   a. ideas for new products
   b. employees
   c. customers
   d. money

4. Szaky ____ a machine that fed waste to worms on a conveyor belt.
   a. invented
   b. won
   c. bought
   d. illegally took

5. "Bottle brigades" collected bottles in their neighborhoods mainly because ____.
   a. they wanted to earn a little money
   b. they wanted to donate their time to protecting the environment
   c. Szaky was friends with their leaders
   d. Szaky didn't want to collect any bottles on his own

6. TerraCycle brought juice pouches from Canada because ____.
   a. the Canadian officials asked TerraCycle to take the juice pouches away
   b. the Canadians didn't have enough space to store the juice pouches
   c. it couldn't get enough juice pouches locally in time to make a large order of tote bags and pencil cases
   d. the juice pouches available in the United States weren't of a high enough quality to make the tote bags and pencil cases

7. TerraCycle lost money on the ReTote because ___.

   a. the ReTote was not a popular item and did not sell well

   b. TerraCycle manufactured the ReTote for more than the product sold for

   c. TerraCycle had to shift production of the ReTote to Mexico

   d. TerraCycle decided not to manufacture the ReTote in the United States

8. Szaky wanted $3 million to release a further $2 million so that TerraCycle could ___.

   a. make a TV show about the company

   b. repay some investors

   c. raise Szaky's salary

   d. stay in business

WHAT DO YOU THINK?

A. Discuss the questions in a group. Then choose one question and write one or two paragraphs in response.

1. Which product developed by Tom Szaky's company do you think is the most creative? Is this a product that you would ever buy and use?

2. Why might many large corporations want to work with Tom Szaky and TerraCycle?

3. The article states that TerraCycle's success is unstable and that it is on the edge of bankruptcy yet a huge success at the same time. Do you think this company will be in business in twenty years? Why or why not?

B. Think about both Reading 1 and Reading 2 as you discuss these questions.

1. Two different methods of turning trash into treasure were presented by the readings in this unit: (1) incinerating waste and creating an artificial island and (2) creating new products from the waste of other products. What are some positive and negative aspects of each of these solutions?

2. Do you think governments or entrepreneurs are more effective at disposing of trash or finding ways to turn it into treasure? Why?

A **suffix** is an ending that is added to a root word. There are several **suffixes that form nouns**. Some of them indicate people or concrete objects or things, and others indicate more abstract nouns. The *Oxford Advanced American Dictionary for learners of English* has a list of suffixes with their meanings and uses. Understanding the meaning of suffixes will help you build your vocabulary by giving you clues to the meaning and function of new words.

Noun suffixes	Suffix meaning	Examples
-ation, -tion	an action or process, or the result of it	conservation, production
-er / -or	a person or thing that	manufacturer, actor
-ist	a person who does or believes in something	ecotourist
-ty, -ity	the quality or state of	biodiversity, clarity
-ment	the action or result of	agreement

A. Complete the chart with the correct form of each noun by using the most appropriate suffix from the skill box. Use your dictionary to help you.

Verb	Not a person / abstract idea	Person or thing
1. incinerate	incineration	incinerator
2. present		
3. fertilize		
4. invest		
5. invent		

B. Read the paragraph. Write the correct noun form of each word to complete the sentence.

Waste disposal is a big issue all around the world. Many countries have

created new _____regulations_____ (regulate) about recycling that encourage
            1

_____ (retail) and _____ (manufacture)
     2   3

to recycle their waste. This recycling keeps waste materials from being

burned in _____ (incinerate) or dumped into landfills. The
             4

_____ (eliminate) of a large amount of garbage helps to
     5

protect the environment and the _____ (pure) of nearby lakes
                      6

and rivers. Many of these retail and manufacturing companies have now

started working with people such as _____ (environmental)
                         7

to think of more ways to lower the amount of waste they produce. Also,

_____ (invest) are putting their money into recycling
     8

companies. With the increase in environmental awareness around the world,

their _____ (invest) are starting to make a profit. As greater
        9

numbers of _____ (corporate) become aware of the importance
        10

of recycling, recycling programs are sure to become more popular.

WRITING

Paraphrasing means putting someone else's words into your own words. A good paraphrase keeps the same meaning and is about the same length as the original text. Paraphrasing is a useful skill for both studying and integrating other people's ideas into your writing. However, it is important to cite the sources for any ideas that you use in your writing, even when you are paraphrasing.

Here are some tips for effective paraphrasing. Use a combination of these tips, but remember that a good paraphrase sounds natural.

- Read over the text you want to paraphrase several times in order to completely understand it.
- Take notes in your own words.
- Find good synonyms for some of the key vocabulary in the text.

> Szaky has **agreements** with **nearly** 50 **corporations**.
> Szaky has **contracts** with **almost** 50 **companies**.

- Write the paraphrase using your own notes without looking at the original.
- Change the grammatical structure of your paraphrase by:

Changing the order of the clauses

> **Since its independence from Malaysia**, Singapore has become wealthy.
> Singapore has become wealthy **since its independence from Malaysia**.

Changing to active or passive voice

> Szaky **convinced** Safeway, Target, and Walgreens to order the bags and cases.
> Safeway, Target, and Walgreens **were convinced** to order the bags and cases.

Changing the word forms

> Pulau Semakau is quite a **success**.
> Pulau Semakau is quite **successful**.

Check your paraphrases against the original texts to make sure that they are similar in content, but different in terms of vocabulary and grammar.

A. In your notebooks, rewrite each sentence according to the instructions. (Read each sentence carefully in order to fully understand the meaning.)

1. Find synonyms for the underlined words. Change from active to passive voice where possible.

   Singapore <u>incinerates</u> more than 90 percent of its <u>garbage</u> and disposes of the ashes on a <u>man-made</u> island. This island may become an important <u>home</u> for rare species of plants and animals in the future.

2. Find synonyms for the underlined words. Change the order of the clauses.

   Despite having a <u>good</u> business <u>model</u>, TerraCycle is <u>very</u> low on <u>cash</u> and might <u>go out of business</u>.

3. Find synonyms for the underlined words. Change from the active to the passive voice. Move the prepositional phrase "in the future" to the end of the paraphrased sentence.

   In the future, ecotourists will <u>visit</u> the island of Pulau Semakau on <u>specially arranged</u> guided <u>tours</u>.

4. Find a synonym for the underlined word. Change from active to passive voice. Change the word form of the word in bold and change the grammar accordingly.

   TerraCycle shouldn't <u>need</u> more than $3 million in order to avoid **bankruptcy**.

B. Paraphrase each pair of sentences. Begin by reading the sentences carefully and taking notes in your notebook. Then write the paraphrase in your notebook without looking at the original. Use a variety of techniques as appropriate.

1. All the trash from Singapore's 4.4 million residents is dumped on an artificial island. This island could become one of Singapore's main tourist attractions in the near future.

2. Singapore burns more than 90 percent of its garbage for reasons of space. Singapore will need to recycle more of its garbage to lower carbon emissions in the atmosphere.

3. Their ideas include bending the toothbrushes into bracelets, purse handles, and toothbrush holders. Retailers may want to sell these products close to their new toothbrushes.

4. TerraCycle's capital levels are always trailing behind Szaky's restless ambition, and the company's short history is filled with crises. However, the company shouldn't go out of business because it is such a great idea.

Tip for Success

When paraphrasing someone else's words or ideas in your writing, you should always reference the source, or tell the reader where the ideas came from. This will help you avoid plagiarism.

We use modals to talk about possibilities in the future and to make predictions. The choice of modal depends on how certain you are about the possibility of something happening in the future.

Absolutely certain	The local landfill **will** be full in ten years. People **won't** be able to get free bags in grocery stores anymore. We **cannot** keep making more and more garbage without hurting the environment. With the building of the new nature reserve, the environmentalists **couldn't** be happier.
Very certain	With the new recycling laws, people **should** start recycling at least half of their garbage. The fertilizer company **should not** go bankrupt, because new investors have been found. People are very concerned about the environment, so our new company **ought to** make a lot of money on our green products.
Somewhat certain	More people **may** start buying reusable tote bags if they become cheaper. Students **may not** buy our new recycled paper products because they are more expensive than regular paper products.
Less certain	The business **could** be making bracelets out of recycled toothbrushes by next year. Unrecyclable plastic **might** be banned in the next few years. Consumers **might not** buy nonrecyclable products in the future.

A. How certain is each prediction? Check (✓) the most appropriate level of certainty.

	Absolutely	Very	Somewhat	Less
1. The environment cannot be saved unless everyone starts recycling waste.	☐	☐	☐	☐
2. A lot of recyclable products might be banned from landfills soon.	☐	☐	☐	☐
3. Old-fashioned incandescent lightbulbs won't be sold in stores by 2050.	☐	☐	☐	☐
4. The city should start seeing the benefits of its new recycling program soon.	☐	☐	☐	☐

	Absolutely	Very	Somewhat	Less
5. If something isn't done soon, the landfill ought to fill up quickly.	☐	☐	☐	☐
6. Consumers may be more interested in buying recycled products if they become less expensive.	☐	☐	☐	☐
7. The recycling program is a big success, and the mayor couldn't be happier with the results.	☐	☐	☐	☐
8. A recycling depot could be built in the neighborhood if more people wanted one.	☐	☐	☐	☐

B. Read each green business idea and write a prediction about the success or failure of the business. Then write a reason for your prediction. Use modals of possibility in your predictions and reasons.

1. Recycle used toothbrushes into fashion bracelets for women.

   Prediction: _This idea might not be successful._

   Reason: _People may not want to wear somebody else's old toothbrush_

   around their wrists.

2. Make umbrellas out of recycled newspaper.

   Prediction: _____

   Reason: _____

3. Pay people to recycle their garbage (a garbage recycling company).

   Prediction: _____

   Reason: _____

4. Collect used coffee grounds from coffee shops and sell them to gardeners as fertilizer.

   Prediction: _____

   Reason: _____

5. Turn used cooking oil into gasoline for cars.

   Prediction: _____

   Reason: _____

C. You live in a large city, and the only landfill in the area is almost full. What is the future going to be like in this city? Write five sentences in your notebook predicting the future. Each sentence should contain a different modal of possibility.

A new landfill might be built on a farm outside of the city.

Unit Assignment   Write a business plan

 In this assignment, you will pretend to start an innovative new company that reuses or recycles garbage. You must find investors for your company. As you prepare your business plan, think about the Unit Question, "How can we turn trash into treasure?" and refer to the Self-Assessment checklist on page 190. Use information from Readings 1 and 2 and your work in this unit to support your ideas.

For alternative unit assignments, see the *Q: Skills for Success Teacher's Handbook.*

PLAN AND WRITE

Tip) Critical Thinking

The Unit Assignment asks you to develop a business plan for an innovative new company. In developing this plan, you will synthesize the information from the unit with your own ideas and prior knowledge to create something new.

A. **BRAINSTORM** What kind of businesses turn trash into treasure? In a group or with a partner, discuss these questions. Then use a cluster diagram like the one below to map your ideas.

1. What are three possible businesses that recycle or reuse trash?

2. What kind of services or products would each company provide?

3. Why would each business be attractive to potential investors?

4. Who would the customers be and how would they buy the product or service?

Trash into treasure

B. **PLAN** Choose a business from Activity A. Follow these steps to prepare to write your business plan for the new company that you want to start.

1. These are questions commonly asked by investors before they put money into a new business. With a partner, answer each question.

    1. What is the name of your business? _____

    2. What kind of business is it? _____

    3. What product or service are you going to provide? _____

    4. Why is this business a great idea? _____

       _____

    5. What are the main goals for this business? _____

       _____

    6. Who are the customers going to be? _____

    7. Where will you sell the product or service? _____

       _____

2. Use this outline to organize your business plan in your notebook. Add or subtract supporting points as needed. Include examples from the readings in this unit to support your business plan.

    Business Plan: Turning Trash into Treasure

    1. **Introduction**
        a. name of business
        b. kind of business

    2. **Business Description**
        a. product or service
        b. why this is a good investment
        c. main goals

    3. **Sales and Marketing**
        a. potential customers
        b. where you will sell the service or product

    4. **Conclusion and Summary**
        a. most important aspects of this plan

C. **WRITE** Write your business plan. Look at the Self-Assessment checklist below to guide your writing.

REVISE AND EDIT

A. **PEER REVIEW** Read a partner's business plan. Consider it from the point of view of a possible investor. Would this business plan convince an investor to learn more about and possibly support the company? Answer the questions and discuss them with your partner.

1. What kind of business is described in the business plan?

2. Is this business a great idea? Why or why not?

3. Are you clear about the company's main goals? Why or why not?

4. What information would you add or delete to improve the business plan?

5. Does the business plan use any ideas from other sources, such as the readings in this unit? Are they paraphrased effectively?

B. **REWRITE** Review the answers to the questions in Activity A. You may want to revise and rewrite your business plan.

C. **EDIT** Complete the Self-Assessment checklist as you prepare to write the final draft of your business plan. Be prepared to hand in your work or discuss it in class.

Yes	No	SELF-ASSESSMENT
☐	☐	Does the business plan build a convincing argument using facts, reasons, and examples?
☐	☐	Has information from Reading 1 and Reading 2 been paraphrased correctly where appropriate?
☐	☐	Are modals of possibility used correctly to express predictions?
☐	☐	Do nouns have the correct suffixes where appropriate?
☐	☐	Does the business plan include vocabulary from the unit?
☐	☐	Did you check the essay for punctuation, spelling, and grammar?

Track Your Success

Circle the words you learned in this unit.

Nouns
bankruptcy
conservation
constraint AWL
consultant AWL
corporation AWL
deficit
desperation
disposal AWL

elimination AWL
entrepreneur
fertilizer
founder
habitat
investor AWL
retailer
revenue AWL

Verbs
anticipate 🔑 AWL
commit 🔑 AWL
incinerate
thrive

Adjectives
abundant
contaminated
obsolete
sustainable AWL

🔑 Oxford 3000™ words

AWL Academic Word List

Check (✓) the skills you learned. If you need more work on a skill, refer to the pages in parentheses.

READING	●	I can anticipate content through questions. (p. 168)
VOCABULARY	●	I can recognize noun suffixes. (p. 182)
WRITING	●	I can paraphrase. (p. 184)
GRAMMAR	●	I can recognize and use modals of possibility. (p. 186)
LEARNING OUTCOME	●	I can prepare a business plan that describes an innovative new garbage recycling company to potential investors.

UNIT **8**

Change

READING ● identifying the author's intent
VOCABULARY ● using the dictionary
WRITING ● summarizing
GRAMMAR ● subject-verb agreement

LEARNING OUTCOME •

Develop a summary and response essay based on an informational text.

Unit QUESTION

Why do people want to change who they are?

PREVIEW THE UNIT

A Discuss these questions with your classmates.

If you could change any aspect of your personality, what would it be? How would this improve your life?

Have you ever changed or wanted to change your physical appearance? What did you change or want to change?

Look at the photo. What is the man changing? Why do you think he wants to change?

B Discuss the Unit Question above with your classmates.

Listen to *The Q Classroom*, Track 11 on CD 2, to hear other answers.

C Read the list of changes. Check (✓) whether you think each change would affect a person's appearance, personality, or both. Discuss your answers in a group.

Change	Appearance	Personality
1. Dye one's hair brown, blond, or black.	☐	☐
2. Learn a new language.	☐	☐
3. Smile more.	☐	☐
4. Dye one's hair purple, blue, or green.	☐	☐
5. Go to a tanning salon.	☐	☐
6. Live abroad for a year.	☐	☐
7. Lose or gain weight.	☐	☐
8. Shave one's head.	☐	☐

D Work with a partner. Describe the personality and lifestyle of each person below. Give reasons for your descriptions. Try to be as detailed as possible.

E The people above want to change. Read what each person wants and write some advice in your notebook. Discuss your answers with a partner or a group. Would it be easy for them to change?

1. I think I'm too shy. I want to be more outgoing.

2. I want to look professional, but not too conservative.

3. I want to look the way I feel: young!

4. I want to live and work in another country.

READING

READING 1 | Set in Our Ways: Why Change Is So Hard

VOCABULARY

Here are some words and phrases from Reading 1. Read their definitions. Then complete each sentence. You may need to change the form of the word or phrase to make the sentence grammatically correct.

> **competence** (*n.*) the ability to do something well
>
> **conceivable** (*adj.*) that you can imagine or believe
>
> **conduct** (*v.*) to organize and/or do a particular activity
>
> **conscientious** (*adj.*) taking care to do things carefully and correctly
>
> **consistency** (*n.*) the quality of always behaving in the same way
>
> **impulsive** (*adj.*) likely to act suddenly without thinking carefully about what might happen
>
> **intention** (*n.*) what you intend or plan to do; your aim
>
> **lose one's appetite** (*phr.*) to lose interest
>
> **novelty** (*n.*) the quality of being new, different, and interesting
>
> **the jury is still out** (*phr.*) used when you are saying that something is still not certain
>
> **transformation** (*n.*) a complete change in somebody or something
>
> **undertake** (*v.*) to make yourself responsible for something and start doing it

1. Some people read self-help books because they are not happy with their lives and are looking for personal _____.

2. The researchers are responsible for organizing the experiments, but their assistants actually _____ them.

3. People don't like too much change because familiar experiences give them a feeling of _____ and control over their lives.

4. Many people start a diet with the best _____ of achieving a healthy weight, but they find it difficult to change their behavior.

5. Some scientists believe personality characteristics are genetic, but _____ on this issue because no research has proved this to be true.

6. As a person gets older, he may start to _____ for change and adventure, instead preferring to be comfortable and safe.

7. Some people are _____ workers and always try to do a good job.

8. Many young people are _____ and make quick decisions that are not based on a lot of thought.

9. Some people think that their hair needs to look different, so they style it in every _____ way.

10. When you _____ a diet or exercise program, you are also responsible for making a long-term change in behavior.

11. A person's ability to communicate information and ideas in a foreign language is called communicative _____.

12. The _____ of visiting a foreign country and experiencing a lot of new things can be very exciting.

PREVIEW READING 1

You are going to read an article by Nikolas Westerhoff from the magazine *Scientific American Mind* that looks at why it is so difficult for people to change their lives and their personalities as they become older.

Why is change so difficult for some people? List three reasons that people may not be able to change their lives or enjoy new experiences.

1. _____

2. _____

3. _____

Set in Our Ways: Why Change Is So Hard

Millions of us dream of transforming our lives, but few of us are able to make major changes after our 20s. Here's why.

1   *"The shortest path to oneself leads around the world."* So wrote German philosopher Count Hermann Keyserling, who believed that travel was the best way to discover who you are.

2   That was how 22-year-old Christopher McCandless was thinking in the summer of 1990, when he decided to leave everything behind—including his family, friends, and career plans. He gave his bank balance of $24,000 to the charity Oxfam International and hitchhiked around the country, ending up in Alaska. There he survived for about four months in the wilderness before dying of starvation in August 1992. His life became the subject of writer Jon Krakauer's 1996 book *Into the Wild*, which inspired the 2007 film of the same name.

3   Not every newly minted college graduate is as **impulsive** and restless as McCandless was, but studies **conducted** since the 1970s by personality researchers Paul Costa and Robert R. McCrae of the National Institutes of Health confirm that people tend to be open to new experiences during their teens and early 20s. Young people fantasize about becoming an adventurer like McCandless rather than following in the footsteps of a grandparent who spent decades working for the same company. But after a person's early 20s, the fascination with **novelty** declines, and resistance to change increases. As Costa and McCrae found, this pattern holds true regardless of cultural background.

People tend to be open to new experiences during their teens and early 20s.

4   Although people typically **lose their appetite** for novelty as they age, many continue to claim a passion for it. Voters cheer on politicians who pledge change. Dieters flock to nutritional programs advertising a dream figure in only five weeks. Consumers embrace self-help books promising personal **transformation**. And scientists tell us that novel stimuli[1] are good for our brains, promoting learning and memory.

5   Yet even as people older than 30 yearn for what is new, many find themselves unable or unwilling to make fundamental changes in their lives. Researchers say this paradox can be largely explained by the demands of adult responsibilities and that unrealistic expectations may also play a part in thwarting[2] our best **intentions**. Change is rarely as easy as we think it will be.

Nature or nurture?

6   Psychologists have long identified openness to new experiences as one of the "Big Five" personality traits, which also include

---

[1] **stimuli:** (*pl. for stimulus*) something that helps somebody or something to develop better or more quickly
[2] **thwart:** to prevent somebody from doing what they want to do

extroversion[3], agreeableness, conscientiousness, and neuroticism[4]. Considerable disagreement exists about how much these personality traits change after age 30, but most research suggests that openness declines in adulthood.

7   The fact that an age-dependent pattern of decreasing openness appears around the globe and in all cultures suggests, according to biopsychologists, a genetic basis. But **the jury is still out**. As psychologist and personality researcher Rainer Riemann of Bielefeld University in Germany points out, it is **conceivable** that people all over the globe are simply confronted with similar life demands and societal expectations. Young men and women everywhere have to go out into the world and find a partner and a livelihood. Later, they have to care for their children and grandchildren. These life tasks require commitment and **consistency** and may serve as a catalyst for personality change.

8   Once a family and career are in place, novelty may no longer be as welcome. New experiences may bring innovation and awakening but also chaos and insecurity. And so most people dream of novelty but hold fast to the familiar. Over time we become creatures of habit: enjoying the same dishes when we eat out, vacationing in favorite spots, and falling into daily routines.

9   "The brain is always trying to automate things and to create habits, which it imbues[5] with feelings of pleasure. Holding to the tried and true gives us a feeling of security, safety, and **competence** while at the same time reducing our fear of the future and of failure," writes brain researcher Gerhard Roth of the University of Bremen in Germany in his 2007 book whose title translates as *Personality, Decision, and Behavior*.

10   But even negative events may have thoroughly positive results, according to sociologist Deborah Carr of Rutgers University. For example, many widows are able to start life over again and to develop talents they never knew they had. People who have been diagnosed with cancer learn to redefine themselves as a result of the disease—and may even conquer their cancer in the process. Survivors of natural catastrophes often discover new strengths. But we should not draw sweeping conclusions from these examples, says psychologist William R. Miller of the University of New Mexico. Many older people report that they have changed little in spite of major life experiences.

Over time we become creatures of habit.

11   The structure of one's personality becomes increasingly stable until about age 60. "That means that a person who is particularly **conscientious** at the age of 40 will be conscientious at 60 as well," says psychologist Peter Borkenau of Martin Luther University Halle-Wittenberg in Germany. Stability decreases again, however, after the age of 60. It seems that people are only able to become more open to new experiences once they have fulfilled their life obligations—that is, after they have retired from their careers and their children have flown the nest.

False hope springs eternal

12   Even after age 60 it is difficult to completely reframe your life. In fact, those who seek to

---

[3] **extroversion:** liveliness and confidence; enjoying being with other people

[4] **neuroticism:** the state of not behaving in a reasonable, calm way, because you are worried about something

[5] **imbue:** to fill with strong feelings, opinions, or values

make large changes often end up failing even to make the most minor corrections. The more an individual believes he can set his own rudder[6] as he pleases, the more likely he is to run aground[7]. That's one reason why so many smokers who tell you that they can quit whenever they want are still smoking 20 years later.

13 In 1999 psychologists Janet Polivy and C. Peter Herman of the University of Toronto Mississauga coined a term for this phenomenon: false hope syndrome. Over and over, they say, people **undertake** both small and large changes in their lives. Most of these attempts never get anywhere, thanks to overblown expectations.

14 Take the woman who believes that if she can lose 20 pounds she will finally meet the man of her dreams and live happily ever after. This fantasy is based on the notion that one positive change—losing weight—automatically brings with it other desired changes. But the reality is that it is difficult to keep weight off over the long term, and finding an ideal life partner is often dependent on luck. Even if dieting proves successful, other goals may remain out of reach. But the false hope syndrome seduces people into trying to overhaul their entire lives all at once: the smoker and couch potato is suddenly inspired to become a nonsmoker and marathon runner, but because he attempts too much too fast, he is doomed to fail.

15 The cure for false hope is to set more reasonable goals and recognize that achieving even modest change will be difficult. And if you are older than 30, remember that your openness to new experiences is slowly declining, so you are better off making a new start today than postponing it until later. Perhaps most important of all, try to appreciate the person that you already are.

16 As the ancient Greek philosopher Epicurus put it: "Do not spoil what you have by desiring what you have not; but remember that what you now have was once among the things only hoped for."

---

[6] **rudder:** a piece of wood used to control the direction of a boat; figurative meaning: control your life

[7] **run aground:** when a ship touches the ground and cannot move; figurative meaning: to have trouble

MAIN IDEAS

A. Match each section of the article with its main ideas.

a. Introduction (Paragraphs 1–5)

b. Nature or Nurture? (Paragraphs 6–11)

c. False Hope Springs Eternal (Paragraphs 12–14)

d. Conclusion (Paragraphs 15–16)

_____ 1. People need to set reasonable goals, as even small changes are difficult. It is more important to be happy with who you are.

_____ 2. As people become older, they are less open to change. This is true around the world and in all cultures, suggesting that resistance to change has a genetic basis. However, it may also indicate that people all over the world simply have similar life demands and societal expectations.

_____ 3. While young people are usually open to new experiences, older people are less interested in new experiences and are more unwilling to change.

_____ 4. People who try to make big changes in their lives often end up failing to make even small changes. Their hopes are too high. Their desire for change is unrealistic.

B. What is the main idea of Reading 1? Write your ideas and compare ideas with a partner.

_____

_____

DETAILS

Answer these questions.

Introduction (Paragraphs 1–5)

1. What did Christopher McCandless do that is an extreme example of the impulsiveness and restlessness of youth?

_____

_____

2. How do the examples of voters, dieters, and consumers show that people continue to claim a passion for novelty as they get older?

_____

_____

Nature or nurture? (Paragraphs 6–11)

3. What evidence is there for a genetic basis to declining openness in adulthood?

_____

_____

4. What is the argument that there isn't a genetic basis to declining openness in adulthood?

_____

_____

5. According to the article, when are people able to become open to new experiences again?

_____

_____

False hope springs eternal (Paragraphs 12–14)

6. What is false hope syndrome?

_____

_____

7. Why will the woman who believes that if she loses 20 pounds, she'll meet the man of her dreams and be happy probably not succeed?

_____

_____

Conclusion (Paragraphs 15–16)

8. What advice does the article give to people over the age of 30 who might want to change?

_____

_____

WHAT DO YOU THINK?

Discuss the questions in a group. Then choose one question and write freely for five to ten minutes in response.

1. How open to new experiences are you? What are some examples of new experiences you have had?

2. Do you agree that the older people become, the harder it is for them to change? How does this idea compare with the experiences of people you know?

3. Based on what you have read and your own experiences, do you feel that the global pattern of being less open to change is genetic or because of the societal pressures everyone faces?

Authors can have many different reasons for what they choose to write. These reasons are the author's **intent**, or purpose. Everything you read has a purpose, and authors may have more than one purpose for writing something. They may want to inform, persuade, and/or entertain their readers. Authors do this through a combination of their writing style, the inclusion of certain facts and ideas, and their choice of particular words.

This chart gives the three basic reasons authors have for writing something. Use the key indicators and examples to help guide you in judging an author's intent. Learning how to identify an author's intent will help you better analyze texts and become a more critical reader.

	Information	Persuasion	Entertainment
Intent	explains, describes, or informs the reader about something	tries to make the reader believe a particular idea, think in a certain way, or take action	entertains the reader
Style	expository writing	persuasive writing	narrative and descriptive writing
Key indicators	provides mostly factual information or gives instructions on how to do something	contains opinions, feelings, and beliefs	paints a picture in the reader's mind that may make the reader feel a strong emotion; can be an interesting story or anecdote
Examples	science textbooks, educational materials, lab reports, directions, cookbooks, some newspaper and magazine articles, some websites	some newspaper and magazine articles, editorials, blog entries, advertisements, opinion essays, academic essays	fiction, short stories, novels, poetry, comics, graphic novels

A. Read these excerpts from Reading 1. Decide if the author is trying to inform (*I*), persuade (*P*), or entertain (*E*). More than one answer may be correct, so be prepared to defend your choice.

_____ 1. He gave his bank balance of $24,000 to the charity Oxfam International and hitchhiked around the country, ending up in Alaska. There he survived for about four months in the wilderness before dying of starvation in August 1992.

_____ 2. Studies conducted since the 1970s by personality researchers Paul Costa and Robert R. McCrae of the National Institutes of Health confirm that people tend to be open to new experiences during their teens and early 20s.

_____ 3. Psychologists have long identified openness to new experiences as one of the "Big Five" personality traits, which also include extroversion, agreeableness, conscientiousness, and neuroticism.

_____ 4. Over time we become creatures of habit: enjoying the same dishes when we eat out, vacationing in favorite spots, and falling into daily routines.

_____ 5. In 1999 psychologists Janet Polivy and C. Peter Herman of the University of Toronto Mississauga coined a term for this phenomenon: false hope syndrome.

_____ 6. The smoker and couch potato is suddenly inspired to become a nonsmoker and marathon runner, but because he attempts too much too fast, he is doomed to fail.

_____ 7. As the ancient Greek philosopher Epicurus put it: "Do not spoil what you have by desiring what you have not; but remember that what you now have was once among the things only hoped for."

 Tip for Success

When you read a newspaper or a magazine, thinking about the author's intent will help you to decide on the trustworthiness and reliability of what you are reading.

B. Work in a group. Discuss these questions about the author's intent. Be sure to give reasons for your answers.

1. In your opinion, why did Nikolas Westerhoff write this article about the difficulty of change?

2. Find examples from the article to support your opinion of the author's purpose(s).

3. How does identifying the author's intent help you to become a better reader?

READING 2 | Kids Want to Tan

VOCABULARY

Here are some words and phrases from Reading 2. Read the sentences. Then match each bold word or phrase with its definition.

_____ 1. In the summer, Norah-Jean loves to stay outside in order to keep her **sun-kissed** glow.

_____ 2. The Canadian **Dermatology** Association says that sun tanning is bad for the skin.

_____ 3. Young people in North America have started tanning **with a vengeance**.

_____ 4. The American Academy of Dermatology reported that older white men have a higher **incidence** of skin cancer.

a. to a greater degree than is expected or usual

b. made warm or brown by the sun

c. the scientific study of skin diseases

d. the extent to which something happens or has an effect

_____ 5. In the last 20 years, the tanning-salon market has shown **phenomenal** growth.

_____ 6. Skin cancer is the most common form of cancer, accounting for one-third of all **diagnoses** of the disease.

_____ 7. Cases of skin cancer are **projected** to increase this year by five percent.

_____ 8. Some people with **olive-toned** skin don't think they need to worry about sunburns.

e. yellowish-brown in color

f. the act of discovering or identifying the exact cause of an illness or a problem

g. very great or impressive

h. to estimate what the size, cost, or amount of something will be in the future based on what is happening now

9. Toxic chemicals can harm our cells and **trigger** the growth of cancer in our bodies.

10. Last year, the World Health Organization **urged** governments to control artificial tanning.

11. The summer sun can be **scorching**, so it is important to protect your skin from burning.

12. Some people feel they are **doomed** to having skin cancer if their parents have had it.

i. to recommend something strongly

j. to make something happen suddenly

k. certain to fail, suffer, die, or experience a terrible event that cannot be avoided

l. very hot

PREVIEW READING 2

This article from the weekly newsmagazine *Maclean's* considers why some people like to tan. It also discusses some of the drawbacks of getting too much sun. What do you think are some of the possible dangers of sun tanning? Write your ideas.

_____

_____

 CD 2
Track 13   **Read the article.**

Kids Want to Tan

Sun is the new tobacco: Why the young, especially, just can't quit

1   In winter, if there's something special going on—a friend's birthday party, say, or a family gathering at Christmas—Norah-Jean Howard, 19, heads to the tanning salon for a little color. In summer, though, Howard might join friends around the pool, or maybe at the trampoline in the backyard, to make sure she keeps that **sun-kissed** glow. The alternative—pallor[1]—is no alternative at all, and she doesn't spend a lot of time worrying about skin cancer.

---

[1] **pallor:** pale coloring of the face

2   Nevertheless, the Canadian **Dermatology** Association says, "No tan is a good tan," since all exposure to solar radiation[2]—whether from the sun or a tanning lamp—damages the skin to some extent. To the sun-obsessed, you might as well be saying, "No air is good air." Young people, especially, have embraced tanning **with a vengeance**, heading to tanning salons and, in warm weather, soaking up the sun. Last month, the American Academy of Dermatology released a survey indicating 79 percent of youths between 12 and 17 know sun tanning can be dangerous. Furthermore, 81 percent recognize that sunburns during childhood up the risk of skin cancer, yet 60 percent said they burned last summer. It gets worse: while more than a third of those surveyed said they knew someone who had skin cancer, almost half said people with tans look healthier.

3   Teenage boys are the worst offenders, with only 32 percent of those 15 to 17 reporting they're either very or somewhat careful under the sun. "This lax[3] behavior could explain findings from a previous study published in the January 2003 issue of the *Journal of the American Academy of Dermatology* in which older white men had a higher **incidence** of skin cancer," the academy reported.

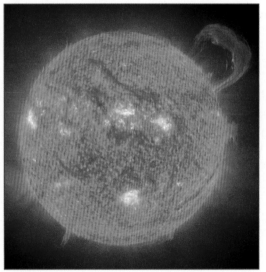

4   North Americans are chasing ultraviolet radiation[4] more vigorously than ever. According to Statistics Canada, Canadians last year made almost 1.5 million trips to countries in the Caribbean for stays of one night or more, a searing 74 percent increase over the 860,000 visits made in 2000. Similarly, the US 5-billion-dollar tanning-salon market in North America has shown **phenomenal** growth, going from fewer than 10,000 outlets in the early 1990s to about 50,000 today. "Gold equals healthy and white equals ill," says Daniel Maes, vice president of global research and development for Estée Lauder in Melville, N.Y. "Nobody wants to deal with people who look ill. This is what pushes people to go lie down on a beach and get burned. They look around and everybody looks better than them."

5   Skin cancer is the most common type of cancer in Canada, accounting for one-third of all **diagnoses** of the disease, with 82,400 cases forecast for this year. There are three kinds: basal, squamous, and melanoma. Basal and squamous are less serious and far more common than melanoma, and will account for roughly 78,000 cases in 2005. They're usually treated without hospitalization. However, the incidence of melanoma, with 4,400 diagnoses and 880 deaths **projected** for this year, has risen alarmingly—an average of 2.4 percent a year in men and 1.8 percent in women since 1992. Various cancer agencies agree: since sun exposure is linked to most skin cancers, reduced exposure to ultraviolet radiation would cut the number of new cancer cases to the same extent that quitting smoking cuts cancer in tobacco addicts.

6   Deborah Kellett grew up in Ontario and spent a lot of time sunning herself in cottage country north of Toronto. Kellett, 47, has **olive-toned** skin and

[2] **solar radiation:** powerful and dangerous rays that are sent out from the sun

[3] **lax:** not strict, severe, or careful enough about work, rules, or standards of behavior

[4] **ultraviolet radiation:** radiation that causes the skin to darken

generally didn't burn. Today, she lives in Bedford, Nova Scotia, and has had a year to think about her cancer. She had been keeping an eye[5] on a spot on her back, just below her armpit, for a few years when her family physician noticed it had grown. Kellett was in to see a specialist within a week, and a week after that, the dermatologist used a local anaesthetic and removed the growth, which was about the size of a baby fingernail. Her prognosis[6]—like any melanoma caught early—is very good. "I always thought I was safe—I was proud of the way I would tan—but I basically tell people that it's not worth it," says Kellett.

7   Sun suppresses the immune system. It works this way: dendritic cells with amoeba-like arms fight infections and are found in tissues throughout the body. They surround and swallow the infectious agent and deliver it to T cells[7], which **trigger** an all-out attack on the infection and also immunize the body against future assaults. The sun, however, "down regulates" dendritic cells, preventing their activation, says Bhagirath Singh, scientific director of the Institute of Infection and Immunity in London, Ontario. "Dendritic cells are really the central mechanism of the immune orchestra," says Singh. "They control how the immune system will mobilize."

> " *Gold equals healthy and white equals ill. . . . This is what pushes people to go lie down on a beach and get burned.* "

8   Even when people put on sunscreen, they often don't put on enough to get the desired SPF[8] rating. That's why Canadian dermatologists have upped their recommendation of SPF 15 to SPF 30, says Dr. Jason Rivers, a professor of dermatology at the University of British Columbia and former national director of the sun awareness program for the Canadian Dermatology Association. "You can lead by example as a parent, so early education is important," suggests Rivers. In fact, it's not all bad news. The tanning-bed industry is under mounting pressure. In March, the World Health Organization—noting that more than two million cases of skin cancer, of which 132,000 are malignant melanomas, occur worldwide each year—**urged** regulators to restrict artificial tanning with UV light to those 18 and older. Early this year, Health Canada took steps that will require manufacturers to toughen warning labels on tanning equipment.

9   Under a **scorching** noonday sun in Toronto's Beaches neighbourhood, Jason Remenda, 34, languidly[9] pushes his 21-month-old son Jaydn on a swing. Remenda, a parts manager for a Japanese car manufacturer, has a rare day off. He's wearing shorts, a baseball cap, and a thick gold chain around his neck. The only SPF lotion anywhere near him is on his son. It's his first time out this year, and he never uses sunscreen. Thoughts of skin cancer cross his mind only when someone asks him about it. "I'm getting up there in age," shrugs Remenda. "I'm going to die of some kind of cancer, right?"

10   A few feet away, lying in the sand along the north shore of Lake Ontario, Gillian Parker feels guilty for being caught out in the sun. The 24-year-old TV production assistant—fair-skinned, strawberry blond and freckled—usually doesn't sunbathe. Nevertheless, here she is, although she says she's watching the time carefully. "I already know that I'll probably get skin cancer," says Parker, explaining how she's burned throughout her life. Four years ago, she fell asleep for 45 minutes in the sun and

---

[5] **keep an eye on something:** to take care of something and make sure it is not harmful

[6] **prognosis:** an opinion, based on medical experience, of the likely development of a disease or an illness

[7] **T cell:** a kind of white blood cell that plays an important role in the human immune system

[8] **SPF:** sun protection factor

[9] **languidly:** moving slowly in an elegant manner, not needing energy or effort

ended up with blisters all over her chin. Her mother has already had skin cancer—twice. "That's why I feel I'm pretty much **doomed**."

11 It's the cry of a tan addict. Many of us, especially young people, just can't say no to the kiss of the sun, even though it could be the kiss of death.

MAIN IDEAS

Answer these questions.

1. What is the main issue in the article?

   _____

2. Why do some people want to tan?

   _____

3. What is the biggest danger associated with tanning?

   _____

DETAILS

Read the statements. Write _T_ (true) or _F_ (false). Then correct each false statement to make it true.

_____ 1. Tanning under a solar lamp isn't as dangerous as tanning in the sun.

_____ 2. Few people between 12 and 17 realize that tanning can be dangerous.

_____ 3. The majority of youths between 12 and 17 got burned by the sun the summer before they answered a survey about tanning habits.

_____ 4. A research study from 2003 indicated that older white men had a lower rate of skin cancer than others.

_____ 5. Today there are fewer than 50,000 tanning salons in North America.

_____ 6. At the time the article was written, melanoma was less common than the other two types of skin cancers.

_____ 7. The incidence of melanoma is higher among women than men.

_____ 8. Although olive-skinned people may believe they are not at risk for skin cancer, they actually are.

_____ 9. A lot of sun exposure is good for the immune system.

_____ 10. The World Health Organization is in favor of limiting tanning with UV light to people over the age of 18.

WHAT DO YOU THINK?

A. Discuss the questions in a group. Then choose one question and write one to two paragraphs in response.

1. Why do people continue to tan despite the dangers of skin cancer?

2. Should governments control the amount of time people can use a tanning bed? Why or why not?

3. What determines whether or not someone is beautiful? Are attitudes towards physical beauty the same all around the world? Is the desire to change the way we look universal?

B. Think about both Reading 1 and Reading 2 as you discuss the questions.

1. Which is more difficult to change: your life (as in Reading 1) or your appearance (as in Reading 2)? Explain your choice.

2. Can changing your physical appearance change your personality or improve your life? Why or why not?

It is important to **make appropriate word choices** when you are writing. The first word that you think of when you are writing isn't always the best word to express your ideas. By looking critically at your vocabulary choices, you can choose words that are the best fit for your writing purpose.

Synonyms

Synonyms may be misleading, as no two words are exactly the same. A synonym may be slightly different from the exact meaning you want, or it may be accurate, but inappropriate for the **audience** or **register and genre** of your writing. If you are not sure of the exact definition or how to use the word, look it up in the dictionary.

Audience

The vocabulary choices you make need to match the audience for your writing. Who is the target audience? American English speakers? British? Academic scholars? The dictionary gives specific information about this sort of usage.

Register and genre

You should always be aware of the level of formality of a word or phrase. Formal and informal writing often require different vocabulary choices. Are you writing an article for a fashion magazine or for an academic journal? Are you posting a blog entry online? You can check your dictionary to see if the word you are using is appropriate or if a more suitable word exists.

---

ex·ac·er·bate /ɪgˈzæsərˌbeɪt/ *verb* ~ **sth** (*formal*) to make something worse, especially a disease or problem **SYN** AGGRAVATE: *The symptoms may be exacerbated by certain drugs.* ▶ **ex·ac·er·ba·tion** /ɪgˌzæsərˈbeɪʃn/ *noun* [U, C]

From the example, you can see that *exacerbate* is a verb that means "to make something worse" and the noun form is *exacerbation*. You can also see that this word is used in formal language and that it is used when talking about diseases and problems, as in the example sentence. If you are writing or speaking in an informal way, it is more natural to say "made worse" than "exacerbated."

All dictionary entries are from the *Oxford Advanced American Dictionary for learners of English* © Oxford University Press 2011.

A. Circle the most appropriate word or phrase to complete each sentence in a formal piece of writing in a magazine. Use your dictionary to help you.

1. Many physicians (beg / urge) tanning-salon owners to set strict rules for use of tanning beds by teenagers.

2. Some self-tanning lotions contain (bad things / toxic chemicals).

3. Consumers love self-help books that promise complete personal (transformation / change).

4. People who are able to make a big change in their lives at an older age are not afraid of (new stuff / innovation).

5. Because of false hope syndrome, people often (fail / mess up) when making big changes in their lives.

6. Couch potatoes who suddenly (are inspired / want) to become marathon runners may not have too much success.

B. Replace the words in bold with a more academic vocabulary word from Reading 1 or Reading 2.

scorching
1. The sun's rays are **really hot**, so it is very important to protect your skin.

2. It is important to clearly define your goals before you **do** an experiment.

3. It's **possible** that skin cancer rates will increase significantly within the next year.

4. People lose their appetite for **new things** as they age.

5. Too much exposure to radiation can **set off** dangerous changes in skin cells.

6. My sister is thinking about becoming a doctor that specializes in **the study of the skin**.

C. Choose ten vocabulary words from this unit. Write a sentence using each word. Be sure to look up the words in the dictionary to see how they are used.

WRITING

A **summary** is a shortened version of a text such as an article or textbook excerpt. It is an objective piece of writing that does not contain any of your opinions or ideas. To write a summary, determine the main ideas in the original text and write a paragraph about them. Summarizing is a useful study aid to help you remember and understand main ideas when you are taking an exam or doing research.

Here are some steps to help you write a summary.

Before You Write: Read the text thoroughly. Use techniques you learned in Unit 1 ("Annotating a text," page 10) and Unit 2 ("Distinguishing main ideas from details," page 38) to determine the main ideas the author is expressing.

As You Write: Write a draft of the summary using your own words. Follow these guidelines:

- **Topic sentence:** Introduce the piece by giving the author's name, the title of the piece, the source, and the general topic of the text.

- **Body:** Write the main ideas of the text in the order they appear. Do not include details.

- **Conclusion:** One way you can end a summary is to briefly restate the main ideas found in the reading.

After You Write: Ensure the summary is much shorter than the original text. Read over your summary to see if it makes sense and expresses the main ideas of the reading. Eliminate any unnecessary details. Then revise and edit your work.

- Always use your own words. Never copy the author's words. (See "Paraphrasing," page 184, in Unit 7.)

- Do not overuse quotes. Use mostly indirect speech. A short quotation of a key phrase may be included.

- Do not add your own ideas or opinions, and do not change the writer's ideas and opinions.

A. Read this article from the British newspaper *The Guardian* about the dangers of sunbeds for children and teenagers. As you read, annotate the text and underline the main ideas.

Children As Young As 11 Use Sunbed Salons

By Sam Jones

a teenager in a sunbed

1   Health campaigners have called for the rules governing tanning salons to be tightened after a study showed that up to 8% of 11- to 12-year-olds have used sunbeds in the past year, with some children visiting tanning shops daily after school. The survey, based in Merseyside, England, also found that some salons allowed mothers to take their babies into the booths while they used sunbeds, and one even offered children's parties.

2   Philomena Zilinski of the campaign group Health in Knowsley said: "We surveyed young people because we wanted to find out why they were using sunbeds and how many times a week. Some were going in every day after school and many were using them four times a week. People don't seem to realize the health risks." Ms. Zilinski said many children were ignoring the damage they were doing to their skin because they thought tanning made them look better and slimmer, or helped clear up complaints such as acne. "The problem is that schoolchildren can afford to use them. Parents don't have to give consent," she added.

3   The research has also prompted a crackdown on tanning salons by local authority officers in Knowsley's public health protection division. They have carried out an assessment of all 38 sunbed salons in the area and have sent written warnings to those that need to make changes. Any that fail to comply could be prosecuted.

4   Richard Fontana, Knowsley council's principal environmental health officer, said the survey had also revealed that some young people were refusing to wear goggles because they do not want white patches on their face, even though tanning without them can cause problems including eye cancer. "We were told one shop was holding tanning parties inviting people to hire out the venue and turn it into a social event," he said.

5   Calls are growing for tighter restrictions on young people visiting tanning salons because the number of people with skin cancer has doubled in the past 10 years. Legally there is nothing to prevent children from using sunbeds but the guidelines recommend they are only used by over-16s. Nina Goad of the British Skin Foundation said: "The advice of the World Health Organization is that people under 18 should not use sunbeds. It is widely reported that there are a number of short- and long-term health risks associated with using sunbeds. Some users have also reported dry, bumpy or itchy skin. However, of more consequence are the potential long-term risks of sunbed use, of which skin cancer is the most significant."

6   The popularity of tanning parlors among young people was highlighted this year when a 15-year-old girl was warned by doctors that she was likely to develop skin cancer by the age of 30 if she did not stop using sunbeds five times a week. Hayley Barlow, from Liverpool, was

dubbed a "tanorexic"[1] after experts found her skin was closer to that of a 25-year-old than a teenager. She has tried to give up visiting tanning salons but still goes at least three times a month.

"All the girls you see in magazines are tanned and lots of my friends use sunbeds as well," she said. "But I'd like to warn other teenagers not to use them."

[1] **tanorexic:** someone who tans obsessively, to the point of making herself sick

Tip **Critical Thinking**

Activity B asks you to assess whether the summary is effective or not. When you assess, you use your own knowledge and opinions to judge another's ideas. People can form different, but equally valid assessments. Making judgments based on the information available and your own values and beliefs can help you understand a topic better.

B. **Read the summaries and answer the questions. Discuss your answers with a partner.**

> The article "Children as young as 11 use sunbed salons" by Sam Jones tells us that 8 percent of 11- to 12-year-olds have used sunbeds in the past year. The article reports that children were ignoring the damage they were doing to their skin because they thought tanning made them look better and slimmer. There are 38 sunbed salons in the area, and some have been sent written warnings. Some young people were refusing to wear goggles because they do not want white patches on their face. The advice of the World Health Organization was that people under 18 should not use sunbeds. A 15-year-old girl was warned by doctors that she was likely to develop skin cancer by the age of 30 if she did not stop using sunbeds five times a week. She is a tanorexic, and she still goes at least three times a month to tanning salons.

1. Is this an effective summary? Why or why not?

_____

_____

> The article from *The Guardian* newspaper "Children as young as 11 use sunbed salons" by Sam Jones looks at the use of tanning salons by children and teenagers. A survey has led health campaigners to ask for stronger government rules and has caused local authorities to crack down on salons. The survey showed that up to 8 percent of 11- to 12-year-olds have used sunbeds in the past year and that children are not protecting themselves properly in the salons because they want to look good. Another factor is that the number of people with skin cancer has doubled in the last ten years. Right now, children can use tanning salons, but government and World Health Organization guidelines state they should be restricted to people over ages 16 and 18, respectively. Children may be using tanning salons now, but health campaigners are working hard at changing the rules.

2. Is this an effective summary? Why or why not?

_____

_____

Sam Jones, in the article "Children as young as 11 use sunbed salons," informs us that many young people are using sunbeds. Some mothers are even taking their babies into the booths with them. This is very dangerous, and they are not good mothers. A survey was carried out that revealed a lot of children are using tanning salons because they think a tan makes them look better and slimmer. They have probably been reading magazines with tanned movie stars and television actors. These kinds of magazines make children think that being tanned is fashionable, but it is very dangerous. The number of people with skin cancer has doubled in the last 10 years. I think there are going to be even more people getting skin cancer in the future because of tanning. I hope Hayley Barlow from Liverpool will stop tanning and realize that she is beautiful just the way she is.

---

3. Is this an effective summary? Why or why not?

_____

_____

4. Which summary is the best? Why?

_____

_____

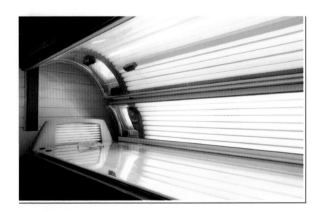

In every sentence, the main subject and verb must agree with each other. Singular subjects agree with singular verbs, and plural subjects agree with plural verbs. To avoid errors when writing, identify the main subject of the sentence and the subjects of any clauses and check that they each have a verb that agrees. Prepositional phrases, relative clauses, and noun clauses can be tricky.

Prepositional Phrases A plural noun at the end of a prepositional phrase modifying a singular subject can cause writers to make subject-verb agreement errors. The subject, not the noun at the end of the prepositional phrase, determines if the verb is singular or plural.

> Sunbed **use** among young people **is** a public health concern.
> prepositional phrase

Subject Relative Clauses The verb in a subject relative clause (see "Adjective phrases," Unit 1, page 23) agrees in number with the noun that the clause modifies. The main verb of the sentence also agrees with the noun.

> Many **physicians** who **are** against the use of sunbeds **treat** people with cancer.
> subject relative clause

Noun Clauses A noun clause can be the subject of a sentence. Use a singular verb in these sentences.

> **What personality studies have shown** **is** that openness to change declines
> noun clause
> with age.

Quantifiers When quantifiers (see Unit 4, page 102) are used, they usually precede a noun. Look at the noun and check that the main verb agrees with it.

> Almost **every teenager is** open to new experiences. (singular)
> I want to diet because **most of my money is spent** on fast food. (noncount)
> **Most of my friends like** to travel to new places and **experience** new cultures.
> (plural)

A. Underline the main subject in each clause of each sentence. Choose the correct verb.

1. Many people (wants / want) to make big changes in their lives, but most of these attempts never (gets / get) anywhere.

2. Openness (is / are) one of the "Big Five" personality traits, which also (includes / include) extroversion, agreeableness, conscientiousness, and neuroticism.

3. Voters often (votes / vote) for the politicians in an election who (pledges / pledge) change.

4. How much people desire trying new things (declines / decline) as people become older.

5. Not every new college graduate (is / are) impulsive and restless.

6. Recommendations for stronger sunscreen use (was made / were made) by the Canadian Dermatologists' Association.

7. Many patients' prognoses for a complete recovery from cancer (depends / depend) on the type of cancer they (has / have).

B. Read the summary. Underline the twelve subject-verb agreement errors and correct each error.

The article by Sam Jones, "Children as young as 11 use sunbed salons," <u>reveal</u> how young people, some as young as 11 or 12, goes to tanning salons. ^s Because so many young people in northern England is using tanning salons, health campaigners wants stronger rules to control these places. A survey about the effects of using sunbeds show that many young people is ignoring the risks. They think that tanning in sunbeds improve the way they look. In response to the survey, local authorities are making sure tanning salons in this part of England is obeying the law. Another thing the survey reveals are that some young people are not wearing protective goggles because they want to look good. Additionally, the number of people who has skin cancer have doubled in the last ten years. As a result, people are asking the government for rules that controls the use of tanning salons by young people.

Unit Assignment   Write a summary and response essay

In this assignment, you will write a summary and response essay for Reading 1 or Reading 2. As you prepare your essay, think about the Unit Question, "Why do people want to change who they are?" and refer to the Self-Assessment checklist on page 220. Use your work in this unit to support your ideas.

For alternative unit assignments, see the *Q: Skills for Success Teacher's Handbook*.

PLAN AND WRITE

A. BRAINSTORM You may respond to one of the following questions in your summary and response essay: 1) Can people change who they are? or 2) Why do people want to change who they are? Decide which question you will address. Then choose Reading 1 or Reading 2 and complete these tasks.

1. Reread the article you chose and annotate as you read. Use these questions to guide you.

   a. How does the article relate to the question you chose?

   b. What are the main ideas of the article?

   c. What main ideas in the article do you agree or disagree with? Why?

   d. What information in the article supports or disagrees with your point of view?

   e. Do you have any personal experience with or prior knowledge of this topic? What facts and examples support or disprove the main ideas in the article?

2. Discuss your answers with a partner who chose the same article.

B. PLAN Choose three main ideas from the article and write them below. Write your personal reaction to each one and how each relates to the question you are going to address in the response part of your essay.

1. Main idea 1 _____

   _____

   Personal reaction _____

   _____

   Relation to question _____

   _____

2. Main idea 2 _____

   _____

   Personal reaction _____

   _____

   Relation to question _____

   _____

3. Main idea 3 _____

_____

Personal reaction _____

_____

Relation to question _____

_____

C. **WRITE** Write your summary and response essay. Use the outline below to organize your essay. Look at the Self-Assessment checklist on page 220 to guide your writing.

1. Introduction

   A. Give the author, title, and source of the article.

   B. State the overall idea of the article.

   C. Write a thesis expressing your reaction and response to the article.

2. Summary Paragraph

   A. Follow the guidelines in the Writing Skill on page 212 for writing a good summary.

   B. Keep your summary to one paragraph in length.

3. Response

   A. Use the answers to the activities in the Brainstorm and Plan sections above to help you write your response to the ideas in the article.

   B. Write one paragraph about each of the main points you identified in the Plan section above.

   C. Support your position in each paragraph by including facts and examples from the reading as well as from your personal experience and prior knowledge.

4. Conclusion

   A. Restate your thesis.

   B. Restate the main ideas from your summary and your response to them.

REVISE AND EDIT

A. PEER REVIEW **Read a partner's summary and response essay. Answer the questions and discuss them with your partner.**

1. Has the writer stated the overall idea of the article in the introduction?

2. Is it clear which question the writer is going to address in the essay? ("Can people change who they are?" or "Why do people want to change who they are?")

3. Is there a clear thesis in the introduction? What is it?

4. How well does the writer summarize the article? Would the main ideas of the article be clear to someone who hadn't read it?

5. Is the response section of the essay well organized? Is only one main idea addressed in each paragraph?

6. Does the writer provide adequate support for his or her main ideas in the response?

7. Does the conclusion provide an effective closing to the essay? Why or why not?

8. What advice can you give to improve any part of the essay?

B. REWRITE **Review the answers to the questions in Activity A. You may want to revise and rewrite your summary and response essay.**

 for Success

One of the best ways to improve your spelling when writing is to consistently look up words in the dictionary if you are not sure of their spelling.

C. EDIT **Complete the Self-Assessment checklist as you prepare to write the final draft of your summary and response essay. Be prepared to hand in your work or discuss it in class.**

		SELF-ASSESSMENT
Yes	**No**	
☐	☐	Does the essay build a convincing argument using facts, reasons, and examples?
☐	☐	Has information from Reading 1 and Reading 2 been summarized correctly where appropriate?
☐	☐	Have you made sure there are no subject-verb agreement errors?
☐	☐	Did you use the dictionary to make appropriate word choices?
☐	☐	Does the essay include vocabulary from the unit?
☐	☐	Did you check the essay for punctuation, spelling, and grammar?

Track Your Success

Circle the words you learned in this unit.

Nouns
competence
consistency AWL
dermatology
diagnosis
incidence AWL
intention 🔑
novelty
transformation AWL

Verbs
conduct 🔑 AWL
doom
project 🔑 AWL
trigger AWL
undertake AWL
urge 🔑

Adjectives
conceivable AWL
conscientious
impulsive
olive-toned
phenomenal AWL
scorching
sun-kissed

Phrases
lose one's appetite
the jury is still out
with a vengeance

🔑 Oxford 3000™ words
AWL Academic Word List

Check (✓) the skills you learned. If you need more work on a skill, refer to the pages in parentheses.

READING	●	I can identify the author's intent. (p. 202)
VOCABULARY	●	I can use the dictionary to make appropriate word choices. (p. 210)
WRITING	●	I can write a summary. (p. 212)
GRAMMAR	●	I can recognize and correct subject-verb agreement errors. (p. 216)
LEARNING OUTCOME	●	I can develop a summary and response essay based on an informational text.

READING ● organizing notes and annotations in a chart
VOCABULARY ● adjective/verb + preposition collocations
WRITING ● writing a cause-and-effect essay
GRAMMAR ● cause-and-effect connectors

Prepare a cause-and-effect essay analyzing two or three methods for boosting energy levels.

Q

Unit QUESTION

What energizes people?

PREVIEW THE UNIT

A Discuss these questions with your classmates.

When do you have the most energy? Are you a morning person or a night owl?

What causes people to suffer from low energy levels?

Look at the photo. What are the people doing? How do you think they feel?

B Read and discuss the Unit Question above with your classmates.

Listen to *The Q Classroom*, Track 2 on CD 3, to hear other answers.

C Answer the questionnaire. Check (√) the ways that you use to feel more energetic.

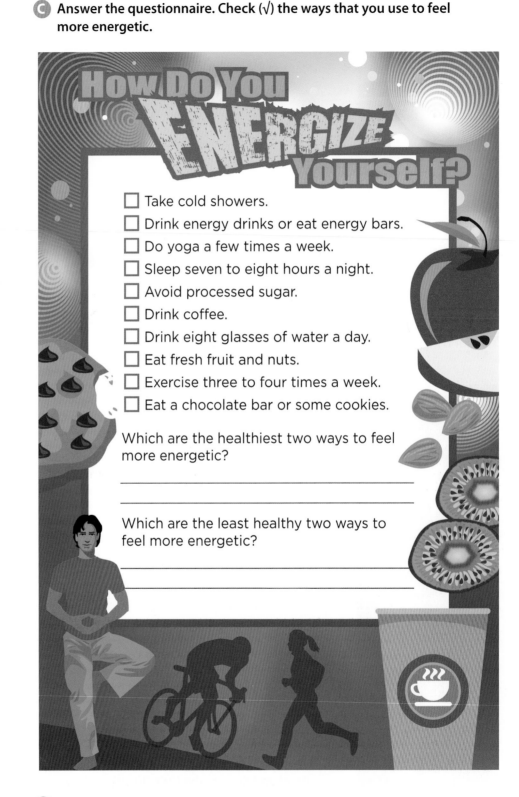

How Do You ENERGIZE Yourself?

- ☐ Take cold showers.
- ☐ Drink energy drinks or eat energy bars.
- ☐ Do yoga a few times a week.
- ☐ Sleep seven to eight hours a night.
- ☐ Avoid processed sugar.
- ☐ Drink coffee.
- ☐ Drink eight glasses of water a day.
- ☐ Eat fresh fruit and nuts.
- ☐ Exercise three to four times a week.
- ☐ Eat a chocolate bar or some cookies.

Which are the healthiest two ways to feel more energetic?

_____

_____

Which are the least healthy two ways to feel more energetic?

_____

_____

D Work in a group. Compare your results from Activity C. Choose the two best ways to boost energy immediately. Choose the two best ways to boost energy over a longer time period.

READING 1 | A Healthy Lifestyle Can Reduce Fatigue, Boost Energy

VOCABULARY

Here are some words and a phrase from Reading 1. Read their definitions. Then complete each sentence.

> **alleviate** (*v.*) to make something less severe
>
> **carbohydrates** (*n.*) foods, such as bread, potatoes, and rice, that provide the body with energy
>
> **digest** (*v.*) to change food into substances that your body can use
>
> **dilemma** (*n.*) a problem, especially a situation in which you have to make a very difficult choice between equally undesirable things
>
> **fatigue** (*n.*) a feeling of being extremely tired, usually because of hard work or exercise
>
> **hormone** (*n.*) a chemical substance produced in the body that encourages growth or regulates how the cells and tissues function
>
> **immune system** (*n.*) the system in your body that produces substances to help it fight against infection and disease
>
> **metabolism** (*n.*) the chemical processes in living things that change food, etc., into energy and materials for growth
>
> **protein** (*n.*) a natural substance found in meat, eggs, fish, etc. Proteins are important for humans and animals to eat to help them grow and stay healthy.
>
> **refined** (*adj.*) made pure by having other substances taken out of it
>
> **restore** (*v.*) to bring somebody or something back to a previous condition
>
> **stamina** (*n.*) the physical or mental strength that enables you to do something difficult for long periods of time

1. Chicken and beef are two foods that contain a lot of _____.

2. Some runners eat pasta or other foods with a lot of _____ because they believe it will give them energy for a big race.

3. Too much caffeine and sugar can affect a person's _____, speeding up nerve activities.

4. You need a lot of _____ to be able to run a marathon.

5. A good diet and plenty of rest can help _____ the symptoms of minor illnesses and make you feel better.

6. After eating, you should allow your body time to _____ the food before you start any exercise.

7. After exercising, you should drink water to _____ the fluids lost during your workout.

8. Severe _____ can be caused by too much exercise or a poor diet, resulting in the desire to sleep all the time.

9. Many adults face a _____ when they must choose whether or not to take time away from work and family in order to exercise.

10. Stress can reduce the effectiveness of your _____ and make it easier for you to become sick.

11. An area of the brain called the pineal gland produces a _____ called melatonin that helps people get the right amount of sleep.

12. Soft drinks and candy bars often contain a lot of _____ sugar, which is not as healthy as the natural sugars in fruits.

PREVIEW READING 1

Tip for Success

As you read, pay attention to how new vocabulary words are used in a sentence in order to learn common collocations and grammatical patterns.

CD 3
Track 3

You are going to read a newspaper article from the *St. Petersburg Times* that looks at three main reasons why many people often feel tired and worn out.

What do you think the reasons are? Check (✓) three answers.

☐ lack of sleep   ☐ financial problems

☐ overwork   ☐ poor diet

☐ too much stress   ☐ too much TV and too many video games

Read the article.

A Healthy Lifestyle Can Reduce Fatigue, Boost Energy

By David Norrie

1   Look around you at the gym. Can you be the only one wondering, "How can I get the energy to do this?" And as you get older, it doesn't get any easier. Little wonder we are besieged[1] by

Does your energy level crash during the day?

---

[1] **besieged:** (especially of something unpleasant or annoying) to surround somebody or something in large numbers

commercials for products that promise to boost our energy. Why the obsession with energy? Are we working harder, not taking care of ourselves, or simply expecting more out of each 24-hour day?

Experts generally agree on three culprits: sleep, stress, and diet

2   Quality, uninterrupted sleep is essential in helping the body repair tissue and **restore** itself, especially in people who exercise. Lack of sleep can impede your concentration levels and cause depression. Dr. John Brown, a sleep specialist at the James A. Haley Veterans Hospital, refers to this lack of quality sleep as "sleep debt," comparable, he says, to our society's financial debt.

3   Quality sleep has five stages, with the fifth (rapid eye movement, or REM) commonly associated with a deep sleep or dream state. It is important to get into the later stages of sleep because that is when the body produces growth **hormone**. Growth hormone, secreted by the pituitary gland, affects all aspects of cellular **metabolism**, including protein synthesis and breaking down fats. A lack of it lowers metabolism, causing fatigue and weight gain.

4   While humans typically need seven to eight hours of sleep each night, "what might be acceptable and tolerable for one might not be for another," Brown says. If you log a normal amount of sleep and continue to experience an abnormal lack of energy during the day, you might want to consult a physician. You might suffer from chronic fatigue syndrome (CFS), which is far more distressful[2] than feeling sluggish[3] in the morning.

5   While CFS can follow a severe illness, abnormal stress, or death in the family, symptoms also can result from sleep apnea. Sleep apnea is characterized by temporary breathing interruptions during sleep, often lasting from 10 to 20 seconds. The pauses in breathing can occur dozens or hundreds of times a night and put a tremendous amount of stress on the respiratory system. Loud snoring, gasping for air during sleep, and excessive daytime napping are signs of sleep apnea. Typically a spouse or bed partner first becomes aware of the situation. Obesity is one major cause of sleep apnea. While obese white males have been studied most thoroughly, the condition can affect anyone.

Stressed out

6   When I was young there was little to worry about other than getting good grades and staying fit. Stress rarely becomes a **dilemma** until we become adults, when work, dating, family, and financial matters expand exponentially. While these common stress factors affect everybody's life, some have a more difficult time coping and the stress manifests itself physically.

7   Stress inhibits the **immune system**, detracts from our focus and often leads us back to the first problem, lack of sleep. Exercise is one good way to **alleviate** stress. But if your mind is cluttered with worries during a weightlifting session or fitness class it becomes difficult to reach your potential and reap the benefits of a successful workout.

8   You've seen ads for weight-loss products that include some derivative of the word cortisol. While I do not endorse these products, the hormone cortisol plays a critical part in how the body deals with stress. Cortisol itself, produced in the adrenal cortex, does not pose a threat to the body; its purpose is to help our bodies deal

[2] **distressful:** causing pain, upsetting
[3] **sluggish:** moving, reacting, or working more slowly than normal and in a way that seems lazy

with stress and maintain a healthy immune system. But prolonged stress can induce an overproduction of cortisol, leading to an increase in blood pressure, blood sugar levels, and abdominal fat while suppressing the body's ability to fight cold and infection.

9   Extended anxiety puts the adrenal gland under enormous pressure to try to keep up with the production of cortisol. This can eventually lead to a group of symptoms that some medical practitioners call adrenal **fatigue**. People with adrenal fatigue typically feel drained[4] in the morning and don't feel fully awake until noon, with lulls in energy all day. Other symptoms include inability to lose weight, difficulty remembering things, colds, and lightheadedness.

Eating yourself to exhaustion

10   As a trainer, the two biggest mistakes I see people make are: 1) going into a good evening workout session having had their last meal around noon, or 2) the reverse, a person who hurried a meal on his way to the gym thinking that would give him proper energy to work out.

11   When and how often you eat are just as important to your energy levels as what you eat. Long periods without food tell our bodies to shut down and conserve energy. That fact has been programmed into our DNA, and it makes perfect sense when you think about it. In the days of Neanderthal Man, food was more scarce. For early man to survive during wintertime or periods of food scarcity, the body's metabolism would slow down dramatically in what you would call "survival mode."

12   To not so great an extent, when we go without food for even five to seven hours, we experience a similar drop in metabolism, a halt in the burning of fuel, and a lull in energy. But eating just before exercise will do nothing but drain your body of its ability to function at an optimum level, as your organs are using energy to process and **digest** food. That is why we feel tired after a large meal.

13   For your body to function as the well-oiled machine it should be, it is better to eat small meals throughout the day, every two to three hours. Consider three basic meals a day with small snacks in between. And by snacks, I mean fruits, nuts, energy bars, etc. Complex **carbohydrates** are the body's preferred source of energy.

14   But perhaps one reason some of us experience fatigue is a diet skewed toward consuming **protein** in large quantities. High-protein meals build muscle and restore our bodies on a cellular level, but a lack of quality carbohydrates makes it much more difficult for our bodies to produce energy. Here's the catch: not all carbohydrates are good for sustained energy. **Refined** sugars, found in sodas and candy bars, give you a quick energy fix but do not provide a good source of long-lasting fuel, typically leaving the body in what's referred to as a "crash" state after they rush through the digestive system.

15   In addition to simple sugars, beware of processed or refined foods, as they are more difficult to break down in digestion. What's more, the foods' molecular structure has changed, robbing them of their true nutrients. Processed and refined foods are higher on the glycemic index, a scale that ranks carbohydrate-rich foods by how much they raise blood glucose levels. Foods high on the index burn quickly and release a rapid shot of energy to the body. Again, this is not good for **stamina** and leaves the body in a crash state. Foods low on the glycemic index release energy more slowly and combat fatigue. Low-index foods are typically lower in calories and fat and higher in fiber.

---

[4] **drained:** weaker with less energy

MAIN IDEAS

Circle the answer that best completes each statement.

1. The main causes of low energy levels are ___.
    a. carbohydrate-rich foods and refined sugars
    b. poor sleep, too much stress, and bad diet
    c. a lack of concentration and depression
    d. working too hard and not taking care of ourselves

2. People need good-quality, uninterrupted sleep in order to ___.
    a. help the body repair tissue and restore itself
    b. digest their food efficiently
    c. stop producing growth hormone
    d. have enough energy to exercise

3. Stress and energy levels are related because ___.
    a. exercise helps to get rid of stress
    b. some people suffer from adrenal fatigue
    c. too much stress has negative physical effects on the body
    d. cortisol is not produced sufficiently when the body is under stress

4. When you eat, how often you eat, and what you eat ___.
    a. affect the glycemic index
    b. are not important for digestion
    c. are programmed into your DNA
    d. have a major effect on your energy level

DETAILS

Rewrite these false statements with the correct information.

1. It is better to eat large meals three times a day at breakfast, lunch, and dinner.

    _____

2. People feel tired and lose weight when they have enough growth hormone.

    _____

3. Exercise is a bad way to deal with stress if you are not too worried about things.

    _____

4. Food choices high on the glycemic index combat fatigue because they
    release energy very quickly in the body.

    _____

5. Sleep apnea can result from chronic fatigue syndrome.

    _____

6. Going without food for several hours results in an increase in metabolism
    and higher energy levels.

    _____

7. Refined sugars provide long-lasting energy.

    _____

8. High levels of cortisol have several positive effects on the body.

    _____

Q WHAT DO YOU THINK?

**Discuss the questions in a group. Then choose one question and write freely
for five to ten minutes in response.**

1. Are getting enough quality sleep, lowering stress, and eating well realistic
    ways to boost energy levels for people in today's world? Why or why not?

2. Do you have enough energy to do the things you want to do? What are you
    doing, or could you be doing, to boost your energy levels?

3. Are most people you know too busy? Do busy people suffer from fatigue
    and low energy? Why or why not?

Reading Skill | **Organizing notes and annotations in a chart** | web

A chart is a useful tool for organizing your notes and annotations from a reading.
Creating such a chart makes studying easier. Charts can also make it easier to
paraphrase and summarize a text for a report or essay. There are various charts
you can use depending on the type of text and the type of writing you plan to do.

Main ideas and details chart

This type of chart helps you identify and understand the relationship between main ideas and details. Record the main ideas in the reading on one side of the chart and the most important details on the other.

Main ideas	Details
Lack of quality sleep decreases energy.	• produce growth hormone when sleeping • sleep apnea causes chronic fatigue syndrome

Cause and effect chart

This type of chart helps you identify and understand the **causes** (the events in a story or the steps in a process) and the **effects** (the results of those events or steps).

Cause	Effect
too much caffeine	nervousness, very alert

Connections to the text chart

This type of chart helps you remember and understand the text in a more meaningful way because you are connecting the text with something you already know.

You can make connections between the reading and:

- things or events in your own life (**text to self**)
- other things you have read (**text to text**)
- issues, events, general knowledge in the world (**text to world**)

Ideas in Reading 1	Connections
One reason some of us experience fatigue is a diet skewed toward consuming protein in large quantities.	**Text to self:** I always feel tired after eating a lot of protein—especially after eating a lot of meat.
	Text to text: I read an online article that said high-protein diets were unhealthy and might cause kidney problems.
	Text to world: High-protein diets are still popular with people who want to lose a lot of weight.

A. Write the number of each corrected statement from the Details activity (page 229) next to the main idea that it supports.

Main ideas	Details
a. Good-quality sleep can reduce fatigue and boost energy.	
b. Dealing with stress can reduce fatigue and boost energy.	
c. Having a healthy diet can reduce fatigue and boost energy.	1,

B. Complete this cause-and-effect chart for Reading 1 with the missing cause or effect.

Cause	Effect
1. quality uninterrupted sleep	body repairs tissue and restores itself
2. lack of sleep	
3.	lower metabolism, fatigue, weight gain
4. sleep apnea	
5.	sleep apnea
6. worrying during exercise	
7.	increase in blood pressure, blood sugar, and abdominal fat; harder to fight cold and infection
8. no food for five to seven hours	
9.	fatigue
10. refined sugars	

C. Complete the connections-to-text chart by identifying text to self, text to text, and text to world connections you can make to the information found in Reading 1.

Ideas in Reading 1	Connections
Poor sleep leads to fatigue.	Text to self:
	Text to text:
	Text to world:

Ideas in Reading 1	Connections
High stress levels lead to fatigue.	Text to self:
	Text to text:
	Text to world:
Poor diet leads to fatigue.	Text to self:
	Text to text:
	Text to world:

READING 2 | A Jolt of Caffeine, by the Can

VOCABULARY

Here are some words and phrases from Reading 2. Read their definitions. Then complete each sentence. You may need to change the form of the word or phrase to make the sentence grammatically correct.

agitated (*adj.*) showing in your behavior that you are anxious and nervous

bar (*v.*) to ban or prevent somebody from doing something

component (*n.*) one of several parts of which something is made

concentration (*n.*) the ability to direct all your effort and attention on one thing, without thinking of other things

contend (*v.*) to say that something is true, especially in an argument

disclaimer (*n.*) a statement in which a company says that it is not connected with or responsible for something

foster (*v.*) to encourage something to develop

minimal (*adj.*) very small in size or amount; as small as possible

mystique (*n.*) the quality of being mysterious or secret that makes somebody or something seem interesting or attractive

relative to (*phr.*) considered according to its position or connection with something else

take issue (*phr.*) to disagree or argue with somebody about something

unfounded (*adj.*) not based on reason or fact

1. Some energy drinks contain a large amount of caffeine _____ the amount in coffee and tea.

2. Vitamins are one important _____ of many energy drinks.

3. Energy drink companies create a _____ about their drinks by making the ingredients sound like little-known medicines.

4. People who drink too much coffee can become _____, restless, and nervous.

5. Regular users of energy drinks _____ with people who believe the drinks should be banned.

6. Some governments _____ the sale of energy drinks because they want to keep people from using drinks that may be harmful.

7. Some people say that energy drinks improve their _____, so they can pay attention and think better.

8. People who criticize energy drinks _____ that the drinks have too much caffeine in them.

9. Scientists caution that energy drinks can start or _____ an addiction to the caffeine in the drinks.

10. The advertiser made claims that were _____, with no research to support them.

11. For some people the effects are _____, but others suffer severe headaches during caffeine withdrawal.

12. Energy drinks often carry a _____ on their label warning that the drink is not suitable for children or pregnant women.

PREVIEW READING 2

You are going to read an article from *The New York Times* that discusses the growing popularity of energy drinks. What do you think the article will say about the caffeine in energy drinks? Check (✓) your answer.

☐ An energy drink has about the same amount of caffeine as a cup of coffee.
☐ An energy drink has much more caffeine than coffee.
☐ An energy drink has more caffeine than coffee but less than most sodas.

A Jolt of Caffeine, by the Can

By Melanie Warner

energy drinks

1   Every day Tom Cabrera, a 27-year-old auto mechanic who lives in Middletown, Rhode Island, drinks a can of SoBe No Fear energy drink on his way to work. Later in the day, if he goes to the gym, he downs another before his workout.

2   He says he probably could not get through the day without one. "It lifts me up. One minute I'm dragging and then it's like 'Pow!'" he said, widening his eyes.

3   Loyal and enthusiastic customers like Mr. Cabrera have helped propel caffeinated energy drinks into the fastest-growing sector of the $93 billion domestic beverage industry. Sales of energy drinks, which sell for $2 to $3 a can, have grown a torrid[1] 61 percent this year in the United States, according to *Beverage Digest*.

4   But that has scientists and nutritionists worried. Energy drinks have as much sugar and roughly three times the caffeine of soda, and some experts peg their popularity to their addictiveness. And with racy[2] names like Full Throttle, Rockstar, and Adrenaline Rush, critics say these drinks are **fostering** caffeine addiction among teenagers.

5   Caffeine can cause hyperactivity and restlessness among children and is known to increase the excretion of calcium, a mineral much needed while bones are still growing.

6   Energy drink manufacturers say they do not market to children and their products have no more caffeine than a typical cup of coffee. But the debate persists. Four countries have **barred** the sale of energy drinks with current levels of caffeine: France, Denmark, Norway, and, two months ago, Argentina.

7   Critics **contend** that much of the skyrocketing growth of energy drinks comes because consumers are getting physically addicted, either by consuming the concoctions[3] daily or guzzling several at a time to elevate their mood.

8   Roland Griffiths, a professor of behavioral biology at Johns Hopkins University School of Medicine, says the amount of caffeine necessary to produce dependency and withdrawal symptoms is about 100 milligrams a day. A can of energy drink has 80 to 160 milligrams, depending on the size, though such information is not listed on any cans. An eight-ounce cup of coffee typically has 100 to 150 milligrams.

9   Some energy brands go so far as to promote their addictiveness as a selling point. "Meet your new addiction! 16 oz's of super charged energy with advanced **components** and a great berry-passion fruit flavor," reads the front page of Pepsi's SoBe No Fear website. Cans of Kronik Energy, made by an Arizona company, warn

---

[1] **torrid:** very hot; (figuratively) fast and strong
[2] **racy:** having a style that is exciting and amusing

[3] **concoction:** a strange or unusual mixture of things, especially a kind of drink or medicine

customers, "Caution: May Be Psychologically Addicting," meant as a daring come-on, not a serious warning.

10　Nutritionists say that while it may be fine for adults to have their dose of caffeine, they worry about children becoming hooked. "I suspect that busy, driven teenagers are grabbing one of these energy drinks instead of eating real food, which I would be concerned about," said Lola O'Rourke, a registered dietitian in Seattle and a spokeswoman for the American Dietetic Association.

11　Cans of SoBe, Monster, Rockstar, and others carry a voluntary **disclaimer**, warning that the fizzy liquid inside is "not recommended for children, pregnant women, or people sensitive to caffeine."

12　But the definition of "children" is not always clear. Coke and Pepsi say they aim their products at those older than 20. Rodney C. Sacks, chief executive of the Hansen Natural Corporation, which sells the popular Monster brand, says that his product is appropriate for anyone over 13.

13　In addition to caffeine, other purportedly energy-enhancing ingredients in energy drinks have attracted the attention of European health officials. When France banned Red Bull in 2000, health officials cited uncertainties about the interaction of caffeine, the amino acid taurine, and glucuronolactone, a type of sugar that is produced by human cells and used in metabolism.

14　Beverage companies say energy drinks have been safely consumed around the world for more than a decade and that such concerns are **unfounded**. But they acknowledge that there have been few studies looking at the particular combinations of these compounds. In addition to taurine and glucuronolactone, energy drinks have other unusual ingredients: guarana, a Brazilian herb that contains caffeine; inositol, a sugar alcohol; D-Ribose, another sugar used in metabolism; carnitine, arginine, and creatine, three amino acids; and ginseng, an Asian herb said to have antioxidant benefits.

15　Red Bull, the Austrian company that makes the original energy drink, makes ambitious assertions about its particular blend of these ingredients. The company's website boasts that Red Bull "improves performance, especially during times of increased stress or strain," "increases **concentration**," and "stimulates the metabolism."

16　Other manufacturers, however, are more circumspect[4] in their claims. Mary Merrill, group director for sports and energy drinks at Coca-Cola, says the reason taurine, guarana, carnitine, and ginseng are in Full Throttle is because customers want them there.

17　"Energy drinks contain ingredients that consumers have come to expect and want to see," Ms. Merrill said. "We make no claims about any of them. We believe in marketing our brand by focusing on the brand's personality, rather than the ingredients."

18　Mr. Cabrera, the auto mechanic, says he likes it that his can of No Fear has strange-sounding ingredients, listed on the top of the can, but he admits he has no idea what taurine, creatine, and arginine are.

19　Kristi Hinck, a spokeswoman for SoBe beverages, says that if consumers are curious about ingredients, they should do research. "We encourage people to do their homework and look it up," she said. "It's part of the whole **mystique** about energy drinks."

20　Some scientists say this mystique amounts to little more than shrewd marketing of overpriced, caffeinated sugar water. "These are just caffeine delivery systems," said Professor Griffiths at Johns Hopkins. "They're being marketed cleverly to imply they have other ingredients that may be useful to some end."

21　Henk Smit, a researcher in the department of experimental psychology at the University

---

[4] **circumspect:** thinking very carefully about something before doing it because there may be risks

of Bristol in Britain, decided to test the effectiveness of energy drinks. In a study published in the medical journal *Nutritional Neuroscience* last year, Mr. Smit found that energy drinks were effective at improving mood and performance, but he concluded that caffeine was the crucial component.

22 "Any additional benefits of taurine, glucuronolactone, or other ingredients are **minimal** compared to those of caffeine, and from what I know, are speculative at best for most of these ingredients," he wrote in an e-mail message.

23 Mr. Sacks, the Hansen chief executive, **takes issue** with these findings. He says Monster is carefully made to deliver a smoother burst of energy than other forms of caffeine. "When you drink coffee you get jittery, **agitated**, and fidgety," he said. "Our experience is that you don't get the same effect with an energy drink."

24 Mr. Sacks says that if his aim were to simply get customers revved up on caffeine, he would have added more of it. "If I wanted to promote sales, I could have doubled the caffeine," he said. "It's a cheap ingredient **relative** to the others. Why would I spend dollars and dollars per case for these other ingredients when I could just put in 2 more cents and double the caffeine?"

25 It is these other, more expensive ingredients that allow manufacturers to charge $2 to $3 a can when a 20-ounce bottle of soda can be had for $1 to $1.50. And that, says Mr. Pirko of Bevmark, has everything to do with marketing. "You're selling images to people who want to be powerful," he said. "It's a head trip[5]."

[5] **head trip:** a feeling resulting from an action done mostly for your own selfish pleasure

MAIN IDEAS

Read the statements. Write *T* (true) or *F* (false).

_____ 1. Beverage companies claim that energy drinks are safe and can have a number of benefits.

_____ 2. Many scientists consider energy drinks a healthy and safe alternative to coffee.

_____ 3. There are worries about the negative effects of high levels of caffeine in energy drinks, especially for children.

_____ 4. Energy drinks are big business, and their sales are growing fast.

_____ 5. The benefits of taurine, glucuronolactone, and other ingredients in energy drinks have been scientifically proven to be much greater than those of caffeine.

_____ 6. According to one study, the additional ingredients in energy drinks have few benefits compared to caffeine, the most important ingredient.

_____ 7. Scientists are worried that people who drink energy drinks are becoming addicted because of the high amounts of caffeine.

DETAILS

A. Write the paragraph number in Reading 2 where each detail can be found.

Main idea	Details	Paragraph
1. Energy drinks are very popular.	a. Some people drink one or two energy drinks every day.	
	b. Energy drinks are the fastest-growing sector of the beverage industry.	
	c. Sales grew 61 percent in one year.	
2. Energy drinks contain high levels of caffeine.	d. Critics say energy drinks encourage caffeine addiction among teenagers.	
	e. Caffeine causes hyperactivity, restlessness, and loss of calcium in children.	
	f. France, Denmark, Norway, and Argentina have stopped the sale of energy drinks with current levels of caffeine.	

B. Use this chart to record your notes on the final part of the reading. Remember to write only the most important details.

Main idea	Details
1. Consumers are becoming addicted to energy drinks.	
2. Energy drinks contain other energy-enhancing ingredients.	
3. Scientists say caffeine is the most important ingredient in energy drinks.	
4. Energy drink companies feel the other ingredients are important.	

WHAT DO YOU THINK?

A. Discuss the questions in a group. Then choose one question and write one or two paragraphs in response.

1. Have you ever tried an energy drink? If yes, how did it make you feel? If you haven't tried one, would you?

2. A number of countries do not allow the sale of energy drinks with high levels of caffeine. Do you think the government should step in and control the consumption of these drinks? Why or why not?

3. Is the popularity of energy drinks mainly due to marketing or to their beneficial effects? Explain your opinion.

Tip for Success

When you research a topic, you can bring together ideas from different sources and synthesize this information to understand the topic in a new way.

B. Think about both Reading 1 and Reading 2 as you discuss the questions.

1. If people know that a good night's sleep, reducing stress, and eating well are sensible lifestyle choices that help to increase energy levels, why do some people choose to use energy drinks instead?

2. Which method of boosting energy do you prefer: lifestyle changes as in Reading 1 or energy drinks as in Reading 2? Why?

| **Vocabulary Skill** | **Adjective/verb + preposition collocations** |

Some **adjectives and verbs** are often **followed by certain prepositions**. These common word combinations are called **collocations**. Being familiar with these patterns can increase your accuracy as you write and speed up your reading comprehension. These charts show some common collocations found in Readings 1 and 2.

Adjective + preposition

Adjective	Preposition	Example
curious	about	Consumers who are **curious about** the ingredients in energy drinks can do some research.
appropriate	for	The chief executive says the energy drink is **appropriate for** anyone over the age of 13.
aware	of	My spouse first became **aware of** my sleep apnea when I started snoring loudly.
sensitive	to	Some people are **sensitive to** caffeine.

Verb + preposition

Verb	Preposition	Example
worry	about	Many university students **worry about** getting good grades.
focus	on	Some energy drink companies like to **focus on** the brand's personality rather than the ingredients.
refer	to	The tired feeling after a quick sugar rush is **referred to** as a crash state.
deal	with	Cortisol helps our bodies **deal with** stress.

Cause or effect

The collocations *result from* and *be caused by* are used to express cause. *Lead to* and *result in* are used to express effect. They are all common in academic writing.

Low energy levels **result from** people not getting enough exercise.
 effect   cause

Not getting enough exercise **results in** low energy levels.
 cause   effect

A. Complete each sentence with the appropriate preposition. If you need help, look at the Skill Box or scan Readings 1 and 2. Then check (✓) the sentences with collocations used to express cause or effect.

1. Some doctors refer ＿＿ a lack of quality sleep as a sleep debt.

2. Too much stress can result ＿＿ many problems, such as having low energy and not being able to lose weight.

3. Busy people find it difficult to deal ＿＿ making healthy meals on a daily basis.

4. Energy drinks are often marketed ＿＿ young adults who are looking for a quick boost.

5. Sometimes, children's behavioral problems result ＿＿ the effects of too much caffeine.

6. Are consumers curious ＿＿ the strange-sounding ingredients found in energy drinks?

B. Combine the phrases (cause, effect, and collocation) into one sentence. Change the verbs and nouns as necessary to create a grammatical sentence.

1. not get enough quality sleep / feel tired all the time / result from

    Feeling tired all the time results from not getting enough quality sleep.

2. be obese / sleep apnea / can result from

    _____

3. high levels of caffeine / France, Denmark, Norway, and Argentina bar the sale of energy drinks / lead to

    _____

4. eat a large, high-protein meal / feel tired / can be caused by

    _____

5. companies spend a lot of money on marketing them / an increase in sales of energy drinks / may be caused by

    _____

6. drink an energy drink / feel wide awake and alert / can result in

    _____

C. Find five new adjective + preposition or verb + preposition collocations in Reading 1 and Reading 2. Then write a sentence in your own words for each new collocation in your notebook.

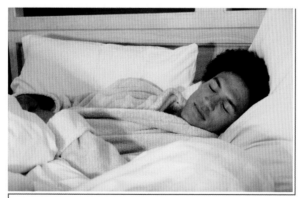

Seven to eight hours of sleep can boost energy.

People often write to understand the reasons behind something or the results of something: causes and effects. The piece of writing can either focus on the causes of a situation or event or it can focus on the results of a situation or event.

The **causal analysis essay** looks at multiple causes leading to one major result. It usually begins by describing a particular situation and then analyzing all of the causes.

Thesis statement: Poor sleep, high stress, and a bad diet can lead to a lack of energy.

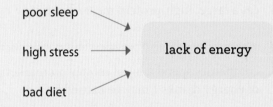

The **effect analysis essay** examines how one major reason has a number of different results. It usually begins by describing a particular situation and then analyzing all of the effects.

Thesis statement: Too much caffeine can result in difficulty sleeping, headaches, and nervousness.

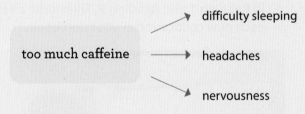

There are two common problems to watch for in a causal analysis or effect analysis essay.

1. The relationships between cause and effect must exist and be logical. Avoid mistaken causal relationships—jumping to conclusions without first checking the logic of your argument.

   ✗ Drinking the right energy drink leads to happiness and love.
   ✗ Eating a large meal with too much protein immediately results in illness.

2. The causal relationships must be supportable with details such as facts, examples, statistics, quotations, and anecdotes.

A. Read the student essay, which was written in response to an English composition class assignment. Then answer the questions with a partner.

English Composition 101 Midterm Essay Assignment:

Why do some students have very low energy and difficulty concentrating? Write an essay analyzing why some students have trouble staying awake during class.

Class Time Is Often Sleepy Time

1   There is a serious problem that is growing on university campuses. Undergraduate students are finding it difficult to stay focused in class in ever greater numbers. It is routine to see students closing their eyes during lectures or staring out the window. While some students hide behind their books, other students move around in their chairs, trying to keep alert. Why are students struggling to make the most of their class time? The reasons for this struggle to stay awake lie in student jobs and university classes.

2   One culprit for this epidemic of lack of focus in class is the increasing number of students who are holding down part-time or even full-time jobs while they are in school. As the cost of living continues to rise and tuition fees become higher, students are finding it necessary to have a job in order to make ends meet. However, as students, often the only jobs available to them are low-paying ones that require long hours in order to make the money necessary to go to school. The long hours cut into study time, forcing students to study later and later into the night. It is not rare for a student to arrive home from a part-time job at 9 p.m. and then to be faced with another four or five hours of homework. It is hard to imagine being bright and energetic for an early morning class after that.

3   Another explanation for why students are not focusing in class has to be the classes themselves. It is easy to hide in a class of 400 students. If students are tired, they have only to sit in the back or at the side of the lecture hall. In addition, classes can often be boring affairs that students must endure. One reason may be that most professors are excellent researchers, but not necessarily the best teachers. They are unable to engage students in learning and instead lecture from prepared notes in a traditional manner. Students today are what have been called digital natives, used to multitasking on the Internet, listening to their iPods, and watching TV in a 500-channel universe. To suddenly ask them to listen to lectures read aloud in a monotone leads to wandering minds.

4   Schedules packed with work and study, along with classes that do not engage students' attention, lead to difficulties focusing in class. Something must change if university students are going to get the most possible out of their programs of study. Students need to make a commitment to work fewer hours, and universities need to make a commitment to improve classroom lectures.

1. What type of essay is this?

   ☐ causal analysis essay   ☐ effect analysis essay

2. What is the thesis statement for this essay? Underline it.

3. What is the first topic sentence? Underline it twice.

4. Make note of the first major cause and its effect in the margin beside their place in the essay.

5. What is the second topic sentence? Underline it twice.

6. Make note of the second major cause and its effect in the margin beside their place in the essay.

7. What is the concluding statement? Underline it.

B. Complete this cause-and-effect chart for each main body paragraph of the essay in Activity A.

Working part-time or full-time jobs is making students tired and unable to focus.	
Cause	**Effect**
1. rising cost of living	
2.	students need a job
3. usually have low-paying jobs	
4.	have to study late at night
5. study late at night	

The classes don't keep students' attention.	
Cause	**Effect**
6.	
7.	
8.	
9.	
10.	

Tip Critical Thinking

In Activity C, you will create a cause-and-effect chart. To do this, you will use your understanding of the readings, as well as the relationship between ideas to organize information in a new way. This can help you remember material better, and use it more effectively to express your own ideas.

C. Imagine you have been assigned to write an essay based on one of the readings in this unit. Choose Reading 1 or Reading 2 and create a cause-and-effect chart in answer to one of these essay questions.

1. What are some reasons why people feel tired during the day?

2. What can people do in order to boost their energy?

3. What are some of the effects of consuming energy drinks?

4. Why are energy drinks becoming so popular?

Grammar Cause-and-effect connectors web

Cause-and-effect connectors show the exact relationship between your ideas and give your writing coherence.

The **coordinating conjunction** *so* follows the cause and is connected to the effect in a sentence. It does not usually start a sentence in formal academic writing.

People do not get enough exercise, **so** they suffer from low energy levels.

The **subordinators** *because*, *due to the fact that*, and *since* connect to the cause in a sentence. They are used in dependent (adverbial) clauses. Notice the use of the comma when the dependent clause comes first.

Some people have low energy **because** they do not get enough exercise.

I have low energy levels **due to the fact that** I don't eat enough complex carbohydrates.

Since you feel so tired, you can stay home and rest.

The **transitions** *as a consequence, as a result, because of this, consequently, for this (that) reason*, and *therefore* all follow the cause and are connected to the effect.

People do not get enough exercise. **Consequently**, they suffer from low energy.

People do not get enough exercise; **for this reason**, they suffer from low energy.

A. Underline the cause once and the effect twice.

1. Jody says his high energy level is **due to the fact that** he drinks an energy drink every morning.

2. France, Denmark, Norway, and Argentina banned the sale of some energy drinks **because** they contain high levels of caffeine.

3. Many customers like strange-sounding ingredients. **Consequently**, energy drink companies add ingredients like guarana, inositol, D-Ribose, and carnitine to their beverages.

4. Energy drinks contain caffeine. One study noted that **because of this**, they can improve mood and performance.

5. Energy drinks have a loyal, enthusiastic customer base. **For this reason**, sales of energy drinks have grown quickly.

B. Read each pair of sentences and draw an arrow from the cause to the effect.

Cause and Effect		
1. She feels tired every day.	←	She's not getting enough sleep.
2. I feel energetic while I work.		I drink coffee in the morning.
3. People eat too many processed and refined food items.		People suffer from low energy levels and fatigue.
4. There is a lot of caffeine in energy drinks.		People are becoming addicted to energy drinks.
5. Energy drinks can give a boost of energy.		People working long shifts buy energy drinks.
6. Adults cope with work, dating, family, and financial matters.		Adults usually have more stress than children.
7. He has symptoms of chronic fatigue syndrome.		He has sleep apnea.
8. People need quality, uninterrupted sleep.		The body repairs tissue and restores itself during sleep.
9. TV ads for energy drinks show popular sports figures enjoying them.		People buy energy drinks.
10. I eat fresh fruit and nuts for snacks.		I feel energetic.

C. In your notebook, rewrite the sentences in Activity B using the connectors below. Change nouns to pronouns as needed to make your sentences sound more natural.

1. for this reason
2. because
3. as
4. due to the fact that
5. because of this

6. consequently
7. as a consequence
8. since
9. so
10. because of this

In this assignment, you will write a cause-and-effect essay that examines the best methods for boosting energy levels. As you prepare your essay, think about the Unit Question, "What energizes people?" and refer to the Self-Assessment checklist on page 249. Use information from Readings 1 and 2 and your work in this unit to support your ideas.

For alternative unit assignments, see the *Q: Skills for Success Teacher's Handbook*.

PLAN AND WRITE

A. BRAINSTORM Brainstorm a list of all the different ways of increasing energy that you read about in this unit. Then complete the activities.

1. Use the chart to describe the positive and negative effects each energy booster has on people.

Energy booster	Positive effects	Negative effects
coffee	helps people wake up in the morning	may make people jittery and nervous

2. Review each energy booster in the chart and decide whether the positive effects outweigh the negative effects. Then decide which energy boosters are best.

B. PLAN Choose two or three energy boosters to examine in your essay. Give reasons for using these methods along with an analysis of their positive effects. Use the chart below to add supporting details, such as facts, examples, statistics, quotations, and anecdotes.

Main causes (energy booster)		Supporting details	Effect
1.	a.		*feeling more energetic*
	b.		
	c.		
2.	a.		
	b.		
	c.		
3.	a.		
	b.		
	c.		

Tip for Success

In order to sound natural, use connectors only when you need to demonstrate a clear relationship between ideas.

C. WRITE Write a cause-and-effect essay on the best methods for boosting energy levels. Look at the Self-Assessment checklist on page 249 to guide your writing.

REVISE AND EDIT

A. PEER REVIEW Read a partner's essay. Answer the questions and discuss them with your partner.

1. Does the essay clearly answer the unit question?

2. What causes of increased energy levels are covered by this essay?

3. Are these energy boosters healthy or not?

4. Are the cause-and-effect relationships in the essay sound and logical?

5. Are the cause-and-effect relationships well supported with details, such as facts, examples, statistics, and anecdotes?

6. Does the essay avoid overgeneralization?

B. REWRITE Review the answers to the questions in Activity A. You may want to revise and rewrite your essay.

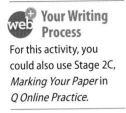

C. **EDIT** Complete the Self-Assessment checklist as you prepare to write the final draft of your essay. Be prepared to hand in your work or discuss it in class.

SELF-ASSESSMENT		
Yes	**No**	
☐	☐	Does the essay build a convincing argument using facts, reasons, and examples?
☐	☐	Does the essay use cause-and-effect connectors?
☐	☐	Are collocations with prepositions used correctly?
☐	☐	Does the essay include vocabulary from the unit?
☐	☐	Did you check the essay for punctuation, spelling, and grammar?

Track Your Success

Circle the words you learned in this unit.

Nouns
carbohydrate
component 🔑 AWL
concentration 🔑 AWL
dilemma
disclaimer
fatigue
hormone
immune system
metabolism

mystique
protein
stamina

Verbs
alleviate
bar
contend
digest
foster
restore 🔑 AWL

Adjectives
agitated
minimal AWL
refined AWL
unfounded AWL

Phrases
relative to
take issue

🔑 Oxford 3000™ words
AWL Academic Word List

Check (✓) the skills you learned. If you need more work on a skill, refer to the page(s) in parentheses.

READING	●	I can organize my notes and annotations in a chart. (p. 230)
VOCABULARY	●	I can use adjective/verb + preposition collocations. (pp. 239–240)
WRITING	●	I can write a cause-and-effect essay. (p. 242)
GRAMMAR	●	I can use cause-and-effect connectors. (p. 245)
LEARNING OUTCOME	●	I can prepare a cause-and-effect essay analyzing two or three methods for boosting energy levels.

UNIT 10
Size and Scale

READING ●	understanding narrative structure
VOCABULARY ●	metaphorical language
WRITING ●	using symbolism
GRAMMAR ●	tense shifts in narratives

Unit QUESTION

Does the size of a country matter?

PREVIEW THE UNIT

A Discuss these questions with your classmates.

Are you from a large country or a small country? What are some advantages and disadvantages of its size?

Are the countries around your country of a similar size? How might this size difference affect the relationships between the countries and people?

Look at the photo. Do you think these people come from a large country or a small country?

B Discuss the Unit Question above with your classmates.

🔊 Listen to *The Q Classroom*, Track 5 on CD 3, to hear other answers.

C Take the geography quiz. Check (✓) the names of the real countries. Write the continent where they are located.

What is your geography IQ?

Identify the real countries and their locations.

Country	Real country?		Continent
1. Andorra	☐ Yes	☐ No	
2. Champina	☐ Yes	☐ No	
3. Florin	☐ Yes	☐ No	
4. Freedonia	☐ Yes	☐ No	
5. Grenada	☐ Yes	☐ No	
6. Luxembourg	☐ Yes	☐ No	
7. Nauru	☐ Yes	☐ No	
8. Pala	☐ Yes	☐ No	
9. San Marino	☐ Yes	☐ No	
10. Tuvalu	☐ Yes	☐ No	
11. Vanuatu	☐ Yes	☐ No	
12. Zambezi	☐ Yes	☐ No	

10-12 correct answers: You are a geography genius!
8-9 correct answers: Good effort!
6-7 correct answers: You should review your geography!

D Do you think it's important to know about the small countries of the world? Why or why not?

READING 1 | "Small Country," Part I

VOCABULARY

Hear are some words and phrases from Reading 1. Read the sentences. Circle the answer that best explains the meaning of each bold word or phrase.

1. Since she wasn't sure about her plans for improving the community, the mayor just **shrugged** when asked about them.
   a. She moved her shoulders up and down because she didn't have an answer.
   b. She touched her ear because she couldn't hear the question.

2. It was difficult to watch TV because the picture kept **flickering**.
   a. The TV picture was shining too brightly.
   b. The TV picture kept going on and off.

3. We got lost because I **pretended** I knew where the house was when I really did not.
   a. I kept it a secret that I knew where the house was.
   b. I acted like I knew where the house was.

4. When you enjoying sharing information about your life with your friends, it can feel like **torture** to keep a secret from them.
   a. It feels like an extreme punishment.
   b. It feels like a special reward.

5. The town's website **boasts** that it was voted the best place to live in the country.
   a. The website talks about the town with pride.
   b. The website talks about the town with embarrassment.

6. When the child misbehaved, his freedom to go out was **withdrawn** and he had to stay home.
   a. His freedom was increased.
   b. His freedom was taken away.

7. I had complained all afternoon and my mother was finally **getting sick of** hearing me, so she went out.
   a. My mother began to feel ill.
   b. My mother became annoyed.

8. I joined the team **as a favor** to my friends because they did not have enough players.

   a. I joined the team mainly to help my friends.

   b. I joined the team because I really wanted to play.

9. The city provides a lot of services that citizens seem to **take for granted**, without realizing how much the services cost.

   a. The citizens ignore the value of the services.

   b. The citizens express thanks for the services.

10. The boy played football when he was **supposed to** do his homework, so his parents were very angry.

    a. The boy was finished with his homework.

    b. The boy should have been doing his homework.

11. I didn't think I could **get away with** missing the town meeting; someone would scold me about it if I didn't go.

    a. I could not escape punishment for missing the meeting.

    b. I could not be unhappy about missing the meeting.

12. My parents have always been very supportive, so I didn't want them to be **ashamed of** my bad football playing.

    a. I didn't want my parents to be embarrassed by how badly I played.

    b. I didn't want my parents to laugh at my bad football playing.

Author Nick Hornby

PREVIEW READING 1

You are going to read a complete short story in two parts. The story is "Small Country," by the best-selling British author Nick Hornby. Part I introduces Stefan, a boy who is surprised to discover that the country he lives in is much smaller than he realized.

How do you think Stefan will feel after he learns that his country is extremely small?

☐ amused   ☐ disgusted   ☐ protective

☐ angry   ☐ embarrassed   ☐ proud

Small Country, Part I
By Nick Hornby

British English	American English
football	soccer
American football	football
mum	mom
(football) pitch	(soccer) field
rubbish (*adj.*)	useless
path	sidewalk

There are small differences among British English, American English, and other varieties (Canadian, Australian, etc.) in vocabulary, grammar, punctuation, and pronunciation.

1   I was six or seven when I found out how small our country was. I was the last one to know in my class. The teacher pinned a big map of Europe up on the
5   wall and showed us the countries around us—France, Switzerland, Italy. And I put my hand up and said, "Where are we? Where's Champina on the map?" And everyone, even the teacher, laughed at me.
10   "You can't see Champina on the map, Stefan," she said.

"Why not?"

"Because we're too small."

"But we must be there somewhere."

15   "Of course we are. But you can't see us," the teacher said.

"How can you not see a whole country on a map?" I asked her.

I could feel my ears getting red. The
20   other kids knew something I didn't, I could tell.

"Do you know why we're called Champina?" the teacher asked me.

I **shrugged**. "No. I thought it was
25   because we were champions of something."

All the other kids laughed again.

"And what would we be champions of?" said the teacher. "No. *Champ* is
30   French for field. We're called Champina because our whole country is no bigger than a field. Champina used to *be* a field, until we built the village on it."

"You mean we're the only village in the
35   country?" I couldn't believe it. Our village is tiny.

You could walk across our country in less than a minute.

You could do it while holding your
40   breath, if you wanted to.

"Why didn't you tell me we lived in the smallest country in the world?" I asked my mum when I got home.

"I thought you knew," she said.

45   "How am I **supposed** to know," I asked her, "if no one tells me?"

"What difference does it make, anyway?" she said.

"I know everyone who lives in our
50   whole country," I said. "There's no one who lives in Champina who I don't know."

"That's nice, isn't it?" my mother asked me. "It's nice to live in a country with no strangers in it."

I wasn't sure about that. I thought I might get bored of looking at the same faces if I lived in this country all my life.

"Anyway, don't countries have presidents and prime ministers and things?"

"Of course," said my mother. "We're no different."

"Okay. So who's the president of Champina?"

"I am," she said.

I looked at her face to see if she was joking, but she wasn't.

"You're the president of Champina? You?"

"Yes," she said. "I thought you knew that, too."

"You don't . . . You don't *do* anything. You just make our sandwiches and do the washing."

"I go to a meeting once a month in Monsieur[1] Grimandi's bar," she said.

"But what about saluting soldiers?" I asked her. You have to remember that I was very young.

"We don't have any soldiers," she said.

"What about putting people in prison?"

"We don't have a prison," she said.

And we went on like that for a little while, until I understood that Champina isn't really a country in the same way that Italy is a country, or France, or America. It doesn't have its own stamps, or money, or television, or prisons, or soldiers, or air force, or navy. But even though we didn't have most things you'd find in normal countries, we did have our own football team.

My dad broke his leg because of football. He wasn't playing, though. What happened was that he was watching a game of football on TV, and the TV suddenly started **flickering**, and then smoke came out of it and the screen went black. I wasn't watching. I was reading on the sofa. I hate all sports, especially football, because football is the one that people talk about the most.

He was really annoyed that the TV was broken. He stood up and he kicked his chair.

"What about the old one?" my mother said. "The little one? It worked perfectly well."

"Where is it?" my father asked grumpily.

"It's in the attic," said my mother.

He was in too much of a hurry because he didn't want to miss any of the game. He got the ladder, climbed into the attic, and then fell when he was trying to carry the TV down.

We all heard the crack. We knew straightaway[2] that he'd broken something.

Three days later, when he was pushing himself into the kitchen on his crutches at breakfast, he said to me, "You know what this means, don't you?" And I **pretended** I didn't, but I did.

"It means you have to play," he said.

"I don't," I said. "There's no law that says so."

Including my dad, there are exactly eleven men and boys in Champina who can run up and down a football pitch,

---

[1] **Monsieur:** the French term of address for an adult man, equivalent to Mr. (Mister) in English

[2] **straightaway:** immediately

and they all play for the national team. No one has ever refused, even though it's **torture**. We should be playing against other villages, but because we are a country, we play against other countries. They're not big countries—we play against San Marino, and the Vatican, and places like that—but all these places have more than eleven players to choose from, and they all beat us hollow[3].

No one seems to care, though. Some people in Champina even seem to like it that way. It gets us some attention, because once or twice a year a sports journalist from another country comes to watch our team and then writes a funny piece about how bad we are. Everyone always makes the same joke when they see one of these newspaper articles. "That will put us on the map," someone will say. But of course nothing can put us on the map.

The truth is, though, that even people who love the game are **getting sick of** playing for Champina. It's no fun being beaten like that all the time.

"How many kids of your age can say they've played football for their country?" my dad asked.

"It's not really much to **boast** about, is it?" I said. "You're only asking me because there's no one else. If there was one other boy or man of the right age in the whole of Champina, you wouldn't be asking me."

"Everyone plays," said Dad. "Nobody has ever said no. It's your duty, Stefan. Your duty as a citizen of Champina."

"I can't do it, Dad," I said. "I'll just make an idiot of myself."

"But if you don't, none of us will be allowed to play," he said. "Play **as a favor** to me," he said. "To make me feel proud of you."

"But that's just the thing," I said. "If I play, you'll be **ashamed of** me."

And then I went into my bedroom and shut the door and read a book.

A few days later, I was at home watching TV when there was a knock at the door. Mum and Dad were in the cafe, having one of their meetings. It was Monsieur Grimandi.

"The president wants to see you," he said.

I laughed. "I'll see the president later," I said.

"It's not funny," he said. "She wants you to come to the cafe. Immediately."

All the grown-ups were in the cafe. My mother was sitting on her own in the middle of the room, like the teacher used to do in kindergarten when she read us a story, with everyone else arranged around her.

"Ah," she said. "Stefan. Take a seat."

"This is so stupid," I said.

Somebody tutted[4], probably because I'd been rude to the president.

"I'll ignore that last remark," she said.

---

[3] **beat hollow:** to beat by a large margin

[4] **tut:** a sound that indicates disapproval

I looked at her. I didn't want to have an argument in front of everyone, but I wouldn't forget it.

"You know why we've asked you to come here?" she said.

"I guess because of the football," I said.

"You guess right," said my mother the president. "Because of the football. You have been given the honor of representing your country, and you said no. Is that correct?"

"That is correct."

"And you're aware that if you don't play, nobody can play?"

"I suppose."

"And you haven't changed your mind?"

"No. I hate football, and I'm rubbish at it. As you know," I told her.

"Right," said my mother. "Okay then. Will you wait outside for a few moments, please, Stefan? The council needs to talk in private."

I stared at her, saw that she was serious, and left the cafe.

When I was let back in, I could see that my mother had a very serious expression on her face, and for a moment I almost believed that she was a president.

"Stefan," she said. "We respect your decision not to play for our national team. But you must understand that living in our small country . . . Well, as a citizen of Champina, you're entitled to many things, things you probably **take for granted**. You attend our school. You use this cafe. You buy candy and cookies in the shop. You walk on our roads and paths. Those rights are now **withdrawn**."

For a moment, I couldn't understand what she was saying.

"You mean . . . I can't go to school!?"

"No."

"You're not joking?"

"No."

"You're not going to let me walk on the roads?"

"No."

I'd been given a prison sentence. I'd be stuck in my house forever.

"I'm sorry if this seems unkind, or unfair," my mother said. "But when you live in a small place, you have responsibilities. What you choose to do, or choose not to do, has much more of an effect than it would in a bigger country. We don't think you should be allowed to take without giving something back."

"Okay," I said. "I'm in. I'll play. But only because no one gave me a choice."

They didn't hear the last part, though, because they were all clapping.

I didn't have to train. I told them I wasn't going to, and that was the one thing they let me **get away with**.

MAIN IDEAS

Answer these questions in your notebook.

1. How is Champina unique?

2. What does Stefan find out about his mother?

3. What happens to Stefan's father?

4. What unpleasant situation does Stefan find himself in? Why?

5. Why does Stefan agree to his mother's demands?

DETAILS

Read the sentences. What do you think the speaker is feeling? Match an emotion with the statement. Then explain what you think the speaker is trying to say. Look back at the story and read the lines in context to help you.

anger	humor	pride	sadness	sarcasm	~~surprise~~

1. Stefan's teacher: "You can't see Champina on the map, Stefan." (line 10)

   Emotion: _____ surprise _____

   She means: _Champina is too small to be seen on the map._

2. Stefan: "I know everyone who lives in our whole country. There's no one who lives in Champina who I don't know." (line 49)

   Emotion: _____

   He means: _____

3. Someone in Champina: "That will put us on the map." (line 149)

   Emotion: _____

   He means: _____

4. "How many kids of your age can say they've played football for their country?" (line 156)

   Emotion: _____

   He means: _____

5. Stefan: "I'll see the president later." (line 184)

   Emotion: _____

   He means: _____

6. Stefan: "Okay," I said. "I'm in. I'll play. But only because no one gave me a choice." (line 256)

   Emotion: _____

   He means: _____

Q WHAT DO YOU THINK?

Discuss the questions in a group. Then choose one question and write freely for five to ten minutes in response.

1. Why does the president force Stefan to play? Do you agree with her decision and her reasons?

2. What is your impression of Stefan and his reaction? How would you feel in a similar situation?

3. Can you gain anything from playing for a losing team? Can you be proud? Why or why not?

Reading Skill | **Understanding narrative structure** web

Reading a short story is different from reading a newspaper article or a textbook. Knowing what to expect will make you a more effective reader. An essay or article is built around a main idea, but fiction is built around a plot. The **plot** is the series of events in the story. In a good plot, all the elements are necessary and connected in some way. If you can understand the sequence and connections, you will understand the the story.

Plots generally follow this pattern:

Exposition: introducing the characters, setting, and time of the story

Initial action: the first event or discovery that sets the plot in motion

Complication(s): one or more actions that arise from the initial action; it puts some of the characters in difficult, dangerous, or comic situations

Climax: the point of maximum tension, interest, or humor, when the characters have to face the complications

Resolution: the end of the plot, when the climax is solved or ends

Analyze the plot of the first half of "Small Country" by answering the questions. Discuss your answers with a partner. Do you agree?

1. What do we learn in the exposition about the setting and main characters?

    a. Champina: _____

    b. Stefan: _____

    c. Stefan's mother: _____

2. What is the initial action of the plot? Circle the best answer.
   a. Stefan learns that his country is very small.
   b. Stefan's dad breaks his leg.
   c. Champina plays football matches against other countries.

3. How does the initial action become a complication in Stefan's life?

   _____

   _____

   _____

4. What do you think the climax of the story will be? You will read the rest
   of the story in Reading 2, but make a guess now based on the first part of
   the plot.

   _____

   _____

   _____

5. What do you think the resolution will be? Why?

   _____

   _____

   _____

READING 2 | "Small Country," Part II

VOCABULARY

**Here are some words and phrases from Reading 2. Read their definitions.
Then complete each sentence.**

> **captain** (*n.*) the leader of a group of people, especially a sports team
>
> **chant** (*v.*) to sing or shout the same words or phrases many times
>
> **fault** (*n.*) responsibility for something wrong that has happened or been done
>
> **feel guilty** (*phr. v.*) to feel ashamed because you have done something that you know is
> wrong or have not done something that you should have done
>
> **home game** (*n.*) a sports match played in a team's town or country
>
> **it wouldn't have killed me** (*phr.*) something I could have done without much difficulty
>
> **make the effort** (*phr. v.*) attempt to do something seriously and genuinely
>
> **nil** (*n.*) zero

pattern (*n.*) the regular way in which something happens or is done
tackle (*n.*) an act of trying to take the ball from an opponent in soccer
tactical (*adj.*) connected with the particular method you use to achieve something
wander (*v.*) to walk slowly, often without any particular sense of purpose or direction

1. Our goalie missed the ball, so it was his _____
   that the other team won.

2. One of the team's fans stood up and got the crowd to
   _____ the cheer, "We are the champions!"

3. Our team did not score a single goal; we worked hard, but our score was
   still _____.

4. The coach picked the player with the strongest leadership to be the
   _____ of the team.

5. The coach told me I would be a better player if I would just
   _____ to learn some basic skills.

6. I was running toward my goal when a player from the other team tried to
   _____ me and get the ball.

7. The other team uses the same plays over and over again in a very
   predictable _____.

8. Last week's game was out of town, but this week, we're playing
   a _____.

9. I realized _____ to go and watch her game. In
   fact, it would have taken much effort at all.

10. The youngest players do not know where to run, so they just
    _____ around the field.

11. The coach tried to explain her _____ plan for
    winning the big game.

12. You played your best, so you should not _____
    about losing the game.

PREVIEW READING 2

In Part I of "Small Country," Stefan learns that his country, Champina, is the size of a field. When his father breaks his leg, Stefan is forced to agree to play for the Champina national football team in the next game. In Part II of the story, Stefan surprises himself, and his fellow citizens, in the first football game he's ever played.

What do you think will happen in Stefan's first game?

CD 3
Track 7   **Read the conclusion of "Small Country."**

Small Country, Part II

By Nick Hornby

British English	American English
footballer	soccer player
boots	cleats
chap	man
goalie	goalkeeper
lads	boys
had got	had gotten

In the story, you will see words like *midfield* and *wide right*. These are examples of jargon: specialized language used only for a particular subject. You don't need to understand the jargon to follow the story.

1   When you play for a team for the first time, they call it your "debut". Well, I made my debut against San Marino. The last time we'd played them, we'd lost twenty-
5   eight–**nil**, but the general feeling was that it might be even worse this time. No one said this was because of me, but I could tell that's what they were all thinking.

It was a **home game**, which meant that
10   we changed in our homes. The San Marino players changed in the bathrooms at the cafe. My father gave me his red-and-white-striped shirt, and I found a pair of white shorts. I didn't have any boots, so I wore
15   sneakers. Then I put on my denim jacket and walked down to the field with Dad.

"You might enjoy it," he said. I laughed.
"You don't have to watch," I told him.
"It's going to rain. Why don't you go
20   home?"
"Everybody watches," he said. "The whole village. The whole country."
"I've never watched before," I told him.
"No," he said. "You were the only one."
25   That made me feel bad. I felt bad that I didn't know everyone else always watched the team, and I **felt guilty** that I'd never **made the effort**. **It wouldn't have killed me** to do something
30   everyone else did, once in a while.

When we got to the field, Dad patted me on the back and wished me luck, and I

| Reading and Writing   **263**

went to stand with my teammates in the middle of the pitch. The only one who really looked like a footballer was Monsieur Blanc, who worked at a fitness center in Italy. He was our **captain**.

"Stefan," he said. "Welcome." He shook my hand. "We thought we'd play you midfield. Wide right."

I didn't understand a word, and I stared at him with my mouth open.

"You know your left from your right, don't you?"

"Yes, of course."

"So. You stand on the right-hand side of the pitch. You see Michel there?" He was pointing at Monsieur Flamini, who's a painter and gardener. "He's the right back. Stand about twenty meters ahead of him, and try to help him if he needs help."

I nodded, but I didn't understand what he was talking about. What sort of help would he need? I didn't think it was a good idea to ask any more questions, though, and in any case, it was time for the game to start. I knew I wasn't going to be any good, and I knew we'd lose the game, but I was still nervous.

We let in a goal[1] after about a minute. It wasn't my **fault**, because everything happened over on the other side. The tall chap who played in the middle of their defense sort of **wandered** forward with the ball, and then gave it to another man who was standing right on the edge of the pitch. And this edge-man ran very fast with the ball toward our goal, and Monsieur Grimandi, our goalie, ran toward him. So the edge-man just passed it sideways, and someone else, a little guy, kicked the ball into an empty goal.

About three minutes after that, the same thing happened. Tall chap, to edge-man, to little goal-scoring guy . . . goal. And then again, and again. San Marino scored thirteen times in the first half of the game, and nine of those goals came in the same way.

I only touched the ball once in the first half. Monsieur Flamini got the ball and passed it to me, very gently, and the next thing I knew, I was lying on the ground, and every single part of me was ringing, as if I were a bell.

But when I picked myself up and looked around, no one cared. Everyone was just playing on as if nothing had happened.

When there was a break in the play, I said to Monsieur Flamini, "Did you see that?"

"It's called a **tackle**, Stefan. Get used to it."

So that's what it's like being a grown-up, I thought. People can just knock you down whenever they feel like it, and no one says anything. It made me wish that I was getting younger every year, not older.

At halftime, we stood on the pitch, because there was nowhere to go. Monsieur Blanc gathered us around him.

"Well," he said. "It's obvious what's going wrong. We have to stop that little guy from scoring all the goals somehow."

I didn't say anything. I just listened.

"I know what we should do," he said, "We'll have to stop worrying about the left side and pull Michel into the middle."

Michel Garde was the one who was supposed to stop the edge-man, the man who was giving the ball to the goal-scorer

---

[1] **let in a goal:** allow the other team to score

all the time. He wasn't doing a very good job of it, obviously, but it seemed crazy not
115 to have anyone on the left at all. I suddenly realized that, even though I was the worst player in the team, the rest of them didn't understand what was happening in the game. They really couldn't see it. So what
120 was I supposed to do? I was new to the team, and useless at the game, so nobody would listen to me. But if I kept quiet, we could lose by fifty or sixty goals, and everyone would say it was my fault.

125 There was something else I'd noticed. Monsieur Blanc was our captain and our best player, but he didn't do anything. I couldn't understand it.

He saw me looking at him.

130 "Any **tactical** changes you want to make, Stefan?"

Everyone else laughed at his joke, and that annoyed me.

"Yes," I said.

135 What did it matter? The worst that could happen was that they wouldn't ask me to play again.

"It's not the little guy who scores all the goals we should be worrying about,"
140 I said. "It's the edge-man. The one drinking out of the water bottle now."

"Why is he the edge-man?"

"Because he plays on the edge of the pitch."

145 "The winger," said Monsieur Blanc, as if I were stupid. "What about him?"

"He's the one that gives the goal-scorer the ball. Without him, the goal-scorer couldn't do anything."

150 Monsieur Garde nodded.

"He's right. He's been running past me all game, and I can't stop him. I need help."

Monsieur Blanc looked annoyed.

"Anything else, Stefan? Seeing
155 as you're the expert?"

I shrugged. "Okay. I'm not being rude, but . . . what do you do? On this team?"

"I'm the striker. That means I'm supposed to score the goals."

160 "But we're never going to score a goal," I said. "We never have the ball, and we're never at the right end of the field."

This time, a couple more people nodded, and I saw Flamini smile to himself.

165 "But if you wanted a job to do, you could stop the tall man."

"Which tall man?"

"The tall man who plays in defense. He's the one that gives the ball to the
170 edge-man. Every time. So if you, I don't know, got in the way or something . . . it might make it harder for them."

It was weird. I knew I was right. I play chess a lot, and sometimes you
175 can see things, shapes and **patterns**. And also, I take things apart to see how they work. It had never occurred to me that you could take football apart in the same way. I thought people just
180 kicked the ball toward the goal.

But there was still no reason for Monsieur Blanc to listen to me.

Just when I was about to give up and tell them to forget it, my mother the president walked onto the pitch to give us some encouragement.

"Bad luck, lads," she said. "You're playing well."

We all looked at her as if she was mad.

"Any plans to change things in the second half?"

"We're going to double up on the right winger," said Monsieur Blanc. "And I'm going to work harder to close down their centre-back."

It took me a little while to work out that these were my ideas, because I didn't understand the words he was using. But when I understood, I looked at him to see when he'd tell her that these were my ideas.

"Very good," said my mother. "Sounds very sensible." And then she walked off again.

I tried to catch Blanc's eye, but he wouldn't look at me.

The second half was really exciting, because we didn't let another goal in for ages and ages. Every time the tall defender got the ball, Monsieur Blanc ran over to him and stood right in front of him. So the edge-man, the winger, didn't get the ball very often, and when he did, he had to run past two players, not just one, and the second player was sometimes able to take the ball away from him. And even though San Marino was winning thirteen-nil, the longer they went without scoring again, the more embarrassed they became.

And we all started to run faster, and jump higher, and tackle harder. The crowd got excited, too, when they saw that things had got so much better. They knew we couldn't win, and they knew that we weren't even going to get a goal.

But as we went fifteen minutes, and then twenty minutes, even nearly thirty minutes of the second half without letting the other team score, you could tell that they were proud of us.

They even started **chanting** and clapping.

We made three stupid mistakes in the last fifteen minutes, and let in three goals. But when the referee blew the whistle for the end of the game, there were a lot of smiles on our team.

Losing a second half three-nil was Champina's best-ever international result.

"Just think," said Grimandi. "If we could play like that in the first half *and* the second half . . ."

". . . We'd lose every game six-nil," laughed Flamini.

I knew what Grimandi meant, though. Six-nil felt like a football score. Good teams, teams you've heard of, lose six-nil sometimes. Nobody ever loses twenty-six–nil, though.

As we walked off the pitch, the whole crowd—the whole of my country—cheered us. And then my teammates did something I will never forget. They walked quickly to the side of the pitch, stood in two lines, and clapped as I walked between them. Even Monsieur Blanc joined in. It must have looked strange to my mother and father. As far as they knew, I had done nothing, apart from fall over once, in the first half.

That was the last time I ever had to play. The next game, they used Grimandi's ten-year-old son, Robert, in my position, and he was better than me. I was told to watch, and tell them where they were going wrong. I became the coach. "You've got brains," Grimandi said. "We haven't."

In my first game as coach, we lost twelve-nil. At the end of the game, the team did a lap of honor[2].

[2] **lap of honor:** victory run around a field

MAIN IDEAS

Answer these questions.

1. What is the climax of the story?

2. What is the resolution of the story?

3. In your own words, what is the story trying to say to its readers?

DETAILS

Complete the chart. Write the letter of the result (on page 268) that best matches each event. You will need to infer some of the answers.

Event		Result
1. Stefan was playing unwillingly in his first game.		c
2. Stefan realized that he was the only person in his country who didn't support the soccer team.		
3. The tall San Marino defender kept passing the ball to the winger on his right side.	→	
4. Stefan got the ball.		
5. Stefan told the captain why San Marino was scoring so many goals.		

Event		Result
6. San Marino could not score goals easily in the second half.		
7. The crowd realized that the Champina team was playing better.		
8. Champina lost the second half three-nil.	→	
9. The team understood that Stefan had helped them.		
10. Another boy was found to take Stefan's place on the team.		

a. The winger passed the ball to the short striker, who scored.

b. Monsieur Blanc changed the team's tactics for the second half.

c. The people of Champina expected the team to lose by more than 28 goals to nil.

d. They honored Stefan as he left the field.

e. They started chanting and clapping.

f. A San Marino player tackled Stefan and knocked him down.

g. Stefan felt guilty that he had never made an effort.

h. Stefan became the coach of the Champina soccer team.

i. The Champina team began to feel more confident.

j. They felt proud of themselves.

 **WHAT DO YOU THINK?**

Tip Critical Thinking

In Activities A and B, you will react to the story. In expressing your opinion, you are showing your understanding of and opinion about the story. When you respond personally to a text, you make it more meaningful and memorable.

A. Discuss the questions in a group.

1. Why do you think Monsieur Blanc took Stefan's advice?

2. At the end of the story, do you think Stefan's attitude toward Champina has changed? Why or why not?

B. Think about the whole story (Reading 1 and Reading 2) as you discuss the questions.

1. Did you enjoy the story? Why or why not?

2. How do you think Stefan's life would have been different if he had lived in a very large country?

3. Does the size of your home country matter to you? Why or why not?

Many words and phrases from the sports world have become part of everyday English. They are used **metaphorically**, meaning that they are used to describe a situation that is not related to sports.

☐   We need to **tackle the problem**.

The word *tackle* in soccer means to try to take the ball from an opponent. However, metaphorically, to *tackle a problem* means to try very hard to solve it or to beat it as you would beat a soccer player whom you tackle.

Use a dictionary to check the meaning of sports metaphors and learn how they are used and what words they collocate with. Sometimes, the metaphorical meaning will be marked "idiom" because the words are not being used in their literal meaning. Learning the sports meaning can help you remember the metaphorical meaning, and using sports metaphors can make your writing and speaking more interesting.

Tip for Success

Many sports metaphors are used in business communication, probably because business and sports are both competitive.

A. The bold phrase in each sentence is a common collocation using a sports term from "Small Country." Explain its meaning in sports and in the sentence.

1. The company **met** its **goal** for improving quality.

   Scoring a goal is the objective in a soccer game. The goal here is the

   company's objective.

2. She really **scored points** with her teacher by volunteering to read her essay.

   _____

3. I want to **pitch an idea** for the end-of-semester party.

   _____

4. If you know your boss is breaking the law, you should **blow the whistle** on him.

   _____

5. After the presentation, I had to **field** a lot of difficult **questions** from the audience.

   _____

B. Work with a partner. Complete the chart with the phrases from the box. Then check your answers in the dictionary.

a situation that cannot have any possible progress	to make contact
control the ball	on the rebound
drop the ball	to signal that you have lost
just what you expect to happen	~~to do something that is certain to be successful~~
knockout blow	to be unsuccessful

	Sports meaning	Phrase	Metaphorical meaning
1.	(basketball) to jump high and put the ball directly into the hoop	slam dunk	to do something that is certain to be successful
2.	(boxing) a hit so hard that the person can't get up		a problem that means you will certainly fail
3.	(baseball) to fail to hit the ball three times	strike out	
4.	(American football) to lose possession of the ball		to make a mistake
5.	(golf) the average number of strokes a good player will make	par for the course	
6.	(soccer)	on the ball	understanding what is happening and reacting quickly
7.	(baseball) to reach one of the four points on the field	touch base	
8.	(basketball) the ball bouncing back after missing the basket		meeting someone when recovering from the end of a previous relationship
9.	(chess) a game in which neither player can win	stalemate	
10.	(boxing)	throw in the towel	to give up; to stop doing something

WRITING

Writing Skill   Using symbolism   web+

A **symbol** is an image, object, event, or sign that represents a bigger idea. In a story, a window might symbolize the outside world for a particular character. Or the sound of a violin could represent a character's childhood when she used to play music. Authors of fiction use symbolism to make their writing more interesting and give it more meaning.

A. Work with a partner. Read the first paragraph of a student's short story. Answer the questions.

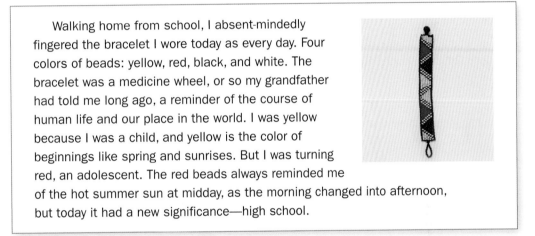

Walking home from school, I absent-mindedly fingered the bracelet I wore today as every day. Four colors of beads: yellow, red, black, and white. The bracelet was a medicine wheel, or so my grandfather had told me long ago, a reminder of the course of human life and our place in the world. I was yellow because I was a child, and yellow is the color of beginnings like spring and sunrises. But I was turning red, an adolescent. The red beads always reminded me of the hot summer sun at midday, as the morning changed into afternoon, but today it had a new significance—high school.

1. What do the colors of the beads in the girl's bracelet symbolize? Complete the table using the information in the paragraph and your own ideas.

	Stage of life	Season	Time of day	Explanation
1. yellow	childhood	spring	dawn	They all represent beginnings.
2. red				
3. black				
4. white				

2. What does the wheel symbolize?

_____

3. How do you think the bracelet will be used in the rest of the story? Make three guesses.

a. _____

b. _____

c. _____

B. Choose an item, color, animal, or number that is symbolic in your culture.

1. What did you choose?

_____

2. What is its original or literal meaning?

_____

_____

3. What is its symbolic meaning or purpose?

_____

_____

4. Write a paragraph in your notebook in which you introduce and explain the symbol.

Grammar   Tense shifts in narratives   web+

Writers use a variety of verb tenses in narratives, both to describe the action clearly and to add comments. Although writers may primarily stick to one tense in a narrative, they may shift tense to create particular effects.

Use **the past** for most storytelling:

- Use **the simple past** for all events that happen in sequence.

  So the edge-man just passed it sideways, and someone else, a little guy, kicked the ball into an empty goal.

- Use **the past continuous** to describe actions that were happening at the same time as the main action.

  What happened was that he was watching a game of football on TV, and the TV suddenly started flickering, and then smoke came out of it and the screen went black.

- Use **the past perfect** for events or states before the main time of the narrative.

  ...I felt guilty that I'd never made the effort.

Shift from **the past tense** to **the present tense**:

- to add an explanation or comment.

  "But what about saluting soldiers?" I asked her. You have to remember that I was very young.

- for a fact, general statement, or regular event

  And we went on like that for a little while, until I understood that Champina isn't really a country in the same way that Italy is a country, or France, or America.

Shift from **the simple past** to **future forms** to look beyond the story.

  And then my teammates did something I will never forget

A. Which tense or tenses are used in these extracts from "Small Country"? Why?

1. Once or twice a year a sports journalist from another country comes to watch our team and then writes a funny piece about how bad we are.

   Tense: _____

   Reason: _____

2. Everyone always makes the same joke when they see one of these newspaper articles. "That will put us on the map," someone will say.

   Tense: _____

   Reason: _____

3. When you play for a team for the first time, they call it your "debut." Well, I made my debut against San Marino.

   Tense: _____

   Reason: _____

4. I knew I was right. I play chess a lot, and sometimes you can see things, shapes and patterns.

   Tense: _____

   Reason: _____

B. Read the first paragraph of another short story. Complete each sentence with the correct form of the verb in parentheses. (More than one choice is possible for some answers.)

It _____ (be) strange how one small decision sometimes

_____ (make) all the difference. For Wei, that decision

_____ (come) in a bookstore. He _____ (look)

through a pile of old, used books when his father _____

(complain), "Wei, you _____ (take) too long!" So Wei just

_____ (grab) the top book off the pile. It _____

(be) a biography of the famous Russian choreographer George Balanchine.

Wei _____ never _____ (hear) of Balanchine before that day, but in the

years to come, he would learn every detail about the great dancer's life

and work.

Unit Assignment | Write a short story

In this assignment, you will write a short story. As you prepare your story, think about the Unit Question, "Does the size of a country matter?" and refer to the Self-Assessment checklist on page 276. Use your work in this unit to support your ideas.

PLAN AND WRITE

A. **BRAINSTORM** Follow these steps to brainstorm ideas for your story.

1. The plot for your short story can be true (nonfiction or autobiographical) or imagined (fiction). Read the questions. Check (✓) at least two to answer. Then write your answers in your notebook.

☐ a. Do you remember an event in your life when you "grew up?" Where and how did it happen? How can you use this experience in a story?

☐ b. Is there a large monument, mountain, or other place that you know well? How could this be a symbol in your story?

☐ c. Is there a small item that you know about that has great significance to you or others? How could this be a symbol in your story?

☐ d. Do you know of a situation in which the size of a country affected the opportunities a person had? How could you use this situation in a story?

2. Read your answers to Activity 1. Which will be most useful when you write? Ask a partner to read your ideas and help you choose. You may also write freely about another idea.

3. Think of two or three main characters for your story. Why are they important to the plot? Name and describe each character briefly in your notebook.

B. PLAN **Choose the narrative point of view you will use for your short story. Then make notes in the chart to plan your story.**

☐ **First-person narrator:** The story is <u>told by one character</u> in the story using the pronoun "I."

☐ **Limited third-person narrator:** The story is <u>told about one character</u> in the story using either "he" or "she."

☐ **Omniscient narrator:** The story is <u>told from the point of view of many characters</u>. The viewpoint can change instantly.

Exposition	
Initial action	
Complication	
Climax	
Resolution	

Your Writing Process

For this activity, you could also use Stage 1C, *Writing a First Draft* in *Q Online Practice*.

C. **WRITE** Write a draft of your short story. Make sure your narrative has an organized plot, interesting characters, and a clear point of view. Look at the Self-Assessment checklist on page 276 to guide your writing.

REVISE AND EDIT

A. **PEER REVIEW** Read one another's stories. Take notes for each story. Then answer the questions and discuss your answers with the group.

1. What do you like about the story?

2. What else do you want to know about the characters or plot?

3. How could the writer improve the structure of the narrative?

4. Are there any sentences that confused you? How can the writer improve them?

5. What else would you like to say to the writer?

B. **REWRITE** Review the answers to the questions in Activity A. You may want to revise and rewrite your short story.

C. **EDIT** Complete the Self-Assessment checklist as you prepare to write the final draft of your short story. Be prepared to hand in your work or discuss it in class.

SELF-ASSESSMENT		
Yes	**No**	
☐	☐	Does the short story have an organized plot, interesting characters, and a clear point of view?
☐	☐	Are verb tense shifts used correctly in the narrative?
☐	☐	Are sports metaphors used appropriately in the story?
☐	☐	Does the short story include vocabulary from the unit?
☐	☐	Did you check the short story for punctuation, spelling, and grammar?

Track Your Success

Circle the words you learned in this unit.

Nouns	Verbs	Phrases
captain 🔑	boast	as a favor
fault 🔑	chant	be ashamed of
home game	flicker	be supposed to
nil	pretend 🔑	feel guilty
pattern 🔑	shrug	get sick of
tackle 🔑	wander 🔑	it wouldn't have killed
torture		me
	Adjectives	make the effort
	tactical	take (something/
	withdrawn	someone) for granted
	Phrasal Verb	
	get away with	

🔑 Oxford 3000™ words

AWL Academic Word List

Check (✓) the skills you learned. If you need more work on a skill, refer to the page(s) in parentheses.

READING	⬤	I can understand narrative structure. (p. 260)
VOCABULARY	⬤	I can use metaphorical language. (p. 269)
WRITING	⬤	I can use symbolism. (p. 271)
GRAMMAR	⬤	I can recognize tense shifts in narratives. (p. 272)
LEARNING OUTCOME	⬤	I can create a short story with an organized plot, interesting characters, and a clear point of view.

ACKNOWLEDGEMENTS

The authors and publisher are grateful to those who have given permission to reproduce the following extracts and adaptations of copyright material: p. 7, from "Blogs and Journalism Need Each Other" by Joseph D. Lasica, *Neiman Reports* 57 (3), 70-74, http://www.jdlasica.com. Used by permission of the author; p. 13, from "Diary-Keeping Pet Projects for Bloggers" by Atsuko Matsumoto, The Daily Yomiuri, January 1, 2008, http://www.yomiuri.co.jp. Adapted by permission of *The Daily Yomiuri;* p. 33, "The History of the Maori Language," from "History of the Maori language - Te Wiki o Te Reo Maori," New Zealand Ministry for Culture and Heritage, http://www.nzhistory.net.nz. Used by permission; p. 42, "When Languages Die," from *When Languages Die: The Extinction of the World's Languages and the Erosion of Human Knowledge* by K. David Harrison, 2007. Used by permission of Oxford University Press, Inc.; p. 47, "Knowledge" adapted from *Oxford Learner's Thesaurus: A dictionary of synonyms* by Diana Lea. © Oxford University Press 2008. Reproduced by permission of Oxford University Press; p. 61, from "Laid-Back Labor: The $140 Homemade Scarf" by Stephen J. Dubner and Steven D. Levitt, *The New York Times,* May 6, 2007. © 2007 The New York Times. All rights reserved. Used by permission and protected by the Copyright Laws of the United States. The printing, copying, redistribution, or retransmission of the Material without express written permission is prohibited; p. 68, "Video Gamers," from "The Land of the Video Geek" from *The New York Times,* October 8, 2006. © 2006 The New York Times. All rights reserved. Used by permission and protected by the Copyright Laws of the United States. The printing, copying, redistribution, or retransmission of the Material without express written permission is prohibited; p. 88, "How Maps Lie," from *How to Lie with Maps, Second Edition* by Mark Monmonier. University of Chicago Press, 1996. Used by permission of University of Chicago Press; p. 94, "Phototruth or Photofiction?" from *Phototruth or Photofiction? Ethics and Media Imagery in the Digital Age* by Thomas H. Wheeler. Copyright © 2002. Reproduced by permission of Taylor and Francis Group, LLC, a division of Informa pic and the author; p. 113, from "In Norway, Global Seed Vault Guards Genetic Resources" by Elisabeth Rosenthal, *The New York Times,* February 28, 2008. © 2008 The New York Times. All rights reserved. Used by permission and protected by the Copyright Laws of the United States. The printing, copying, redistribution, or retransmission of the Material without express written permission is prohibited; p. 121, from "The Long Countdown: For U.S. Astronauts, a Russian Second Home," by John Schwartz, *The New York Times,* October 13, 2008. © 2008 The New York Times. All rights reserved. Used by permission and protected by the Copyright Laws of the United States. The printing, copying, redistribution, or retransmission of the Material without express written permission is prohibited; p. 143, "The New Third Places" from "Where Everybody Knows Your Name" by Mary Newsom, September 24, 2009, http://citiwire.net. Reprinted by permission of *The Charlotte Observer* and Citiwire.net.; p. 143, from "The new oases" in *The Economist.* © The Economist Newspaper Limited, London April 12, 2008. Reproduced by permission; p. 150, from "A Path to Road Safety with No Signposts" by Sarah Lyall, *The New York Times,* January 22, 2005. © 2005 The New York Times. All rights reserved. Used by permission and protected by the Copyright Laws of the United States. The printing, copying, redistribution, or retransmission of the Material without express written permission is prohibited; p. 172, "Garbage of Eden" from "Garbage of Eden: want to be at one with nature? Take a stroll round Singapore's island of trash," by Eric Bland, *New Scientist,* April 14, 2007. © New Science Magazine. Used by permission; p. 179, "Garbage Mogul Makes Millions from Trash," from "Trash Talker," from FORTUNE April 2009. © 2009 Time Inc. All rights reserved. Used by permission and protected by the Copyright Laws of the United States. The printing, copying, redistribution, or retransmission of the Material without express written permission is prohibited; p. 199, from "Set in Our Ways: Why Change Is So Hard" by Nikolas Westerhoff, *Scientific American Mind,* December 2008, http://www.sciam.com. Copyright © 2008 by Scientific American, Inc. All rights reserved. Used by permission; p. 207, from "Cancer be damned, kids wanna tan," by Danylo Hawaleshka from *Maclean's,* June 27, 2005, www.macleans.ca. Used by permission; p. 229, from "A Healthy Lifestyle Can Reduce Fatigue, Boost Energy," by David Norrie, January 7, 2009, http://www.sptimes.com. Used by permission of the author; p. 237, "A Jolt of Caffeine, by the Can," from "A Jolt of Caffeine, by the Can; Caution: Energy Drink Profits May be Addictive" by Melanie Warner, *The New York Times,* November 23, 2005. © 2005 The New York Times. All rights reserved. Used by permission and protected by the Copyright Laws of the United States. The printing, copying, redistribution, or retransmission of the Material without express written permission is prohibited; p. 259, "Small Country, Part 1" and p. 268, "Small Country, Part 2" from "Small Country." Reproduced from *The United States of McSweeney's* © Nick Hornby by permission of United Agents Ltd. (www.unitedagents.co.uk) on behalf of the author; p. 213 "Children as Young as 11 Use Sunbed Salons in Northern England," from "Children as Young as 11 Use Sunbed Salons," by Sam Jones, The Guardian, December 14, 2005, http://www.guardian.co.uk. Copyright Guardian News & Media Ltd., 2005. Used by permission.

Illustrations by: p. 4 Stacy Merlin; p. 11 Barb Bastian; p. 13 Karen Minot; p. 14 Karen Minot; p. 30 Stacy Merlin; p. 84 Karen Minot; p. 89 Karen Minot; p. 90 Karen Minot; p. 102 Marc Kolle; p. 103 Marc Kolle; p. 110 Stacy Merlin; p. 138 Stacy Merlin; p. 166 Stacy Merlin; p. 171 Karen Minot; p. 224 Karen Minot; p. 252 Stacy Merlin; p. 257 Greg Paprocki; p. 265 Greg Paprocki.

We would also like to thank the following for permission to reproduce the following photographs: Cover Yukmin/Asia Images/Getty Images; Jupiter Images/ Workbook Stock/Getty Images; David Anderson/istockphoto; 4x6/ istockphoto; Kuzma/istockphoto; TrapdoorMedia/istockphoto; vi Marcin Krygier/istockphoto; xii Rüstem GÜRLER/istockphoto; p. 2 Shawn Baldwin/ Corbis; p. 7 David Brabyn/Corbis; p. 19 Blend Images/Oxford University Press; p. 28 National Geographic "Enduring Language" project. Photo by Chris Rainier; p. 30 Digital Vision/Getty Images (businessmen); Brian Ziskind (rice); p. 33 AridOcean/Shutterstock; p. 42 Greg Stott/ Masterfile; p. 56 Greg Fahringer; p. 58 OJO Images Ltd/Alamy (video game); Mike Ford/SuperStock (photographer); Marnie Burkhart/Masterfile (grocery); Rick Gomez/Masterfile (knitting); Reflexstock/Blend RM/Ariel Skelley (gardening); PhotoAlto/Alamy (computer); Corbis/Photolibrary (cleaning); Tetra Images/Corbis (reading); Blend Images/SuperStock (exercising); p. 61 Mel Yates/Getty Images; p. 68 CHOI JAE-KU/AFP/Getty Images; p. 72 MBI/Alamy; p. 82 WARNER BROS./ THE KOBAL COLLECTION; p. 84 AP Photo/Robert Klein ("photograph"); ImageZoo/Corbis ("cartoon"); 3LH-B&W ART FILE/Getty Images ("artist drawing"); p. 95 GORDON GAHAN/National Geographic Stock; p. 97 Peter Barrett/Masterfile; p. 108 Sharon Dupuis/Alamy; p. 110 zbruch/istockphoto; p. 113 Paul Nicklen/National Geographic Society/Corbis (seed vault); Stephen Ausmus courtesy of USDA (garlic); p. 114 Bon Appetit/Alamy; p. 121 Roscosmos/Gagarin Cosmonaut Training Center/NASA; p. 125 Photodisc/ Oxford University Press; p. 136 IndexStock/SuperStock; p. 143 AP Photo/ Bizuayehu Tesfaye; p. 145 David Sailors/Corbis (Stata Center); Ambient Images Inc./Alamy (Bryant Park); p. 149 DASfotografie/Sunshine/ZUMA Press; p. 159 Photodisc/Oxford University Press; p. 164 "Springtime Flowers" by Rolando Politi photo by Adriane Sage; p. 168 FOTOSEARCH RM/age fotostock; p. 170 ROSLAN RAHMAN/AFP/Getty Images; p. 174 ROSLAN RAHMAN/AFP/ Getty Images; p. 177 AP Photo/Jose F. Moreno; p. 192 Science Photo Library/ Alamy; p. 194 Emil Pozar/age fotostock (student); Gallo Images/Getty Images (architect); Nancy Falconi/Getty Images (photographer); Cultura/Alamy (backpacker); p. 197 Purestock/Getty Images; p. 198 amana productions inc./Getty Images; p. 206 ESA/NASA/SOHO; p. 213 Flirt/SuperStock; p. 215 Michael Bodmann/istockphoto; p. 222 Chen Haohao/Color China Photo/AP Images; p. 226 Ken Seet/Corbis; p. 235 Richard Levine/Alamy; p. 241 A. Inden/ Corbis; p. 250 TIMOTHY A. CLARY/AFP/Getty Images; p. 252 Map Resources/ Shutterstock; p. 252 Volina/Shutterstock; p. 254 Elisabetta Villa/Getty Images; p. 271 Tarquin Wyeth/istockphoto.